BETTER GOVERNANCE
AND PUBLIC POLICY

D1501436

BETTER GOVERNANCE AND PUBLIC POLICY

Capacity Building for Democratic Renewal in Africa

Editors
Dele Olowu and Soumana Sako

Kumarian
Press, Inc.

Better Governance and Public Policy: Capacity Building and Democratic Renewal in Africa
Published 2002 in the United States of America by Kumarian Press, Inc.
1294 Blue Hills Avenue, Bloomfield, CT 06002 USA

Production and design by Rosanne Pignone, Pro Production
Proofread by Phil Trahan, The Sarov Press
Index by Barbara DeGenero

Printed in the United States of America on acid-free paper by Thomson-Shore, Inc.
Text printed with vegetable oil-based ink.

∞ The paper used in this publication meets the minimum requirements of the American National Standard for Information Sciences—Permanence of Paper for Printed Library Materials, ANSI Z39.48–1984.

Library of Congress Cataloging-in-Publication Data
    Better governance and public policy : capacity building for democratic
renewal in Africa / editors, Dele Olowu and Soumana Sako.
      p. cm.
    Includes bibliographical references and index.
    ISBN 1-56549-160-2 (pbk. : alk. paper) — ISBN 1-56549-161-0
      (hardcover : alk. paper)
      1. Africa—Politics and government—1960– 2. Democratization—Africa.
3. Political planning—Africa. I. Olowu, Dele. II. Sako, Soumana.
JQ1879.A15 B48 2002
320'.6'096—dc21

                                   2002153520

---

11 10 09 08 07 06 05 04 03 02   10 9 8 7 6 5 4 3 2 1 First Printing 2002

Contents

Part III Case Studies

1

Introduction:
Governance and Policy Management Capacity in Africa

Dele Olowu

In the last two decades, governance has become an important issue in development policy discourse and social science research. Yet a lack of conceptual consensus on the term results in a multiplicity of definitions. Moreover, the relationship of governance to development, institutional reforms, and public policy processes and outcomes remains ambiguous. This book brings together analysis of these issues by prominent scholars and practitioners of African development policy. The underlying argument is that governance changes in African polity and economy since the 1990s necessitate the building and sustenance of critical institutional capacities within and outside the state if they are to impact poverty alleviation and development.

If governance is the independent variable that explains African underdevelopment to date, as claimed by the World Bank (1989:60) in its analysis of the region's long-term development, then recent governance changes beget the key questions posed in this book:

- What is governance, and how can it be measured in diverse political and socioeconomic contexts?
- What is the relationship between governance and institutional reforms?
- How do institutional reforms impact public policy processes and outcomes especially in developing countries generally, as well as in specific areas such as economic governance, environment, privatization, and local government reforms and decentralization?
- What is the relationship between economic governance and policy research?

- How effective are capacity-building efforts to boost the capacity of various state and nonstate institutions for effective developmental public policies and good governance?

The book has three major objectives. First, it attempts to *describe* governance changes that have occurred in African countries. As most recent discussions on governance in the last two decades have focused on how to improve governance in developing and transitional countries, even though it is increasingly becoming obvious—as Hyden and Court note in the next chapter—that demand for better or improved governance exists in all countries. Moreover, governance improvement can hardly take place without proper understanding of what governance is and of governance changes and their consequences for state, society, and citizens. The second objective of the book is therefore to *analyze* the consequences of governance change for institutional reforms. To what extent is democratic change leading to good governance in either processes or outcomes or both? Third, the book *highlights the challenge of building different types of institutional capacities* to consolidate the ongoing governance changes in economic and political realms that began in the 1990s.

The paradigm shift from autocracy to democracy in African states since 1989 has led some scholars to refer to 1989 as a watershed in African politics (Hyden, 1992). Our objective here is to help refocus the present discourse on governance, from one perceived as dominated by normative criteria for disbursing aid from rich to poor countries, to analyzing and identifying the critical institutions that are required by African countries if they are to reap the democratic dividend (Dornboos, 2001). The latter is regarded as crucial to improving economic performance and people's welfare as well as reducing poverty within a relatively short time.

In spite of the modest recovery recorded in the 1990s, by 2000 African countries were still the slowest growing economies in the world. Indebtedness and poverty have increased as growth has been impaired by a combination of conflicts and instability, HIV/AIDS, weather, and adverse international terms of trade for African exports (African Development Bank, 2001). Social indicators also show a decrease in basic health and education for many countries even though secondary education has improved. African economies have increasingly relied on aid rather than trade. Such aid is often tied to donor criteria and has made these countries more dependent on donors for credit and policy advice. These arrangements have not enhanced their economic or democratic governance prospects.

An important outcome of democratic governance is that it opens up the political process to make and implement more transparent and responsive public policies, as a result of a variety of new actors participating in the policy process—legislatures, political parties, civil society/interest groups, research centers—and in some cases even civil service and local governments. These inputs make such public policies more rational in terms of factual content and make them more politically acceptable. This positive outcome constitutes the litmus test of good or better governance. Students of African political and economic institutions point to the long time it takes for these political institutions to develop the competence, capacity, and confidence to make positive inputs to the policy process. In fact, they may undermine that very process—leading to paralysis and policies that reflect group or private rather than public interests. Africa's past experiences at democratization in the immediate post-independence periods reinforce these arguments (Barkan & Okumu, 1984; Gyimah-Boadi, 1998; van de Walle, 2002).

This chapter provides a sense of how the authors approach our subject matter: the concept of governance, its links to institutional reform and public policy, and its capacity-building implications. While the framework acknowledges different approaches to studying or analyzing governance, it highlights the congenital link between governance and public policy.

African countries have witnessed profound governance changes since the beginning of the 1990s (Bratton & van de Walle, 1997; African Development Bank, 2001; van de Walle, 2002). As a result of a variety of domestic and external factors, a paradigm change in governance from autocracy to democracy has occurred as Table 1.1 makes evident. While the debates continue on the exact factors responsible for this change and the possibility of sustaining democracy in poor countries, this book poses a different set of questions—how does democratic governance transform into good or better governance? By the latter we mean public policies that are both technically efficient and effective and also responsive to the needs of large sections of the citizenry, if not the whole public. In other words, how do we reconcile political or people's power with expert knowledge? This is an important question as research on African democratic renewal shows that the demand for democracy by the mass of the people falls far short of its supply by African governments (Bratton & Mattes, 2001).

This book argues that democracy will be sustained in Africa only if the critical institutions that positively impact the public policy process are built and sustained. Since building and sustaining such institutional capacities are likely to be costly in real terms, successful capacity building for democracy requires effective development strategies, policies, and institutions. Democracy requires institutions that can make policies that are transparent, accountable, predictable, and participative, i.e. efficient and effective from the society's point of view (Schiavo-Campo & Sundaram, 1999). Without these, African democracies will remain "choiceless democracies" (Mkandawire, 1999).

Table 1.1 Africa's Governance Patterns

Institutions	Criteria	Liberal Democracy	Partial Democracy	Authoritarian
State	Accountability to Citizens	High	Limited	None
	Elections	Free, fair, competitive	Unfree, unfair, competitive	None
Civil Society	Civil & Political Rights	High	Limited	None
	Associational Autonomy	High	Compromised	Nonexistent
Sub-Saharan	1975	3	2	43
Africa	1995	12	16	12
	2001	20	24	4

Source: Base data and typology from Potter et al., 1997; Young, 1999; Bangura, 2000; van de Walle, 2002.

Approaches to Analyzing Governance, Institutional Reforms, and Public Policy

Hyden and Court provide a comprehensive analysis of governance conceptions in chapter two. It is important to note here that two major definitions of governance have gained currency in the rapidly growing academic and policy literature on the subject. In the most popular one, used by the World Bank and most other United Nations institutions, governance is defined as "the manner in which power is exercised in the management of a country's economic and social development" (World Bank, 1994:vii; see also United Nations Development Programme, 1997). Essentially, governance, as conceived by these multilateral organs, emphasizes leadership—the manner in which political (state) leaders manage, use, or misuse power—to promote social and economic development or to pursue agendas that undermine such goals. Good governance is conceived from a process perspective with emphasis on rule of law, accountability, participation, transparency, and human and civil rights. These elements are indistinguishable from governance elements of a mature liberal democracy (World Bank, 1989; Adamolekun, 1999; see Schiavo-Campo & Sundaram, 2000 and Leftwich, 1993 for a full critique).

A second approach to defining governance focuses on sharing authority for public management between state and nonstate organizations. Jan Kooimans (1993:2) and other European researchers define sociopolitical forms of governing as "forms in which public or private actors do not act separately but in conjunction, together, in combination, that is to say, co-arrangements." The school therefore views governance as forms of multi-organizational action rather than exclusively state actions. An important difference from the first approach is that governance is judged as good or bad by both processes as well as by outcomes: the use of state and nonstate institutional resources to solve social problems. This approach is also referred to as the partnership approach to governance.

The definition used in this book is closer to this second school of thought. Governance is approached, as it has always been understood in the political science literature, as the fundamental rules that regulate the relationships between rulers and the ruled, the rules-in-use, or constitutive choice rules and operating at deeper levels of analysis than collective and operational choice rules (Kiser & Ostrom, 1982; Ostrom, 1990; Hyden, 1992). The legal community (Okoth-Ogendo, 2000) refers to these constitutional rules as "ground-norms." Although primarily associated with the analysis of the state, governance is a generic term that can be applied to all forms of human organizations—economic, cultural, religious, or military.

The advantage of this third approach is that it enables us to suspend judgment on whether or not democratic reform is good or bad governance. A process-only approach seems to equate democratic change to good governance. But we know that governance might actually decline in some important respects under democratization—especially if the crucial institutions supposed to perform specific functions are weak or lacking. Process and outcomes are important in this approach, but from a process perspective governance can be classified in terms of the quality of the fundamental rules of the political game. While democratic governance promotes rules that ensure the fundamental equality between rulers and the ruled, autocratic forms assume and reify inequality between them. But the primary criteria for distinguishing between good and bad governance is the outcomes of policies promoted by public organs. Good governance results from the activities of public sector institutions as they work with other societal organizations to formulate public policies and programs, which are implemented to improve the people's welfare, reduce poverty, and realize other public and societal goals.

But this is exactly where these countries experience their most difficult challenges. Countries at incipient stages of democracy do not possess the full array of institutional tools they require to tackle the economic and social challenges they are confronted with. The situation is even worse when these countries are poor and heavily dependent economically, technologically, and in the case of Africa, even fiscally.

According to the African Capacity Building Foundation (ACBF), only a couple of years ago capacity building was widely regarded as the missing link in African development. African countries pursued policies that undermined both the supply and demand of human resource and institutional capacities (Olowu, 1998). This book links this concept with the good governance discourse. If it is possible to identify realms of governance—political, economic, and societal—as argued by the UNDP (1997) using a three-dimensional governance perspective incorporating all three realms, one of the important policy issues raised by the governance discourse is to audit and estimate the capacity of the critical social institutions required to make and implement policies that promote good governance in each of these realms. This book therefore focuses not only on the governance changes taking place but also identifies the capacity available and needed for good or better governance in different realms: in the private as well as the public sector, in the central and local government, in state as well as in civil society, and in economic as well as political realms. If it is indeed the case, as argued by Gene Ogiogio and Grace Ongile that " . . . there is shortage of capacity in virtually every sector and every country in sub-Saharan country," what must be done to transform the situation to ensure a good governance outcome?

Contemporary experience teaches that institutions for coupling knowledge with societal interest are best built from the community level up. However, African countries have attempted to construct these institutions from the top-down, leading to several adverse outcomes (Wunsch & Olowu, 1990). This may explain why African public policy processes in the years before governance change were opaque and increasingly devoid of analytical inputs from the people or knowledgeable experts who could engage the technical aspects of the policy (Mutahaba & Balogun, 1992). The capacity to utilize available institutional resources in tackling social problems must be acquired and calls for new rule systems for managing the whole spectrum of the public policy processes—formulation, implementation, and evaluation—in these countries. This is especially the case because the problems confronting many African countries have both domestic and external dimensions, and it is important these countries respond to these challenges effectively, responsibly, and at times collectively as a region. A number of countries in the region have embraced these fundamental reforms, and some of these are captured in the chapters that follow.

Overview of the Chapters

The book has three parts: conceptual and analytical perspectives, a review of capacity-building challenges, and a set of regional, subregional, and country cases studies. In chapter two, Goran Hyden and Julius Court provide a comprehensive analysis of governance conceptions as well as the methodological problems of measuring governance. They identify four strands that define governance—as activity or process and as rules or controls. They then adapt the structural-functional model to analyze governance for a World Governance survey, currently under way. They also measure governance along six main lines—socialization, aggregation, execution, management, regulation, and adjudication.

In chapter three O. P. Dwivedi distinguishes between common good and good governance. By reviewing the philosophical, policy, and administrative literature, to which he has contributed substantially over the years, he concludes that governance raises not only institutional and constitutional issues but also spiritual, ethical, and moral agendas.

Chapter four, by Dele Olowu, appraises governance changes in Africa in the last two decades and their implications for institutional reform and public policy processes. The chapter highlights a paradox: several of the institutions in many developing countries predicted by democratic theory to lead the policy process are in fact not ineffective or are nonfunctional. Other institutional organs, especially external multilateral agencies, have taken up this role. Olowu argues that, in order to fully realize their potential, countries must focus on five key strategic policy institutions: parliaments, judicial organs, higher education, civil service institutions, and local governments.

Part II contains four chapters on capacity building. Coeditor Sousmana Sako provides a sense of the capacity requirements in the public and private sectors. He also discusses the crucial challenges of boosting institutional capacities of public, private, and civil society organizations in a region where all these institutions are weak.

In chapter six Gene Ogiogio and Grace Ongile discuss how ACBF has helped nurture public policy centers in many African countries, especially since ACBF's mandate was expanded to support noneconomic activities and institutions. ACBF uses a model of capacity building, which focuses on building capacities within and outside economic development or planning ministries. These policy centers or think tanks work within and outside government, but they are also funded as semiautonomous organs, many of which are located in universities. Chapter six focuses on some of the problems of the current model.

In chapter seven, Vasant Moharir reviews the relationship between governance and policy analysis. He suggests the use of six criteria for making decisions that will lead to good governance: effectiveness, efficiency, responsiveness, innovation, political feasibility, and administrative feasibility. These criteria reinforce the links between governance, institutions, and public policies.

The final chapter in Part II, by Paschal Mihyo, combines a regional and global perspective on economic governance as related to African countries. This chapter provides a detailed account of new European Union environmental regulations and reviews their potential impact on access to Africa's exports to European countries.

Chapter nine, by Mohamed Salih, begins Part III of the book, which contains regional, subregional, and national case studies. This chapter focuses on environmental governance in Eastern and Southern Africa and poses a number of questions: Are environmental policies, action plans, and conservation strategies working? What are the main constraints? Are these constraints surmountable? This chapter argues that countries in this region have become increasingly influenced by the resolutions of global forums, negotiations, conventions, treaties, and declarations based on the emerging concept of global environmental governance. Both governmental and nongovernmental institutions are involved in the environmental policy processes but governments have relied on legal rather than economic incentives for the implementation of these policies. Nevertheless, there remains increased awareness on environmental issues at the national level, and new policies are being developed that integrate economic and environmental activities towards sustainable development.

The last four chapters are national case studies of governance changes and their implications for institutional reforms and public policy processes in Ghana, Nigeria, Zambia, and Namibia. In chapter ten, Eloho Otobo examines the policy processes for Nigeria's privatization programme under the present civilian administration. In chapter eleven, Joseph Ayee focuses on governance and policy outcomes in Ghana. Dirk Hansohm in chapter twelve discusses the relationship between research and economic policy in Namibia. In chapter thirteen, Roy Mukwena and Peter Lolojih discuss decentralization and local government reforms in the post–Kaunda Third Republic in Zambia.

The book as a whole provides a broad spectrum of insights for understanding the relationships between governance change, institutional reforms, and policy outcomes. The reality of governance change in most of the African countries is undeniable. The end of cold war, globalization, democratization, and other pressures—demographic changes and the role of external and internal actors in the policy processes—are bound to impact policy outcomes. The available evidence, provided in this book and by other literature, points to the need to focus on developing capacities for crucial institutions of governance at global, regional, national, and community levels. This process of change will not produce results in the short term but over the long haul, democratic change might be transformed into good governance. The opposite is also possible if these lessons are ignored.

References

Adamolekun, L. 1999. *Public Administration in Africa: Main Issues and Selected Countries.* Boulder, Colo.: Westview Press.

African Development Bank. 2001. *African Development Report 2001.* Oxford: Oxford University Press.

Barkan, J. and J. Okumu, eds. 1984. *Politics and Public Policy in Kenya and Tanzania.* New York: Praeger.

Bratton, M. and N. van de Walle. 1997. *Democratic Experiments in Africa: Regime Transitions in Comparative Perspective.* New York: Cambridge University Press.

Bratton, M. and R. Mattes. 2001. "Africans' Surprising Universalism." *Journal of Democracy* 12 (1): 107–121.

Dia, M. 1996. *Africa's Management in the 1990s and Beyond: Reconciling Indigenous and Transplanted Institutions.* Washington D.C.: World Bank.

Dornboos, Martin. 2001. "'Good Governance': The Rise and Decline of a Policy Metaphor?" *Journal of Development Studies* 37 (6): 93–108.

Hyden, G. 1992. "Governance and the Study of Politics" Pp. 1–26 in G. Hyden and M. Bratton, eds. *Governance and Politics in Africa.* Boulder, Colo.: Lynne Rienner.

Hyden, G. D. Olowu, and Okoth-Ogendo, eds. 2000. *African Perspectives on Governance.* North Trenton, N.J.: Red Sea Press.

Kiser, Larry L., and Elinor. 1982. "Three Worlds of Action: A Metaphorical Synthesis of Institutional Approaches." In *Strategies of Political Inquiry*, ed. Elinor Ostrom, pp. 179–222. Beverly Hills, CA: Sage. Reprinted in McGinnis 1999a.

Kooimans, J., ed. 1993. *Modern Governance: New Government–Society Interaction.* London: Sage.

Leftwich A. 1993. "Governance, Democracy and Development in the Third World." *Third World Quarterly* 14 (3): 605–624.

Mkandawire, T. 1993. "Crisis Management and the Making of Choiceless Democracies." Pp. 119–136 in R. Joseph, ed. *State, Conflict, and Democracy in Africa.* Boulder, Colo.: Lynne Rienner.

Mutahaba, G. and J. Balogun, eds. 1992. *Enhancing Policy Management Capacity in Africa.* West Hartford, Conn.: Kumarian Press.

Myers, C. N. 1997. "Policy Research Institutes in Developing Countries." Pp. 177–198 in M. Grindle, ed. *Getting Good Government: Capacity Building in the Public Sectors of Developing Countries.* Cambridge, Mass.: Harvard University Press.

Okoth-Ogendo, W. 2000. "The Quest for Constitutional Government." Pp. 33–60
in G. Hyden, D. Olowu, and W. Okoth-Ogendo, eds. *African Perspectives on
Governance*. Trenton, N.J.: Africa World Press.

Olowu, D. 1998. "Building Critical Capacities for Sustainable Development in
Africa: Matters Arising." *International Journal of Technical Cooperation* 4 (1):
1–19.

Ostrom, E. 1990. *Governing the Commons: The Evolution of Institutions for Collective
Action*. Cambridge: Cambridge University Press.

Ostrom V. 1997. *The Meaning of Democracy and the Vulnerability of Democracies*. Ann
Arbor: University of Michigan Press.

Potter, D., D. Goblatt, M. Kiloh, and P. Lewis. 1997. *Democratization*. Cambridge,
Mass.: Polity Press/Open University.

Schiavo-Campo, S. and P. Sundaram. 2001. *Improving Public Administration in a
Competitive World*. Manila: Asian Development Bank.

United Nations Development Programme. 1997. *Reconceptualizing Governance*.
Discussion Paper No. 2. New York, Management Development and Governance Division.

United Nations Economic Commission for Africa. 1999. *Economic Report for Africa*.
Addis Ababa: UNECA.

van de Walle, N. 2002. "Africa's Range of Regimes." *Journal of Democracy* 13 (2):
66–80.

World Bank. 1989. *From Crisis to Sustainable Development: Africa's Long-Term Perspective*. Washington D.C.: World Bank.

World Bank. 1992. *Governance: The World Bank's Experience*. Washington D.C.:
World Bank.

Wunsch, J. S. and D. Olowu, eds. *The Failure of the Centralized State: Institutions
and Self Governance in Africa*. New York: Westview Press, 1990. (Second Edition, Institute of Contemporary Studies, 1995).

Part I

Conceptual and Analytical Perspectives

2

Comparing Governance Across Countries and Over Time: Conceptual Challenges

Goran Hyden and Julius Court

Governance is by no means a new concept. It has been a recurrent theme in the literature on politics ever since people began to reflect upon how they are being ruled. This theme can be traced to Plato and Aristotle in ancient Greece. Relevant ideas were also at the heart of enlightenment thinking in the eighteenth and nineteenth centuries, followed by the work of Weber and Schumpeter. What is new, however, is the meteoric rise over the last ten years of governance as a key concept in the international development debate. This marks an intriguing transformation in focus from micro to macro issues. It also poses fresh challenges to those interested in relating socioeconomic outcomes to macro interventions.

After ten years of efforts to make sense of governance, many basic challenges remain. What do we really mean by governance? How can we meaningfully measure it? What would a universal scale of measuring the quality of governance look like? How important is governance compared to other factors that may shape development outcomes?

A brief review of the literature highlights governance quality as the most critical variable in promoting development across the world. The development crisis in Africa has been described as a "crisis of governance" (World Bank, 1989). In contrast, the importance of good governance has been highlighted as one of the "big lessons" of the period of rapid growth in East Asia (Root, 1996). A recent report noted, "The reasons for South Asia's colossal human deprivation are rooted in poor governance" (HDC, 1999). Much work on Latin America highlights the challenges of shifting from authoritarian regimes towards building effective democracy (Linz and Stepan, 1996).

These national and regional findings are being buttressed by empirical work. The 1997 World Development Report found evidence that certain governance indicators are important for growth. Data on institutional issues are increasingly included in cross-country growth regressions, giving empirical support to the assertion that "governance matters" (Kaufman et al., 1999a). There is also growing evidence of the consequences of poor governance for ordinary citizens. A recent World Bank–funded study (Narayan et al., 2000) highlights powerlessness and voicelessness as crucial elements of poverty as stated by the poor themselves.

Governance, however, is not only an issue in developing countries. The retreat of communism and the end of the bipolar structure of international relations have not only paved the way for the spread of liberal democratic norms to various corners of the world, but it has also exposed weaknesses in the Western democracies themselves. Many citizens in these countries maintain that current forms of democratic governance are void of content. The Gallup *Millennium Survey* (the largest-ever global public opinion survey, covering sixty countries) highlights strong dissatisfaction around the world with the way democracy works. Even when societies are considered to be democratic, there is often a sense of impotence about the inefficient, unresponsive, and unjust ways in which governance takes place (Sprogard and James, 2000).

This chapter classifies the approaches taken in different strands of the literature as well as by different actors in the international community. It then disaggregates the governance realm into six dimensions—from the extent of participation in the political process to institutions created for dispute resolution, highlights the rationale for a rights-based approach and outlines six emerging principles of good governance; outlines thirty indicators to capture national perceptions of governance; and outlines a framework for analysis.

Defining Governance

Despite the recent popularity of governance at both the practical and theoretical levels, the concept continues to mean different things to different people. Academics and practitioners often talk past one another, as do scholars in different academic disciplines. A review of the literature, however, suggests that these differences tend to crystallize along two separate lines, one regarding the substantive content of governance, the other regarding its character in practice. Along the first line, there are, on the one hand, those who view governance as concerned with the rules of conducting public affairs, and, on the other, those who see it as steering or controlling public affairs. One might say that the rules approach tends to emphasize the institutional determinants of choice, while the steering approach concentrates on how choices get implemented.

For the steering approach, the difference is between governance as activity or as process. Some analysts treat governance as reflected in human intention and action, since it is possible to see the results of governance interventions. Others, however, view governance as an ongoing phenomenon that is hard to pin down but which affects how results are achieved. Practitioners tend to adopt the former approach; academics often end up taking the latter position. As Figure 1 illustrates, one can identify four major positions on how governance has been defined and used. Students of public administration share with analysts and practitioners in international development agencies the notion that governance is about steering and control, but they differ in that the former regard it as a process while the latter see it as an activity. For example, representatives of the donor community wish to see measurable results of governance—hence their concern with developing results-based indicators. Students of public administration, on the other hand, are content with recognizing that managing public affairs—and thus controlling outcomes—is no longer confined to traditional jurisdictions but influenced by processes that transcend such boundaries. International relations scholars share with students of comparative politics the notion that governance is about the rules of the game while they have divergent views on its character, the former treating it as process, the latter as activity. For example, students of international relations recognize that creating new rules for global governance is a process involving multiple actors at different levels, and thus the difficulty of overcoming tendencies among national governments to stick with realist principles. Comparativists, by contrast, especially those studying democratization, look at governance as a voluntarist act that can make a positive difference.

To help sort out the basic issues surrounding the uses of the concept, it may be helpful to elaborate a little on each of these four positions. Beginning with public administration, it is interesting to note that governance has emerged as a popular way of dealing with the fact that conventional jurisdictional boundaries of administration no longer have the same exclusivity as in the past. Substantive issues cut across these boundaries. Formulation and implementation of policy, therefore, often require cooperation among representatives of different organizations. This was first noted by European scholars as they studied the effects of European integration and the growth of new institutional formulas in the social welfare sector. In one of the first and more comprehensive treatments of governance from a public administration perspective, Kooiman (1993) and

Figure 2.1 Different Uses of the Governance Concept

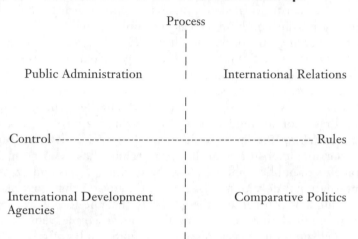

his collaborators argue that governance is composed of purposeful action to guide, steer, and control society. They recognize that this is not achieved with a single measure, but is a process that takes time and involves both governmental and nongovernmental organizations. Governance, they argue, consists of the regularized, institutional patterns that emerge from the interactions of these organizations. Their view of governance reflects the normative change that took place in Europe in the 1980s when economic liberalization reduced the role of the welfare state as the sole agent of policy implementation and paved the way for public-private partnerships. Needs are no longer confined to society, or capacity to govern. Rather, needs and capacities are both public and private. They are embedded in both state and society in their mutual interdependencies.

Thus, governance transcends the conventional boundaries of public administration. This point is also underscored by other students of European governments such as Rhodes (1997) and Pierre and Peters (2000), for whom self-organizing, interorganizational networks constitute the essential ingredients of the governance process. In the context of a disarticulated state, i.e., one with reduced capacity to solve public problems, it is in governance theory that public administration gets to wrestle with problems of representation, political control of bureaucracy, and the democratic legitimacy of institutions and networks.

This view is also shared by a growing number of students of public administration in the United States. Although the impetus for turning to governance has been primarily the issue of the disconnect between the scope of public issues and the jurisdictional boundaries of public agencies, this group tends to approach governance similarly to their European counterparts. Thus, for example, Lynn, Heinrich, and Hill (1999) argue that governance links values and interest of citizens, legislative choice, executive and organizational structures and roles, and judicial oversight in a way that suggests interrelationships among them that can have significant consequences for performance. Governance is a process that brings administrators into new collaborative relations in which the prospect for results is deemed to be better than within conventional organizational settings.

The international relations literature on governance emerged after the collapse of communism and the bipolar world order. This new perspective accepts that interdependence is an increasingly important feature of the new world order and argues that this order calls for commonly accepted norms, rules, and patterns of behavior that facilitate international cooperation (Holsti, 1992). Contrary to the realist or neorealist approach to international politics that stresses the overwhelming importance of perceived national interest, governance is typically associated with a constructivist approach, in which rules as regimes are viewed as key ingredients for stabilizing international relations. Cooperation across both national and issue boundaries requires the initiation of a process involving actors ready to transcend narrow national concerns. Thus governance as, for example, Rosenau (1992) and Redfern and Desai (1997) argue, is a process involving multiple actors in the international arena that produces new norms and rules for working together to solve global problems or conflicts.

Interest in governance among students of comparative politics has also emerged as a result of the collapse of communism. Their study of the rules of the game is associated with the increasing global concern to bring about democracy. In this context, governance is studied as part of regime transition. In a first attempt to delineate the concept, Hyden (1992:7) defines governance as the "conscious management of regime structures with a view to enhancing the legitimacy of the public realm." By focusing on rules as reflected in regime structures and how they are managed, this view of governance emphasizes the normative framework within which public decisions and policies are made. It calls for attention to constitutional and legal issues in ways that are not addressed by conventional political economy studies focusing on how resources are allocated. Governance is a product of human agency—hence an activity—that helps define the relations and interactions between state and society. March and Olsen (1998:6) adopt a similar perspective when they argue that governance "involves affecting the framework within which citizens and [state] officials act and politics occurs." Their view of governance as institutional framework for realizing democratic ideals also tallies with the interpretation by public administration scholars in that it recognizes the revision of rules in order to meet the demands of more complex societal systems.

Governance and International Development Agencies

While international development agencies tend to agree about governance as an activity aimed at steering societies in desired directions, they have typically adopted the concept to suit their own programmatic needs. Their entry points differ. The United Nations Development Programme, for example, has adopted a definition of governance as "the exercise of economic, political, and administrative authority to manage a country's affairs at all levels" (UNDP, 1997:2–3). In this perspective, governance comprises the mechanisms, processes, and institutions through which citizens and groups articulate their interests, exercise their legal rights, meet their obligations, and mediate their conflicts. Governance is said to have three legs: economic, political, and administrative. Economic governance includes decision-making processes that affect a country's economic activities and its relationship with other economies. Political governance involves the formulation of policy, while administrative governance is the system of policy implementation. As can be seen from this and similar definitions used by international development agencies, governance is an all-encompassing concept. It permeates all sectors and makes no distinction between governance, policy-making, and policy implementation.

The World Bank has its own interpretation of governance that is of special interest because its official mandate prevents it from dealing with political issues. To cope with this, the Bank distinguishes between governance as an analytic framework and governance as an operational framework, leading it to identify three aspects of governance: (1) the form of political regime, (2) the process by which authority is exercised in the management of a country's economic and social resources for development, and (3) the capacity of governments to design, formulate, and implement policies and discharge functions (World Bank, 1992). The Bank professes to confine itself only to the second and third aspects of governance, but it has found itself under increasing pressure from Western bilateral donors to address the first as well. Its recent recognition of human rights as an essential aspect of governance seems to manifest this extended operational use of the concept.

The problem with the definitions used by international development agencies is twofold. By being a catch-all concept it fails to make distinctions that are important for any attempt to assess governance. In this way it very much resembles the notion of development management that was employed in the 1970s to identify what governments in developing countries were doing. More specifically, it fails to make a distinction between governance, policy, and administration. Governance folds into the latter two but has no distinct meaning. Thus it is difficult to know whether governance is actually the quality of policy-making and implementation rather than something peculiar known as governance that really is supposed to make a difference. For example, it is quite possible that the same kind of governance set-up in two separate countries may produce different outcomes because of variations in policy formulation or implementation capacity. Secondly, by watering down its political character, governance loses its distinction in relation to the economy. Where does governance begin and end as a variable expected to cause specific outcomes? How can one meaningfully say something about the impact of governance unless it has some specificity? These are the definitional challenges that face any attempt to survey perceptions of governance in a systematic and measurable manner.

For the UNU World Governance Survey project, the definition of governance focuses on the importance of rules rather than results. Governance is treated as both activity and process in the sense that it reflects human intention and agency but is itself a process that sets the parameters for how policy is made and implemented. Analytically speaking, governance becomes a meta activity that influences outcomes, such as reducing transaction costs and protecting human rights, depending on the nature of the rules adopted. With this in mind, we propose the following definition:

> Governance refers to the formation and stewardship of the formal and informal rules that regulate the public realm, the arena in which state as well as economic and societal actors interact to make decisions.

Governance, then, refers to behavioral dispositions rather than technical capacities. It is a quality of the political system that in the current development debate serves as an independent variable, i.e., as an explanatory factor. In this perspective, governance deals with the constitutive side of how a political system operates rather than its distributive or allocative aspects that are more directly a function of policy. Table 2.1 illustrates how governance is conceived and how it relates to other concepts that international development agencies tend to fuse it with.

These different levels are empirically interconnected, but there are good reasons for keeping them analytically apart. Rules are, empirically speaking, set at different levels. For example, a community may decide to change the rules by which its members abide in order to improve the

Table 2.1 Governance and Its Relations to Other Concepts and Activities

Level	Activity	Concept
Meta	Politics	Governance
Macro	Policy	Policy-Making
Meso	Program	Public Administration
Micro	Project	Management

prospects of a better life. Such a revision of rules—the local community regime—bears on how decisions are made and implemented or how singular project activities are managed. Governance is also present at higher levels, ultimately in terms of establishing and managing constitutional principles at national or international levels.

With this definition of the concept, it is also possible to sustain the distinction between a constitutive and distributive side of politics. What is new in the contemporary international setting is that the distributive side is no longer solely important. The classical political economy question, originally attributed to Harold Lasswell, of "who gets what, when, and how?" that underlay previous approaches to development is now being challenged by another important concern: "who sets what rules, when, and how?" This constitutive side of politics needs to be highlighted and emphasized in the name of governance because it is fresh—and overlooked if not differentiated from the concerns derived from policy of how resources are allocated. Governance does not influence such outcomes directly, although by changing the rules for how policies are made, it may do so indirectly. The best analogy to explain our approach is that governance is to policy and administration what road is to car. The nature of the car ride depends on the quality of the road on which it travels. In sum, perceptions of the regime within which policies are made and acted upon will vary depending on the effects of formal and informal rules on what can or cannot be done.

If governance is about rules, the question inevitably arises as to which rules are important for shaping policy processes and, by extension, development outcomes. Given the connection to policy, implementation, and development, the choice made here is to focus on the various dimensions of the political process that produce outcomes. The assumption is that how the political process is structured—how state, society, and economy interact—is important for development.

In deciding what dimensions are important, it may be helpful to examine the functions associated with how policy comes about. This allows us to reduce normative biases associated with the way governance has been applied so far. Yet, by virtue of its inclusivity, this functional approach covers what most analysts and agencies consider relevant and important. It also makes specific references to the various arenas in which these functions are performed and the purpose of the rules associated with each function. The scheme is summarized in Table 2.2.

The following sections elaborate on the rationale and the substantive content of each dimension.

The Socializing Dimension

This dimension refers to the first phase of the political process: how persons get familiar with and interested in public issues and how rules tend to affect the articulation of interests from society. The way rules are constituted to channel participation in public affairs is generally considered an important aspect of governance. For example, much of the recent literature on democratization indicates the important role that citizens have played in reshaping the rules so as to enhance their own input into the making of public policy. Putnam's study (1993) of making democracy work in Italy is a case in point. He emphasizes, like Tocqueville before him, the importance of local associations in building trust and confidence both in institutions and among people.

In Latin America as well as Eastern Europe, political reforms have been the result of political socialization in the context of social movements, intensified political communication, and an enhanced articulation

Table 2.2 The Functional Dimensions of Governance and Their Institutional Arenas

Functional Dimension	Institutional Arena	Purpose of Rules
Socializing	Civil Society	To shape the way citizens raise and become aware of public issues
Aggregating	Political Society	To shape the way issues are combined into policy by political institutions
Executive	Government	To shape the way policies are made by government institutions
Managerial	Bureaucracy	To shape the way policies are administered and implemented by public servants
Regulatory	Economic Society	To shape the way state and market interact to promote development
Adjudicatory	Judicial System	To shape the setting for resolution of disputes and conflicts

of interests that previously were latent for fear of public authority. As Juan Linz and Alfred Stepan (1996) note in their account of the democratic transition and consolidation in these two regions, civil society was rightly considered the celebrity of democratic resistance and transition in many countries. However, the opportunity for articulating citizen voices on public issues is still limited in many countries. A recent global survey also found that not having a voice in policy formulation is a source of frustration even in countries where elections are regularly held (Sprogard and James, 2000). On a more positive note, at the micro level, World Bank research (Isham et al., 1995) shows that water projects with citizen participation are better designed and constructed, and participation enhances the likelihood of sustained support required for long-term maintenance of such schemes. Much more evidence could be garnered for support of the position that it matters how civil society is organized. Suffice it to say here that for any survey of how governance relates to development, this dimension is of doubtless significance.

The Aggregating Dimension

This dimension refers to the ways a political system is organized to facilitate and control the making of public policy. It deals with how ideas and interests are aggregated into specific policy proposals. This arena is often referred to as political society, i.e., the place where public demands get tackled by specific political institutions. Rules for aggregating policy vary. One major distinction in democratic polities is between pluralist (competitive) and corporatist (directive) systems. Many authoritarian regimes find the transition at the political society level especially difficult since rules at this level tend to dictate who gets power. Thus, the design of electoral systems influences the party system, and the party system influences the way the legislature operates. Countries in political transition tend to prefer a presidential system rather than a parliamentary one on the assumption— often mistaken—that a strong executive can control political society and provide greater political stability. Much has been written on this subject based on the experience of a broad range of countries, especially those in Latin America (see Stepan and Skach, 1996). In recent years, many of the governance concerns of the international community have also centered on this dimension. Designing electoral systems, monitoring elections to assess their fairness, as well as strengthening the technical capacity of parliaments to be effective in making policy and holding public officials accountable are measures that the international community has sponsored in developing and transitional countries. Think-tanks and other institutions that try to assess progress toward democracy give particular attention to the rules affecting performance of political society.

The Executive Dimension

Governments do not just make policies. They are also responsible for creating a climate in which people enjoy peace and security. The rules that government set to shape the relation between state and society in the broader security area are of growing importance, not only in societies in transition but also in established political systems. One important issue is how the political leadership structures its relations with the military. In many transitional societies, the military has held political power in the past and is unlikely to relinquish it without setting certain conditions. These rules in turn are likely to affect people's perception of governance. Dealing with violence and poverty in society is another set of issues that transcends the boundaries of individual policy and enters the governance realm. What rules, formal and informal, do governments put in place to meet popular expectations of freedom from fear and want? These are systemic concerns for which government is ultimately responsible. Taking on these issues is not easy, and many governments are unwilling to face the challenge (see Campos and Nugent, 1999).

The Managerial Dimension

This dimension refers to how the policy implementation machinery is organized. The central arena in this context is the bureaucracy. Public servants working in such organizations are engaged in formulating and implementing policy and delivering services. Their public impact, however, comes foremost from their most visible role in carrying out policy. How bureaucracy is structured and how it relates to the political leadership have been issues of great significance to academics and practitioners alike ever since the days of Max Weber some one-hundred years ago. The idea that rules must be legal-rational, i.e. formal and logical, has dominated, especially in modern democracies. Many assume that bureaucracy can function efficiently and effectively only in such conditions (see Blau, 1963, 1964). Others, however, have also pointed to the problems of combining formal rules and procedures with positive substantive outcomes. Bureaucracy in this type of study is viewed in negative terms (see Crozier, 1965). Comparative studies of how bureaucratic rules affect economic development have emerged in recent years (e.g. Evans and Rauch, 2000). They indicate the importance of viewing bureaucracy in the context not only of individual policy implementation but also in governance, since its rules and procedures tend to influence how people perceive the political system at large. As we know, citizens' contacts with government are often with first-level bureaucrats responsible for processing requests for services and assistance.

The Regulatory Dimension

State–market relations have become increasingly important for governance. No less an advocate of the invisible hand of the market than Adam Smith acknowledged that the state is necessary to perform certain economic functions. Most important of these is to deal with market failures—situations when the market fails to aggregate private choices in an optimal fashion. State institutions, therefore, are often created and called upon to regulate the economy. This arena is sometimes referred to as economic society, a term that we borrow from Linz and Stepan (1996). One frequent assumption is that when private firms have an opportunity to influence the way rules are formulated and implemented, this regulatory dimension is more effectively managed, making policy better and also enhancing regime legitimacy among key economic actors. The norms and institutions put in place to regulate how corporations operate, how property is owned and protected, as well as how capital may be transferred and trade conducted are all important aspects of governance. This subject has gained greater prominence in recent years through theorists such as Douglass North (1990). The compatibility of market and democracy is also a subject of study by Przeworski (1991) and Dryzek (1996). This regulatory dimension figures significantly in the strategies of many development agencies, which view economic liberalization as a precondition for political democracy.

The Adjudicatory Dimension

Each political system develops its own structures for conflict and dispute resolution. How such institutions operate has a great bearing on popular perceptions of regime performance. For example, persons who have been maltreated by public officials or find themselves in conflict with others must have an authoritative instance to call upon for a fair hearing. The importance of this dimension has been recognized by political theorists such as John Locke (1946, 1960) and Montesquieu (1970) as well as by anthropologists such as Gluckman (1965). The adjudicatory function, however, goes beyond the boundaries of individual cases to include how conflicts between groups in society, and even conflicts with other countries, are handled. What rules apply to resolving such conflicts is an important governance question. The legal culture that develops as a result of how arbitration in this broader sense is carried out is important for how people perceive not only the judiciary but also the political system at large. While the notion of rule of law is important, many societies also have informal mechanisms for resolving conflicts between government and private actors. Such is the case, for example, in many Asian countries. The adjudicatory dimension is important for governance, particularly in developing and transitional societies where rules are in flux. How rules can be stabilized and turned into institutions that enjoy the confidence of citizens is vital.

Measuring Governance

Measuring governance poses challenges not encountered in the economic or social development fields. It is possible to provide firm indicators of economic growth, level of unemployment, primary school enrollment, and so forth. It is much more difficult to find and agree upon indicators of a political macro phenomenon such as governance. Attempts to do so, such as by Kaufmann, Kraay, and Zoido-Lobaton (1999), confirm this difficulty but also indicate that aggregate measures of such phenomena as rule of law are useful. More and better data are needed to provide a firmer basis for identifying statistically significant differences in governance across countries as well as for country-specific, in-depth governance diagnostics. The World Governance Survey is an attempt to generate coherent and systematic data needed.

What constitutes good governance? The tendency in international development circles has been to treat it as a synonym for liberal democracy. In other words, features found in the political systems of Western societies have been elevated by the dominant international development agencies to the level of being universally desirable. There are understandable reasons for such a move. With the collapse of the communist systems—at least the majority of them—liberal democracies can claim that they have proved to be most sustainable. They continue to enjoy an acceptable level of legitimacy and even though they do not work perfectly, they combine efficiency with justice in ways that other systems do not. Nonetheless, many countries around the world question liberal democratic values as the basis for better governance, and leaders and citizens in these countries see calls for good governance as a cover for extending Western influence. In short, any attempt to measure governance is fraught with controversy about which norms should prevail.

What can be done in these circumstances? The most suitable approach is to turn to the human rights arena, because here, at least officially, the broadest consensus on what constitutes good governance may be found. Although the issue of human rights also generates discussion, there is broad support for the principles that form the basis for a broad range of international declarations in this arena. More specifically, the Universal Declaration of Human Rights (UDHR)—the secular equivalent of the Ten

Commandments or similar statements in other major religions around the world—was signed by 58 Member States of the United Nations in 1948. More recently, 171 countries reaffirmed their commitment to the UDHR at the World Conference on Human Rights in Vienna in 1993. In addition, every country in the world has ratified at least one of the six principal human rights treaties. And over half the countries of the world have ratified all six principal human rights treaties—up from just 10 percent just a decade ago. A special millennium survey conducted by Gallup International indicates that the protection of human rights is of great concern to ordinary people around the world. The same survey also shows that people believe that governments are not doing enough to address human rights problems (Sprogard and James, 2000). Although defining exactly what constitutes universal values will continue to be a source of controversy, there is clearly a growing global consensus to move in that direction. The most suitable basis for any effort to measure governance, therefore, is the growing consensus about the significance of human rights in the development debate.

A rights-based approach to governance and development has a number of advantages. First, it shifts the focus from government to citizen. Good governance is a public good that citizens should be entitled to. Second, by focusing on entitlements, this approach recognizes that poverty is not just a matter of being economically deprived but is defined and sustained by a sense on the part of the poor of helplessness, dependence, lack of opportunities, and lack of self-confidence and self-respect. The language of rights makes clear that the poor are not the subject of charity and benevolence by governments or the rich, that they are entitled to a decent standard of living, and that rights are the vehicles for their participation and empowerment. As Amartya Sen (1999) argues, development should include a broad range of freedoms or rights such as the basic capabilities to avoid starvation, undernourishment, or premature mortality, as well as rights to education and to participation in the political process. This argument is reflected in the 2000 Human Development Report (UNDP, 2000), in the discussion of the relationship between human rights and human development approaches.

Third, a rights-based approach draws attention to the importance of norms and rules. How a society is governed and how it achieves its development is as important in this perspective as what these processes accomplish. Thus the World Governance Survey is justifiably focusing on rules, not just results. In this view, the quantitative indicators of development—social or economic—should be analyzed in terms of how they were achieved. What scope do regimes leave for citizens to enjoy their rights? How these rules, aggregated into a particular political regime, are perceived gives us clues to how good governance is.

The following is a series of basic principles that reflect the emerging global consensus of what should and could constitute good governance:

- Participation: the degree of involvement and ownership of affected stakeholders;
- Fairness: the degree to which rules apply equally to everyone in society regardless of status;
- Transparency: the degree to which decisions made by public officials are clear and open to scrutiny by citizens or their representatives;
- Decency: the degree to which the formation and stewardship of rules are undertaken without humiliation of or harm to the people;
- Accountability: the degree to which public officials, elected as well as appointed, are responsible for their actions and responsive to public demands;
- Efficiency: the degree to which rules facilitate speedy and timely decision-making.

The assumption is that the more governance is undertaken according to the principles outlined above, the better it is. In arriving at the choice of these principles, the World Governance Survey draws on already existing approaches to governance by various development agencies but transcends them by not being tied to specific programmatic concerns. It is meant to provide an independent assessment of governance that may serve as a backdrop against which these agencies can compare their own measures.

Governance Indicators

The World Governance Survey is meant to capture subjective perceptions of governance at the national level and is expected to gather data on the most important meta-level issues relating to governance. Although information on some of these issues is already available through other instruments, this survey is designed to be comprehensive and provide the basis for cross-country comparisons. Data from these other sources, e.g. Freedom House, Transparency International, or the Economist Intelligence Unit, should therefore provide useful points of reference and comparison.

In selecting indicators and creating the basis for systematic and relevant data analysis, two considerations have been of special importance. The first is the number of indicators to include, which affects how detailed or disaggregated any measure will be. In striking a balance between being comprehensive and analytically manageable, the survey consists of thirty indicators, or five indicators per governance dimension. These are inevitably aggregate variables, but we believe that they are meaningful and often more significant in understanding governance than more specific measures. The survey, therefore, is not meant to probe governance issues in depth within individual countries but rather provides the basis for an aggregate assessment of governance over time within (and between) countries. In so doing, it is expected to serve as a springboard for country-specific governance surveys and debates. The second consideration is whether each dimension is of equal importance. Should they be weighted equally? The World Governance Survey is being designed on the premise that each dimension and each indicator does indeed carry the same weight—each is made up of five indicators using the same rating scale. Changing the weighting of governance dimensions would make the analysis more difficult and arbitrary.

The thirty indicators chosen for the pilot phase of the survey are summarized under each dimension.

1. ***The Socializing Dimension***
    i. *Freedom of Expression.* How rules affect people's opportunities to seek, receive, and impart information in public reflecting UDHR Article 19.
    ii. *Freedom of Peaceful Association.* The extent to which citizens can form and belong to associations of their choice, reflecting the content of UDHR Article 20.
    iii. *Freedom from Discrimination.* The level of tolerance between individuals and groups in society, reflecting the concerns raised in UDHR Article 2.
    iv. *Opportunity for Consultation.* The extent to which government engages in consultation with citizens on public issues.
    v. *Public Duties.* The extent to which citizens respect the rules that are necessary to achieve common and public goods.

2. ***The Aggregating Dimension***
    i. *Representativeness of Legislature.* The extent to which the legislature represents society at large, reflecting concerns in UDHR Article 21.
    ii. *Political Competition.* The extent to which power can be contested without fear.
    iii. *Aggregation of Public Preferences.* How effectively and fairly public preferences are aggregated into public policy.
    iv. *Role of Legislative Function.* The influence that the legislature has on the making of public policy.
    v. *Accountability of Elected Officials.* The extent to which elected officials are accountable to their constituents.

3. The Executive Dimension

  i. *Ensuring Freedom from Fear.* The extent to which governments promote rules that reduce threats to personal security, reflecting concerns in UDHR Articles 3–5 and Conventions Against Torture.

  ii. *Ensuring Freedom from Want.* How far social and economic rights are being promoted, reflecting UDHR, especially Articles 23–25 and the International Covenant on Economic, Social and Cultural Rights.

  iii. *Willingness to Make Tough Decisions.* How far rules enable governments to make decisions with the long-term interests of the country in mind as opposed to being led by populist and short-term demands.

  iv. *Political-Military Relations.* How far military is subject to civilian control and largely confined to its professional roles.

  v. *Attitude to Peace.* How seriously government takes the rules of conduct within its borders.

4. The Managerial Dimension

  i. *Scope for Policy Advice.* The extent to which advice by senior civil servants with specialist competence has a bearing on how policy is made.

  ii. *Meritocracy.* How far merit enters into the recruitment and tenure of civil servants.

  iii. *Accountability of Appointed Officials.* The extent to which mechanisms such as audit, courts, or ombudsman operate in holding public servants accountable.

  iv. *Transparency.* The extent to which citizens have access to public documents and can know about rules and procedures that guide public decisions.

  v. *Equal Access to Public Service.* How effectively the state is organized to cope with the principle of equal access to public service, a concern highlighted in UDHR Article 21.

5. The Regulatory Dimension

  i. *Security of Property.* The extent to which property rights—whether private, common, or public—are respected by governments and individual public servants, a concern contained in UDHR Article 17.

  ii. *Equal Treatment.* The extent to which economic regulations are seen as applying equally to all economic actors, regardless of size.

  iii. *Obstacles to Business.* The transactions involved in getting a business license and starting a business.

iv. *Consultation with Private Sector.* The degree to which private sector actors are consulted and involved in shaping economic policy.

v. *International Economic Considerations.* The degree to which governments consider international opportunities and risks in making economic policy.

6. The Adjudicatory Dimension

i. *Equal Access to Justice.* The extent to which society has in place mechanisms for ensuring equal access to justice, reflecting concerns in UDHR Article 7.

ii. *Due Process.* The extent to which proper procedures are followed in every aspect of legal cases.

iii. *Accountability of Judges.* The extent to which society has in place mechanisms such as appeal, judicial review, and special inquiries that serve to make judges accountable.

iv. *Incorporation of International Human Rights Norms.* The extent to which international jurisprudence is being incorporated into national laws.

v. *Predisposition to Conflict Resolution.* How society is structured to preempt and contain conflicts between groups of citizens.

A Framework for Analysis

In conclusion, it is worthwhile outlining a broad analytical framework that guides the analysis—summarized in Figure 2.2. As indicated, governance is treated as both an independent and dependent variable. The determinants (to the left in the figure) are the generic factors likely to influence the quality of governance. The World Governance Survey will generate perceptions of governance in the six dimensions (center of figure).

Governance, however, is also treated as an independent variable influencing various aspects of development, as indicated in the right column of the figure. The analysis would build on existing work that tries to link institutional features to development, such as Knack and Keefer (1995) and LaPorta et al. (1999). The survey is expected to provide additional valuable information that can be meaningfully correlated with the objective development indicators contained in the World Development Report and the Human Development Report. If governance is as important as is assumed in international development circles, one would expect that where governance scores are high, rules enjoying legitimacy should translate into outputs that indicate the effectiveness of the political process in serving economy and society. The analysis would also examine which aspect or

Governance refers to the formation and stewardship of the formal and informal rules that regulate the public realm, the arena in which state as well as economic and societal actors interact to make decisions.

Determinants

1. Historical context

2. Political context—e.g., regime type, civil war

3. Social context—e.g., ethnic fragmentation, education level, religion

4. Economic context

5. International context

Governance Realm

1. Socializing

2. Aggregating

3. Executive

4. Managerial

5. Regulatory

6. Adjudicatory

Intermediate Outcomes

Policy Choices/ Instrumental Arrangements
e.g., macro-stability fiscal discipline—budget deficit basic services vs. military spending

corruption number of NGOs number of newspapers

Public Behavior
paying taxes voting turnout crime rates

constitutive

instrumental

Development
(after Sen, 2000)

1. Political rights

2. Protective security

3. Economic entitlements

4. Social opportunities

5. Trust and transparency guarantees

dimension of governance may show the highest level of correlation with development outputs. In short, it may be possible to identify which aspect of governance may be most critical for enhancing social or economic development.

References

Blau, P. 1963. *The Dynamics of Bureaucracy: A Study of Interpersonal Relations in Two Government Agencies.* Chicago: University of Chicago Press.

Blau, P. 1964. *Exchange and Power in Social Life.* London: J. Wiley.

Campos, N., and J. Nugent. 1999. "Development Performance and the Institutions of Governance: Evidence from East Asia and Latin America." *World Development* 27 (3): 439–52.

Crozier, M. 1964. *The Bureaucratic Phenomenon.* Chicago: University of Chicago Press.

Dryzek, J. 1996. *Democracy in Capitalist Times: Ideals, Limits, and Struggles.* Oxford: Oxford University Press.

Evans, P., and J. Rauch. 2000. "Bureaucratic Structure and Bureaucratic Performance in Less Developed Countries." *Journal of Public Economics* 75 (January 2000): 49–71.

Gluckman, M. 1965. *Politics, Law and Ritual in Tribal Society.* Oxford: Blackwell.

Holsti, K. J. 1992. "Governance without Government: Polyarchy in 19th Century European International Politics," in J. N. Rosenau and E.-O. Cziempel, eds. *Governance Without Government: Order and Change in World Politics.* Cambridge: Cambridge University Press.

Human Development Centre 1999, *Human Development in South Asia 1999: The Crisis of Governance.* Oxford: Oxford University Press.

Hyden, G. 1992. "The Study of Governance." Pp. 1–26 in G. Hyden and M. Bratton, eds. *Governance and Politics in Africa.* Boulder, Colo.: Lynne Rienner Publishers.

Isham J., Narayan D., and Prichett L. 1995. "Does Participation Improve Performance? Establishing Casualty with Subjective Data." In *The World Bank Economic Review*, vol. 9, No. 2: pp. 175–200.

Kaufmann, D., A. Kraay, and P. Zoido-Lobaton. 1999. "Aggregating Governance Indicators." *World Bank Working Paper.* Washington, D.C.: The World Bank.

Kooiman, J., ed. 1993. *Modern Governance: New Government–Society Interactions.* London: Sage.

Knack, S. and O. Keefer. 1995. "Institutions and Economic Performance: Cross-Country Tests Using Alternative Institutional Measures," *Economics and Politics* 7: 207–27.

LaPorta, R., F. Lopez-de-Silanes, A. Shleifer, and R. Vishy. 1999. "The Quality of Government." *NBER Working Paper Series #6727.* Cambridge, Mass.: NBER.

Linz, J. and A. Stepan. 1996. *Problems of Democratic Transition and Consolidation: Southern Europe, South America, and Post-Communist Europe.* Baltimore, Md.: Johns Hopkins University Press.

Locke, J. 1946. *The Second Treatise of Civil Government.* Oxford: Blackwell.

Locke, J. 1960. *Two Treatises of Government.* Cambridge, Cambridge University Press.

Lynn, L. E. Jr., C. and Heinrich, C. J. Hill. 1999. "The Empirical Study of Governance: Theories, Models, Methods." Presented at the Workshop for the Empirical Study of Governance. Tucson: University of Arizona.

March, J. G., and J. P. Olsen. 1998. *Democratic Governance.* New York: Free Press.

Montesquieu, C. 1970 (1748). *Spirit of the Laws.* New York: Free Press.

Narayan, D., R. Patel, K. Schafft, A. Rademacher, and S. Koch-Schulte. 2000. *Voices of the Poor: Can Anyone Hear Us?* Washington, DC: World Bank.

North, D. 1990. *Institutions, Institutional Change and Economic Performance.* Cambridge: Cambridge University Press.

Pierre, J. and G. Peters. 2000. *Governance, Politics and the State.* London: Macmillan.

Przeworski, A. 1991. *Democracy and the Market.* New York: Cambridge University Press.

Putnam, R. 1993. *Making Democracy Work: Civic Traditions in Italy.* Princeton, N.J.: Princeton University Press.

Redfern, P,. and M. Desai. 1997. *Global Governance: Ethics and Economics of the World Order.* New York: Pinter.

Rhodes, R. A. W. 1997. *Understanding Governance: Policy Networks, Governance, and Accountability.* Buckingham: Open University Press.

Root, H. 1996. *Small Countries Big Lessons: Governance and the Rise of East Asia.* Oxford: Oxford University Press.

Rosenau, James N., and E. O. Cziempel, eds. 1992. *Governance Without Government: Order and Change in World Politics.* Cambridge: Cambridge University Press.

Sen, Amartya. 1999. *Development as Freedom.* New York: Random House.

Sprogard, R. and M. James. 2000. "Governance and Democracy: The People's View. A Global Opinion Poll." Presented at the U.N. University's Millennium Conference, Tokyo, January 19–21.

Stepan, A. and C. Skach. 1996. "Constitutional Frameworks and Democratic Consolidation: Parliamentarism versus Presidentialism," *World Politics* 46 (1): 1–22.

United Nations Development Programme. 1997. *Reconceptualizing Governance.* New York: UNDP.

United Nations Development Programme. 2000. *Human Development Report.* New York: Oxford University Press.

World Bank. 1989. *Sub-Saharan Africa: From Crisis to Sustainable Growth.* Washington, D.C.: World Bank.

World Bank. 1992. *Governance and Development.* Washington, D.C.: World Bank.

3

On Common Good and Good Governance: An Alternative Approach

O. P. DWIVEDI

Sustaining the Common Good

The term common good has come to mean several things such as "the good of the whole in which the parts share," "the greatest good of the greatest number," "the commonweal," or "universal happiness," but presently in Western thinking, the term rarely encompasses universality. On the contrary, the Eastern (Hindu and Buddhist) concept of common good emphasizes the care of all instead of the greatest good of the greatest number. For this discussion, the concept means an action or a deed which is beneficial to all, although such benefits or privileges may not be immediately attainable or available, whether or not everyone realizes it. Furthermore, while the benefits may be available to all, it does not mean that *all* the people are entitled to identical or equal benefits. Instead the concept means that everyone should receive or be given their individual and collective *due share*. In other words, the concept includes receiving benefits from others (including the community, state, or other entities, as well as rendering to others whatever is their due share (Dwivedi, 1998).

It is important to distinguish between *a* common good and *the* common good. Examples can be cited about common goods that are exhibited by special groups such as a soccer team (for which winning a tournament is its ultimate common good), an interest group (for which securing a particular

---

This chapter is based on a paper presented at the 25th Congress on Governance of the International Institute of Administrative Sciences, Athens, Greece, July 9–13, 2001.

advantage to its members is the sole purpose of its existence), or a political party (for which winning an election is its ultimate aim). Thus, the meaning of a common good shifts according to its context. On the other hand, according to Yves R. Simon: "The common good, however, refers to a comprehensive set of goods in which the entire civil society participates" (Simon, 1993). Those comprehensive set of goods relate to the material as well as spiritual goods and services of an entire society. We should note that rarely does anyone know in advance how all the components of the common good can be made to fit together; the challenge is how to bring together the individual needs and aspirations within the overarching domain of the common good. Further, the common good should not be perceived as some kind of a rigid or static declaration of values; rather, it is a dynamic affirmation and promotion of values, beliefs, institutions, and cultural determinants which encourage the pursuit of a common endeavor by a society, a nation, or a global community. *The essence of the common good is in securing universal care and welfare by voluntary cooperation of community members.* The common good also requires willingness of individuals in the society to sacrifice a part of their own advantages or privileges to the common good in the name of sustaining universal welfare. Thus, the common good is larger than any individual or group interest and derives its authority from community voluntary cooperation.

The common good takes precedence over a private good (including individual material good, personal or moral goods, or special communal good); further, it moves toward the full realization or development of the potential of individuals as well as of the entire community. Under such a system, a virtuous citizen should always strive for the common good by acting for the fuller development of the potentials of his fellow citizens and of the community at large. Thus, the term has a much wider connotation because it relates to the action resulting in caring for others, including the performance of public duties which ought to be directed towards universal upliftment and welfare. Finally, a person is conscious of his or her duties and moral obligations by sustaining the common good just as the common good persuades people to attain that consciousness and reach for that common good.

It seems that the term common good, because of its basic tenet requiring a universal commitment, is a better concept for good governance than the term public interest. This difference has been amply demonstrated by the planetary environmental crisis that the humanity faces nowadays. For years, since the end of World War II, rapid industrial development, pollution, and other related environmental damages were sidelined precisely because the prevailing public interest could not rise above the aggregation of various individual (private) interests that controlled the public agenda.

In the process, the good of the environment (the good of humanity as well as of nature) would not be permitted by those who controlled the public agenda to take precedence over their private interest. Only belatedly, when the Brundtland Commission report, *Our Common Future*, was released in 1987, the world-wide interest in environmental protection and sustainable development could rise above economic and commercial concerns. Thus, when we compare the two terms, public interest and common good, the term public interest is incapable of covering the good of the humanity while the common good appears to be holistic and spiritual enough to influence not only a specific community but even the world and beyond. The following statement of Saint Thomas Aquinas reflects this idea: "the common good of the whole is God himself in whom consists the happiness of all" (Aquinas, 1995). Nevertheless, we should note that the common good is not cast in stone. The common good can be subject to interpretations given need, time, and place for its deliberation. Furthermore, human spirituality needs to be reawakened so that it becomes a foundation for universal welfare and upliftment which is facilitated by good governance.

Governance

Governance has emerged as a new paradigm denoting something more than government, and replacing the traditional meaning of the term government, which refers to a set of instruments through which people living in a state, believing and sharing a common core of values, govern themselves by the means of laws, rules, and regulations enforced by the state apparatus. In this context, the term state means "an association for securing the common interests and promoting the common purposes of the individuals who are its members" (Corry and Hodgetts, 1957:41). Finally, the term governance denotes a system of values, policies, and institutions by which a society manages its economic, political, and social affairs through interaction within and among the state, civil society, and private sector. In 1992, the World Bank defined the term governance as "the exercise of political power to manage nation's affairs" (World Bank, 1992). Of course, the exercise of that political power entails steering, control, and management functions. Thus, politics, government, and governance are intimately related to each other: the first deals with the allocation of state resources, the second stresses mechanisms of control, while the third encompasses the first two but goes beyond to include other stakeholders in the society. During the late 1980s, the New Public Management movement suggested a new governance paradigm which essentially meant a minimal state with emphasis on less government through privatization of government operations where possible, ensuring debureaucratization, treating citizens as clients, and using private sector techniques in achieving results (Dwivedi and Gow, 1999).

But what constitutes the basic elements of the term governance? Hyden has suggested four basic elements: degree of trust, reciprocity of relationship between government and civil society, degree of accountability, and nature of authority wielded (Hyden and Braton, 1993:7). Degree of trust is essential among elites about the nature and purposes of the state, including rules and practices of sociopolitical behavior. Without trust in the political system, individuals and interest groups have no reason to engage in active political life. Public trust helps to create an environment where multiple stakeholders are able to interact across the public, private, and community sectors to form alliances and seek change in the governing process. Reciprocity is necessary within a civil society because it permits associations, political parties, and other interest groups to promote their interests through competition, negotiations, and conflict resolution. A degree of accountability forces those who govern to be held accountable and act transparently through institutionalized processes such as fair elections, public oversight of governmental operations, and referenda. Finally, it is also important to understand the nature of authority and the power wielded by political leaders with respect to policy-making and implementation; in other words, the capacity to govern depends upon the political legitimacy which is obtained by creating conditions in the polity that sustain the first three criteria. In addition to these four elements, the scope of governance includes five main parts:

1. *Political governance* includes setting policies, marshaling resources, and creating processes of political decision-making institutions, popular participation in governance, fundamental rights and democratic pluralism, rule of law, and socioeconomic consensus and equity.
2. *Economic governance* includes the economic and financial policy of instruments, processes, and systems of economic decision-making, industrial policy and role of the private sector, and impact of globalization and international trade.
3. *Social governance* consists of social norms, values and standard setting, role of culture, religion and civil society, the welfare state, and institutions to control poverty and human deprivation.
4. *Green governance* includes environmental democracy and sustainable development, environmental Bill of Rights, green justice, and eco-spirituality.
5. *Spiritual/Morality-inspired governance* is based on moral leadership, which is an essential requirement of good governance; public confidence and trust in the process of governance can be maintained

only in the presence of a higher moral tone that draws on spirituality and sustains the common good.

Essentially, governance includes a full range of activities involving all stakeholders in a country such as all governmental institutions (legislative, executive, administrative, judicial, and parastatal); political parties; interest groups; nongovernmental organizations including civil society; the private sector; and the public at large (Frederickson, 1997:86). Thus, governance implies a complexity of activities, pluralistic in nature, inclusive in decision-making, set in a multi-institutional organizational context, empowering the weaker sections of society, and geared to achieve the generally accepted common good. Finally, it is founded on the four pillars of legitimacy, transparency, accountability, and morality/spirituality.

Good Governance Leads to Better Sustainability

There is a general misconception in public policy and public administration that the development of public policy and its application is a purely secular endeavor in which moral and spiritual factors have no specific role to play. However, we know that values and morality are not limited only to personal matters. A democratic society is founded on the principle of the dignity and worth of all people. That societal moral principles emanate from the most basic religious value that human life is both sacred and social (in some religious traditions, all life forms are considered sacred). Protection and development of human life with dignity is enshrined in many constitutions. Any constitution in itself is the embodiment of moral values that guarantee us fundamental freedoms, justice, rule of law, and the like. These are the moral dimensions on which any public policy and its management ought to be based. We live in an interdependent world, in which both morality and secularism share and balance each other in the protection and development of human values. There is no need to remove morality and spirituality in the name of secularism, objectivity, or neutrality. In fact, if we continue to do so much longer, the moral vision that has shaped and guided humanity thus far will be eclipsed by immorality, expediency, and corruption.

Emergence of Bad Governance

It is a paradox of history that the empire builders of Europe who started their business in Asia and Africa with naked corruption ended up handing over a relatively clean administration to the leaders of those newly-independent colonies. Without doubt, during the British, French, Dutch, or Belgian rule there was corruption, but compared to the present level colonial corruption pales. Although the leaders of those independent nations began with a higher standard of probity and accountability, the people now find themselves in a cesspool of corruption and bad governance. On the other hand, the major difference between corruption in the industrialized world and in the developing world is that the public office in an industrialized country does not sanctify corrupt or immoral behavior of the officeholder. For example, the presidency could not protect Richard Nixon and he had to resign; nor could it shield Bill Clinton from charges of moral lassitude. In contrast, the office of president or prime minister in a number of developing nations protects its holders against criminal prosecution or being held accountable while in power.

Rise of Amoralism

A persistent problem extant in governance is that of moral leadership. Moral decay and double standards are reportedly pervasive both in the public place and in primary groups. Righteousness in public office is, of course, extremely difficult to define, to draw a line between public morality and private sin, or between public ethics and private conscience. In some cases, ethical lassitude in holders of public office may result partly from the absence of deterrence, but also partly from the increasing tendency to moral relativism that results from rapid change and cultural disintegration. Political leaders frequently justify fraud and deception in the name of self-serving principles of national security, government needs, economic rationality, or community demands. Lack of moral integrity appears more pervasive at the top simply because there is more to be gained or lost. Moral leadership must start at the top because its positive or negative effects are always felt and extended to the entire state and civil society. The absence of such leadership generates hypocrisy, greed, and self-indulgence, ultimately breeding public cynicism and the acceptance of the inevitability of corruption. No governing process of any developing country is immune to this growing moral disarray as people feel that dishonesty and corruption in public life are endemic. In these countries, poverty, failed states, authoritarianism, turmoil, disintegration, and growing human insecurity provide the context for the collapse of moral standards and quality of public service. This is also true in the case of the now transitional (former Soviet socialist) societies of Eastern Europe.

As demonstrated by the annual corruption profile of several countries published by Transparency International, standards of conduct and probity have been steadily declining among political elites. This decline has also profoundly affected the civil service. However, despite charges of overwhelming corruption, the administrative apparatus in many places is still functioning, and statecraft has not become fully contaminated by sectarian and criminal forces. The media continues to project a negative image of bureaucracy as being bloated, inefficient, status-conscious, and authoritarian. The coexistence of corruption and unaccountability with inefficient civil service is eating away the public trust in effective governance. Bureaucratic delays, ambiguous laws, rampant corruption, and a very slow judicial redress mechanism have all effectively accelerated the common person's misery and distress. The will to fight back is minimal, and the desire to surrender and go with the tide is stronger. For common people, there is nothing but a perpetual ordeal, accepted silently.

However, not all public officials are corrupt. There are some honest and ethical administrators in government and politics, but they appear not to influence the overall character and culture of government. The moral relativism resulting from rapid change and cultural disintegration has produced moral decay and double standards both in the public place and in primary groups. As a consequence, an environment of corruption and unethical behavior has been created. Holding public office requires a willingness to acknowledge moral responsibility and personal accountability for one's actions. What is needed is moral leadership from the top. The absence of such leadership breeds cynicism and tolerance of hypocrisy, greed, and self-indulgence. The state and society at large have become the victims of those holding public office who are unable to put the public interest above their own selfish desires. Thus, effective and good governance depends much on the political context of a state.

The Political Context

The analysis thus far could be applied to any country. But what about developing nations, whose machinery of government was shaped primarily by the rule of colonial powers? Since achieving independence many such countries have made extensive reforms in their inherited systems of government, but the basic foundation and main tenets of the administrative process have remained. While these countries continue to profess such administrative values as ministerial responsibility, political neutrality and anonymity of public servants, and the merit principle in recruitment and promotion, political leaders of various developing nations have found that these values were counterproductive if the goal was acceleration of social and economic reforms. Conflict soon emerged between immediacy and expediency of achieving both national objectives and inherited administrative values that put the professionalism of public servants above the ends and means used by politicians. However, in this conflict, politics would emerge as the most important value in the governing of a nation. Ministers claiming the right to shape the destiny of the nation told public servants that the nation would not necessarily uphold the inherited colonial values of professionalism, neutrality, and objectivity if they were not in the public interest. Of course, no one could question the politicians who fought for the nation's freedom and who ostensibly made heavy sacrifices while the public servants continued to work for the colonial masters.

Thus, it was not surprising to see power shifting from administrators to ministers as the latter acquired supremacy in decision-making, including control of public servants. When the power center moved from career administrators to politicians, the foundation and basic values of administration were put under great strain. With this shift in the power base, particularly in civil service appointments, promotions, and the use of discretionary decision-making authority, certain side effects were inevitable. Some examples include politicians acting as brokers between a business concern and government departments; the politicizing of the interpretation and enforcement of laws; the censoring of the mass media so that antiregime views are not circulated; interference in the normal functioning of administration to secure appointments of friends or supporters including loyal civil servants; the influencing of the sale of government property and the issuing of contracts and licenses; the improper use of police, paramilitary, and military forces in peacetime activities of citizens; the manipulation of and intervention in the purchase of machinery, property, equipment, and services for government departments; the misuse of official and confidential information for private gain; and the concentration of extraconstitutional and legal authority in the hands of individuals who may not hold any elected position (Dwivedi, 1978:24). Politicians have become an easy conduit for achieving such ends. Naturally, such an environment has influenced the behavior and attitudes of public servants who, by and large, have seen the benefit of adjusting to the situation; consequently, the bureaucracy in many of these countries has become a pawn in the use and abuse of power and authority. The ascendency of politics over administration has meant that political leaders are now capable of using their power and the state machinery to foster a growing personalization of their authority. However, the myth of political neutrality, noninterference in day-to-day operations, and the merit system continues while politicians seek legitimization of their actions by using the machinery of administration unchecked by any legislative body. As a result, a specific administrative culture has emerged that does not appear to be conducive to responsible, morally accountable, and good governance.

Towards Good Governance

Recognition of the moral dimension of governance raises concern for improving the conduct of public service and government. The broad principles that should govern governmental conduct are not obscure; rather, they mark the direction in which those who govern must channel their efforts if they are to serve society. These principles include a call for individual moral responsibility and obligation, sacrifice, compassion, justice, and an honest effort to achieve the highest good. Morality provides the foundation for the governing process. Public confidence and trust in liberal democracy can be secured only when the governing process exhibits a higher moral tone. And yet that moral tone is only one of several prerequisites of good governance. A broader list of values includes: (a) *Democratic pluralism*: a cornerstone of liberal democracy is based on three implicit values—equality, empathy, and tolerance for cultural diversity—and draws from three basic ideals: fundamental freedom for all, equality of all, and universal participation in the governing process; (b) *legitimacy* of the governing process allows those who govern to derive authority and power from legitimate constitutional instruments of governance; (c) *consensus* among different and differing interests in the society, and *equity* assures all individuals the opportunity to improve their well-being; (d) *public participation* in decision-making; (e) *rule of law* that is enforced impartially; (f) *responsiveness* of institutions to the needs of all stakeholders; (g) *effective and efficient responsibility and accountability* of institutions and the statecraft that meet basic needs of all by using state-controlled resources to their optimum accountability; (h) a *strategic vision* of the leaders for broad-range, long-term perspectives on sustainable human development; (i) *transparency* for access to governing institutions and state information sources; and (j) *moral governance* that reflects such values as the common good, cultural diversity, public service ethics, controlling corruption, seeking spiritual guidance for secular work, and governing elites dedicating their lives for service to the public. Good governance and sustainable human development, especially for developing nations, also requires conscientious attempts at eliminating poverty, sustaining livelihoods, fulfilling basic needs, and offering an administrative system which is clean, accountable, and moral.

Good Governance Requires Both
Procedural and Moral/Spiritual Accountability

A holistic approach to good governance requires that public officials be held responsible and accountable not only for administrative procedures (following rules and regulations and keeping away from illegal activities) but also for the ethical and moral consequences of their deeds.

Procedural accountability in the public service. Of course, public service accountability is the foundation of any governing process, and the effectiveness of that process depends upon how those in authority account for how they have fulfilled their responsibilities, both constitutional and legal. "Accountability is the fundamental prerequisite for preventing the abuse of delegated power and for ensuring instead that power is directed toward the achievement of broadly accepted national goals with the greatest possible degree of efficiency, effectiveness, probity, and prudence" (Canada, Royal Commission, 1979:21). Indeed, the requirement for responsibility and accountability of ministers and public servants lies at the very root of democracy.

Accountability means being answerable for one's actions or behavior. Generally, public officials and their organizations are considered accountable only to the extent that they are legally required to answer for their actions. However, from the public's perspective, other aspects of officials' behavior, such as professional conduct, fair play, justice, equity, and the morality of administrative actions are equally important. Public service accountability involves the methods by which government ministries, departments, public agencies, and public servants fulfill their *legally assigned duties*, and the process by which those departments, agencies, or public officials are required to account for their actions.

Those who believe in procedural accountability assert that the means, processes, and procedures in government administration are just as important as purposes or ends. "Thus the emphasis is on the effects observed, results achieved, and ends met" (Dwivedi and Gow, 1999:168). Public officials who believe in this approach feel that in public policy and administration, most choices are not moral absolutes but rather depend on calculations of costs and benefits, not only to the public but also to politicians and public servants. This approach emphasizes creating institutions of external control (such as the office of auditor general, parliamentary committee on public accounts, or vigilance commission) and procedures to check financial mismanagement and corruption. However, the main weaknesses of this approach are its emphasis on reductionism and lack of a moral imperative. No matter how comprehensive the rules and procedures to check the misuse of power and authority, people will invent the means to bend the rules or use legal loopholes in order to engage in unethical activities.

A moral approach to accountability. A general misconception in public policy and administration is that the development and application of public policy is purely an objective, secular endeavor where moral, subjective, and spiritual factors have no specific role to play. But values and morality are not limited to personal matters. A democratic society is founded on the principle of the dignity and worth of all people, and that moral principle emanates from basic religious values that hold human life to be both sacred and social. Furthermore, most constitutions are the embodiment of moral values that guarantee fundamental freedoms, justice, rule of law, and the like. These are the moral foundations on which public policy and its management must be based, especially in a world of interdependence in which morality and secularism share and balance each other in the protection and development of human values. There is no need to fence out morality and spirituality in the name of secularism, public service objectivity, and neutrality lest the moral vision that has shaped and guided humanity thus far may be compromised by immorality, expediency, and corruption.

Insisting on morality in public policy and governmental decision-making may strengthen the ethical and moral obligations of the people as well as of the organizations they represent. The focus must be on the ethics and morality of the administrator: What sense of duty should the public servant have, towards whom, and how can this sense be operationalized? The moral approach assumes there are correct ways of doing things—standards and rules that should be adhered to. Public servants in this mold believe that administrative responsibility is primarily a moral question (Bernard, 1948). They are moved by a higher cause, believing they have been entrusted with the stewardship of the state and therefore owe special obligations, have specific expectations, and reside in a fiduciary world. It is here where the spiritual approach, discussed in the next section, acquires a holistic tone; ultimately, our public servants exist for the public they are employed to serve. This approach needs to be revitalized in our public service. The commitment to a collective vision for sustaining the common good is one of the cardinal virtues of public servants and is derived from the concept of public service as vocation. For, if the profession of public service is not a calling, then it is merely a job; and in that case, loyalty to that job will depend largely on the material benefits and satisfaction the job provides. Under these circumstances, no one can expect public servants to exhibit the virtues of service to society, prudence in the use of taxpayers' money, and commitment to the common good and collective welfare of the people.

A comprehensive account of the use of power and authority by public officials would be incomplete without procedural as well as moral approaches. By using these twin approaches to good governance, we may be able to create a holistic vision for human governance. In their absence, no number of laws, codes of conduct, external or internal control mechanisms, or threats of punishment can force public officials to behave ethically and morally. Because all of those nations that are the most corrupt, according to Transparency International, do have on their books various laws and mechanisms to control corruption—and yet it continues. Unless public officials are also guided by a sense of vocation, service to others, and accountability, we cannot expect moral government.

> This belief holds that government is a public trust and public service is a vocation for persons who should know how to behave morally. Behavior emanating from ideals associated with service as the highest calling includes possessing and exhibiting such virtues as honesty, impartiality, sincerity, and justice. Further, it is equally desirable that the conduct of public administrators should be beyond reproach, and that they should perform their duties loyally, efficiently, and economically (Dwivedi, 1995:297).

Towards A Moral Governance. The public wants those offering their services to the state to show moral leadership. And those who follow a righteousness in public office commit no sin. In some cases, ethical violations in public places are encouraged by the absence of fear of being caught, by a tendency to sidestep the voice of conscience, or by the view that if caught, there may be only a mild reprimand. The objective of good governance is to create an environment in which public servants as well as politicians in government are able to respond to the challenge of good governance. That challenge for public officials involves a notion of duty as well as acting morally and accountably. If these two dimensions can be brought together in the management of the public service, it may become possible for a public servant to rise above self-interest, by placing the collective good above private interest and greed. The strengthening of such a notion creates a shared feeling or spirit of public duty among those who govern and includes other values such as probity, the universal application of objective standards, a willingness to speak the truth to Ministers, an appreciation of the wider common good over and above narrower political interest, equity, and a sustained concern for democratic ideals. Such is the duty of those who wish to be involved in the difficult and complex world of governance.

Confidence and trust in democracy can be safeguarded only when the governing process exhibits a higher, credible, and ethical stand, based on the trinity of justice, equity, and morality. Only by bringing together the domains of moral and procedural accountability can we wage a strong fight against corruption, mismanagement, and bad governance. For no nation or society, irrespective of its political and religious orientation, can survive in a spiritual or moral vacuum. Furthermore, there must be articles of faith, drawn from societal values, cultural traditions, and moral ideals that govern our lives.

These articles should be encouraged, reinforced, resurrected, and strengthened because good governance is essentially a moral enterprise.

The Spiritual Dimension: An Alternative Approach

Morality can lead to mastery over our baser impulses such as greed, exploitation, abuse of power, and mistreatment of people. Morality requires self-discipline, humility, and above all, the absence of arrogance in holding public office. Morality enables people to center their values around the notion of a cosmic ordinance and divine law that must be maintained. Spirituality serves both as a model and as operative strategy for the transformation of human character by strengthening the genuine, substantive will to serve the common people. If our goal is to serve and protect the common good, then spirituality can provide the incentive for public officials to serve the public with dignity and respect. Could spirituality be an alternative approach towards good governance?

Spirituality means a kind of energy source that (a) is beyond ourselves and transcendent; (b) impels us to search for the purpose of life here and after, as well as why are we here on earth; (c) has an overarching influence on our sense of right and wrong; (d) empowers us to care for others; and (e) inspires us to act for the common good. Willa Bruce and John Novinson, writing on spirituality in public service, suggested that an effort ought to be made to operationalize the concept (Bruce and Novinson, 1999). A similar approach about the place of morality and spirituality in managing statecraft states "The moral dimension of governance represents a concern for an improvement in the quality of public service and the conduct of statecraft" (Dwivedi, 1987:707). Although spirituality is supposed to be an integral part of our religious traditions and beliefs, its secular dimension—which is yet to be particularly acknowledged by secular institutions—is crucial in governance, especially with respect to public service ethics and values. The aforementioned energy source can be converted into a moral force to be used for good governance. How can this be possible? The following two energy sources are offered as essential elements of spiritual governance.

The Karma and Dharma of Public Officials

The term Karma means that each act, willfully performed, leaves a consequence in its wake. The law of Karma tells us that every action performed creates its own chain of reactions and events, some of which are immediately visible, while others may take a long time to surface. In the sphere of Karma, a good or righteous action generates beneficial results, while an unethical action results in harmful effects. For example, in the public domain, the Karmic law is particularly relevant as decisions made by public officials are interrelated with and interconnected to what eventually happens within the society in general, and sometimes even beyond a country's borders. Thus, when an action in the public domain has taken place, those who committed the deed may not face the consequences individually; nevertheless, someone else is going to be burdened with or benefit from their actions. In this context the concept of righteousness, also called Dharma, becomes meaningful.

The term Dharma means righteousness, a system of ethics and moral duty. Applied to governance, while a person performing a public duty may be capable of both good and evil tendencies, as long as she remembers that it is her duty to sustain the general welfare of all people, she will act righteously. But those who deviate from that righteous path will surely endanger the state, resulting in bad governance. For a public official to act in a Dharmic (righteous) manner, it is important for her to act in the service of and to avoid exploiting other human beings. A spiritually oriented public official knows that her Dharma enables her to serve others. In so doing, he will be fulfilling two duties: one to the self, whereby one seeks inner strength through spiritual action; and the other to the community-at-large whereby one works for the common good. As such, Dharma regulates human conduct and casts individuals into the right character mold by inculcating in them spiritual, social, and moral virtues and thereby strengthens the ethos that binds the social and moral fabric of a society by maintaining order in society, building individual and group character, and giving rise to harmony and understanding.

The spiritual path of managing public affairs deriving from the precepts of Karma and Dharma can lead to mastery over our base characteristics such as greed, exploitation, abuse of power, and possibly mistreatment of people. Finally, by understanding the precepts and relevance of Dharma and Karma for the management of statecraft, a common strategy for public service spirituality and good governance can be developed. Such a strategy depends upon how those public officials together (a) perceive a common future for their society; (b) act both individually and collectively towards protecting the common good; and (c) realize that they as individuals have a moral obligation to support their society's goal since their acts will have repercussions on its future.

Demonstrating Social Conscience and Caring Behavior

Demonstration of social conscience and caring behavior by public officials is intertwined with the general concept of common good. It is an obligation that human beings owe not only to each other within a society but also to others living elsewhere. The concept of service can be seen from the religious and the secular dimensions. Historically, world religions have played a vital role in upholding the virtue of serving others. There is ample evidence about this concept in all major religions of the world (such as Christianity, Judaism, Islam, Hinduism, and Buddhism) where people have been exhorted to serve others. This doctrine of service is considered the noblest duty and the ultimate concern of all human beings. Furthermore, examples abound in various religious faiths throughout the history that great souls devoted their lives to serving others. One can look to Buddha, Christ, and Gandhi as examples of such individuals who devoted their lives to the principles of individual self-discipline, sacrifice, compassion, justice, and striving for the highest moral purpose by serving others.

Conclusion: Towards Humane Governance

Governance geared towards a universal human development should lead to developing capacities for humane governance. Humane governance is good governance—the system should foster an enabling environment and the equitable distribution of resources in dealing with poverty and inequality. It empowers voice and participation of poor in governance and decision-making processes; it promotes women's advancement through an economic base, education, and legal rights; it enables governance actors to work collectively in finding broad-based, consensus-building solutions to poverty and inequality; and finally, it promotes the principles of moral and spiritual governance.

From the above, we could assume that humane governance, in a liberal democratic state, is assumed to exist for the sustenance of the common good. This is achieved through certain institutions of the state whose actions and decisions the public accepts. The purpose of such institutions, and of the state itself, is to perform certain duties and fulfill acquired obligations. The justification for the state to pursue the common good is actually the justification of its own existence. The basic thrust of the concept is to motivate people in government so that they can make a full contribution of their capabilities in serving their nation and the community. The objective of good governance is to create an environment so that public servants as well as politicians in government are able to respond to the challenge of good governance. That challenge involves a notion of duty, vocation, and service to the public, as well as the caring responsibility for their welfare. And it strengthens the values of liberal democracy. That ideal, based on vocation, duty, and service also draws upon the concept of sacrifice—a concept that rises above self-interest, placing individualism over collective good, and greed. The concept of service also creates a shared feeling or spirit of public duty among those who govern.

Public service as an ideal is and has been the classical view of good governance. That classical view also includes such values as probity, applying objective standards universally, willingness to speak truth to ministers (but also having readiness to carry out instructions to the contrary if overridden), an appreciation of the wider common good over and above the public interest, equity, and a constant concern for democratic ideals.

That essence and basis of the moral state depends on the triangle of those public policies and actions that ought to be undertaken (a) for the general welfare of society, (b) for maintaining and protecting the common good, and (c) securing universal care for all. However, these prerequisites enunciated in ancient times in all civilizations are sadly missing among many of today's leaders and practitioners of governance. The need to operationalize this cultural wisdom through spirituality in governance is imperative. In this task, both the secular and spiritual forces and institutions must work together rather than one fencing out the other, because good governance is not possible without bringing spirituality in the public domain. Although one deals with the welfare and care of life here and now, while the other strives for the life hereafter, both are essential for the common good and good governance.

Spirituality in governance means that officials must adhere to the principle of serving others by setting a high standard of moral conduct and by considering their jobs as vocation. The objective is to create an atmosphere that motivates officials to respond to the challenges of government by adhering to the notion of duty and service to the community, as well as taking responsibility for the welfare of others. Confidence and trust in the liberal democratic system can be safeguarded only when the governing process demonstrates a higher moral tone. The greatest challenge for liberal democratic governance everywhere, but especially among developing nations, is to rise above a prevailing ethical vacuum that is the Western legacy to public administration. Instead, developing nations should chart their own indigenous model of good governance, which should be interactive, inclusive, and holistic. At the same time, good ideas from the Western system of governance should not be excluded.

Both spirituality and governance have to work together for the common good and good governance. The values of caring and respect for human dignity taught by various religious traditions can be our true guide to managing governance problems. By bringing spiritual and secular domains together we can wage a good fight against corruption, mismanagement, and bad governance. No nation or society, no matter its political and religious orientation, lives in a spiritual or moral vacuum. Some articles of faith, drawn from the societal values, cultural traditions, and spiritual ideals governing our lives, must be encouraged, reinforced, resurrected and strengthened. Good governance is essentially a moral enterprise drawing strength from societal spirituality.

References

Aquinas, Thomas. 1995. *De perfectione vitae spiritualis,* quoted by Michael A Smith, "The Common Advantage and Common Good," *Laval theologique et philosophique* 51 (1):121.

Barnard, Chester I. 1948. *The Functions of the Executive.* Cambridge, Mass: Harvard University Press.

Canada, Royal Commission on Financial Management and Accountability. 1979. *Final Report.* Ottawa: Supply and Services, Government of Canada.

Corry, J. A. and J. E. Hodgetts. 1957. *Democratic Government and Politics.* Toronto, Canada: University of Toronto Press.

Dwivedi, O. P. 1978. *Public Service Ethics.* Brussels: International Institute of Administrative Sciences.

———. (1987). "Moral Dimensions of Statecraft: A Plea for an Administrative Theology." *Canadian Journal of Political Science,* 20 (4):699–709.

———. 1995. "Reflections on Moral Government and Public Service as a Vocation," *Indian Journal of Public Administration.* 41 (July–September):296–306.

———. 1998. "Common Good and Good Governance." *Indian Journal of Public Administration.* 44 (July–September):253–64.

Dwivedi, O. P. and James Iain Gow. 1999. *From Bureaucracy to Public Management: The Administrative Culture of the Government of Canada.* Peterborough, Canada. Broadview Press.

Frederickson, H. George. 1997. *The Spirit of Public Administration.* San Francisco, Calif.: Jossey-Bass Publishers.

Hyden, G. and M. Braton, eds. 1993. *Governance and Politics in Africa.* Boulder, Colo., Lynne Rienner.

Simon, Yves R. 1993. *Philosophy of Democratic Government.* Notre Dame, Ind.: University of Notre Dame Press.

Bruce, Willa, and John Novinson. 1999. "Spirituality in Public Service: A Dialogue." *Public Administration Review* 59 (March/April):163–69.

World Bank. 1992. *The World Development Report.* Washington, DC: World Bank.

4

Governance, Institutional Reforms, and Policy Processes in Africa: Research and Capacity-Building Implications

Dele Olowu

Most close observers of Africa concurred when the World Bank concluded in 1989 that governance was the fundamental problem of Africa. The Berlin Wall fell about that time and many African countries, like their counterparts in other developing and transitional countries, have experienced major governance changes—from autocracy to democracy. Implicit in the discussion of governance change is a simplistic assumption that such democratic change leads to good or better governance. Hence, governance and its qualifiers, such as good, democratic, and participatory governance, are used interchangeably. No clear criteria exist for distinguishing between good, bad, or better governance even when governance has become central in aid discourse and policy (OECD, 1997; Doornbos, 2001).

Governance changes from autocracy to democracy have led to major institutional reforms—the creation or revitalization of democratic structures such as multiparties, legislatures, judiciaries, civic groups, democratic local governments, and media organs. Many such organizations were either abolished or severely constrained under the military or civilian authoritarian governance regimes that held sway in many African countries until the late 1980s. But research in many countries shows that democratization does not necessarily lead to improved policy processes or outcomes (Healey & Tordoff, 1995; Spink, 1999; Suleiman, 1997; Wuyts, 1996).

This chapter reviews the relationships between governance and institutional reforms on the one hand and public policy processes and outcomes in Africa on the other. A model that connects governance to public

53

policy, based on the rich literature on comparative governance and public policy developed in the 1960s, is applied to the African case. The model is then used to evaluate key policy institutions with the aim of identifying those should be focused for capacity building in view of the limited resources available for such efforts in the region. Absence of such strategic choice has led in the past to the misdirection and dissipation of scarce resources on failed institution-building efforts (Haq & Aziz, 1999; Olowu, 1999a).

Governance, Institutional Reforms, and Policy Outcomes

This chapter does not repeat the conceptual distinctions elaborated in chapter one. Rather, it uses these as the framework for analysis of the African case. Although they appear conflictual, the three approaches to defining governance advanced in that chapter are actually complementary. Research on social capital points to the importance of leaders in creating institutions when organizations are young and how these roles become reversed when organizations become more mature (Tocqueville, 1959; Putnam, 1993). Moreover, the deficit of sanguine political leadership, of effective organizations in the public and private sectors, and of legitimate rules have all been identified as problems in Africa. But the most serious of these deficits is the absence of rules or institutions that serve as incentives for human cooperation in problem solving (see Adamolekun, 1986; Wunsch & Olowu, 1990; V. Ostrom, 1990; Mandami, 1996).

A definition of governance as fundamental rules or regime structures is therefore significant in that it focuses on the critical role played by institutions in a polity. And this is important for the analysis of public policy in developing countries. Whereas the institutional framework within which public policy takes place can be and normally is taken for granted in industrialized countries, developing country contexts are usually quite different. Here, the absence of effective and legitimate institutions is often a major reason that policies designed by external actors—at times with the best of intentions—flounder (Grindle, 1996). As we shall show below, among these countries, the African case is a *sui generis*.

Problem-solving communities are at the heart of governance and development. In the Western countries these problem-solving communities have become part of the social capital and the institutional architecture in different areas and scales and constitute the fundamental distinction between state and society, at all levels of the social space (Putnam, 1993). These systems are then nested into one another and form the key elements of the democratic system. This pattern of interaction between citizens and the array of institutions that meet citizens' needs as well as the inter-actions between state and society institutions in ensuring effective and responsive state institutions is the basis on which different governance systems are classified. For instance, Vincent Ostrom (1997) classifies polities broadly into monocentric and polycentric political structures. Monocentric structures centralize the locus of power in one institution (the state) whereas polycentric systems recognize the problem-solving capacities of different institutions in specific areas of human endeavor. The latter institutions possess problem-solving capacities and also exercise veto in interacting with other organs (see also Shivakumar, 1999). Generally, institutions can be evaluated by a set of common criteria: the extent to which they use information in ways that enhance the effectiveness and legitimacy of such institutions and the nature of the rules, which they craft.

Table 1.1 in chapter one is adapted from Potter et. al (1997), which used a three-fold classification of governance forms—liberal democracy, partial democracy, and authoritarianism using the elements identified above—namely accountability, autonomy of organizations, and civil and political rights exercisable by individuals. Most African countries were autocracies in 1975, and one should wonder why this is the case for states that have just emerged from the repression of colonial rule. One explanation is that African countries have been disarticulated since colonial times from their indigenous institutions of problem solving. Instead of Africa's postindependence governments redressing these anomalies, they have further aggravated them by reproducing local despotism at the national level—emerging as forms of authoritarian or patrimonial rule (Davidson, 1992; Bratton & van de Walle, 1997; Bangura, 2000). That these structures of governance have hampered rather than enhanced development is well documented (Hyden, 1983; Wunsch & Olowu, 1990; Davidson, 1992). The only bit of good news is that there are a few exceptions to this general rule (Botswana and Mauritius are regularly cited) and the fact that changes started to occur from 1989, which is regarded as the commencement of Africa's second liberation (Hyden & Bratton, 1992; Bratton & van de Walle, 1997; Young, 1999; Hyden et al., 2000).

The foregoing suggests that without a dense network of effective self-governing organizations operating at local and national levels, in state and nonstate sectors, the task of governance at the national level becomes much more difficult (E. Ostrom, 1990).

An early linkage between governance structures or institutions and policy was made by some political scientists when they developed structural-functional constructs to guide comparative political science research in the 1960s (Almond & Coleman, 1960; Easton, 1965). They did not employ governance as a concept, but several of the issues they raised have found their way into our lexicography today, although under new labels. For instance, interest groups—are now civil society, and policy was categorized under three output functions: rule making, rule-application, and rule adjudication. These output functions are themselves responses to four demands or inputs on the system: socialization, interest articulation, aggregation, and communication by a variety of structures. This impressive effort at comparative study of institutions was unfortunately cut off by the imperatives of the Cold War and it is not completely surprising that the cessation of that war has led to a resumption of this important enterprise, although from a completely unexpected source—economists concerned with structural adjustment and economic recovery and growth rather than political scientists.

Using this four-point criteria—inputs and outputs, state, and society institutions—a set of institutions within and outside the state can be identified that interact to produce public policies (Table 4.1). Democratization would be expected to increase the degrees of freedom of individual citizens and the organizations that serve them. It will also be expected to lead to greater differentiation in the performance of functions by different organizations both within and outside the state.

Whereas all these institutions are involved in the policy processes, four sets of institutional actors play strategic roles in the public policy process (PPP) in most democracies. These are senior politicians (serving in the executive and legislative positions, who articulate ideas, values, or purpose), scientists and researchers (who are preoccupied with the acquisition and analysis of new information in promoting innovation and social renewal), professionals (who combine specific scientific knowledge with social purposes) and senior administrators (who help integrate the activities of all three other actors in the policy process). Even though the work of all four institutional actors are closely intertwined, each has a separate vocation in the PPP and provides special skills to facilitate the making and implementing of policies that are based on facts as well as values. The greater the need for rigor, the weaker is the consideration for purpose and the less the need for social accountability. Hence, researchers and scientists are given the greatest autonomy. Professionals also enjoy autonomy as a group under the law but hold themselves accountable to ethical codes that transcend the organization for which they work, whereas politicians must renew their accountability constantly—through elections and opinion surveys (Price, 1967). Administrators are accountable directly to politicians, although increasingly they are also being subjected to direct accountability to service users through mechanisms such as service delivery surveys, citizens' charters, and so forth (Olowu, 1999b).

Table 4.1 African Institutions and Public Policy Processes

	Function	Structure	Expected Role in PPP (H, M, L)	Actual Role in PPP
Nonstate	Socialization	Educational institutions/	H	L
		Community organs	M	L
	Interest Articulation	Interest groups/Civil society	H	M
	Interest Aggregation	Political	H	M, L
		parties/Private sector	M	
	Political Communication	Media	H	M
State	Rule Making	Legislature	H	L
	Rule Execution	Cabinet/Presidency,	H	M
		Civil service, PEs	H	
		LGs, Regulatory agencies		
	Rule Adjudication	Judiciary, Quasi-Judicial organs, e.g., election bodies	H	M

PE = Public Enterprises; LG = Local Government; H, M, L (High, Medium & Low); PPP = Public Policy Process
Note: Scores based on broad perceptions of performance of most countries in the region. Some countries will not reflect this median performance rating.
Source: Adaptation of Almond & Powell, 1960; Easton, 1965.

In most countries, this four-fold structure has been compacted to only two as the civil service expanded to incorporate large numbers of scientists and professionals in its ranks, leading at times to a generalists vs. professionalists struggle for power for administrative leadership. In addition, direct consultation has made for scientific input into the policy process through the work of study groups, ad hoc commissions, and universities. This then narrows the policy process to the activities of main actors—the senior politicians and civil servants who are required to consult with a wide variety of state and nonstate actors. Indeed, in a major study of some selected Western countries, Aberbach et al. (1981) found that the roles of these two sets of actors have converged over time resulting in the emergence of a new crop of policy makers, which they refer to as political administrators.

Table 4.2 attempts to integrate the governance and policy models. In authoritarian systems, the demand for policy analysis is limited due to the opaque nature of the policy process and the constraints on individuals and groups in making demands. The supply side depends on governance capacity—the existence of institutions that can transform available state

Table 4.2 Model of Governance, Institutional Reform, and Policy Processes

Phases	Governance Models	Institutional Mode	Public Policy Process	Policy Outcomes
Phase 1	Authoritarianism/ Autocracy	Monocracy	Limited demand for policy analysis	Focus on inputs
			Low involvement of key sectors in PPP	Weak implementation
Phase 2	Democratizing	Pluralism of national policy institutions	Increasing demand for policy analysis (transparency, accountability)	Implementation of NPM-type reforms
		Weak community-based institutions	Increasing freedom but resource constraints for policy institutions	
Phase 3	Liberal or Participatory Democracy	Polycentricity	High demand for policy analysis	Focus on outputs
			High involvement of key policy actors in PPP	High implementation as evaluation is driven by policy actors (e.g., civil society, parliament, audit agencies, citizens)

and nonstate resources into goods and services required by the public (Grindle, 1996; Brautigam, 1996).

The African Governance Crisis and Its Policy Implications

Research on whether politicians or senior civil servants dominate the PPP in Africa has produced conflicting results. In some countries, senior bureaucrats used their advantages of long tenure, education, and familiarity with the technical issues relating to public policy to dominate the policy process vis-à-vis other actors (the famous imbalance thesis, see Riggs, 1998). On the other hand, in some other countries, the reverse happened. Single-party leaders and military dictators dominated the policy process, even though they lacked the information that could inform policies and deliberately politicized the top bureaucracy to ensure that only those who value loyalty above all else become senior public officials (Hyden, 1984; Adamolekun, 1986). Countries such as Kenya and Nigeria until 1975 are examples of the former whereas Tanzania, Côte d'Ivoire, Cameroon, and Nigeria—especially after its ill-fated 1988 civil service reform—are examples of the latter. Indeed, whereas some scholars suggest that the PPP in developing countries is marked by an imbalance between bureaucrats and politicians, one African scholar found that both sets of actors—politicians and senior administrators—were ill-equipped to perform expected roles in most countries (Adamolekun, 1986).

By the end of the 1980s, it became evident that African countries were experiencing a severe governance crisis marked by six symptoms:

- A dominant authoritarian/patrimonial rule paradigm. This expressed itself in terms of the widespread use of presidentialism and personalized rule that placed the ruler above any rules. Autocracy led to many abuses—most frequently cited were violation of human rights, systemic clientelism, corruption, and misuse of state resources (Jackson & Rosberg, 1982).
- Breakdown of the public realm, evidenced by creeping decay from petty corruption by low-level bureaucrats to big-time grand corruption by many African leaders. In return, most citizens sought solutions to their problems outside of the regime structures, either through conflicts, community-based security arrangements as robbers worked in collusion with the official security organs, or alternative public service delivery arrangements when state provision fail perpetually, thus underscoring the notion of dual publics (Ekeh,

1975; Hyden, 1992 and 2000; Olowu, 1996 and 1999b; Bratton & van de Walle, 1997; Bangura, 2000). The examples of Mobutu and Abacha were the more widely documented.

- Africa's international boundaries reflect the realities of the territorial interests of their former colonial powers. These artificial boundaries have tended to lump people of diverse cultures together within the ambit of an artificial state while separating people belonging to the same problem-solving communities that have existed for centuries (Asiwaju, 1985). This has several negative implications both for nation-building and state formation. For one, Africa's large number of states results in many states being unsustainable in terms of available natural or human resources, an important factor in the analysis of Africa's persisting poverty (Akyuz & Gore, 2001). On the other hand, locking multiple ethnic groups together within these artificial states has also generated some of the most difficult problems for nation building—the worst cases have been in the Sudan, Nigeria, Rwanda, and Burundi. Some of these groups have had strong antipathies to one another for many generations and this has led in some unfortunate cases to severe and unending violence.

- The persistent tendency for state policy to be guided by urban consumer rather than rural productive interests (Bates, 1981). Africa is increasingly becoming urbanized. More people are moving to her cities and more than half will be living in cities by 2015. Yet, the present cities are poorly resourced in terms of infrastructures—large sections of cities are being ruralized—nor have effective urban governance structures been developed. The result is the increasing immiseration of urban peoples in the continent and the high food dependency on the continent. Basic institutions to govern urban or rural life remain underdeveloped, and it is not surprising that African countries have the least developed local government system and that many cities do not rate property, largely due to the problems associated with urban land management (Stren, 1995; Mabogunje, 1995; Wekwette, 1997).

- Africa's integration into the international global economy as a weak constituent is further reinforced by its very limited capacities to either monitor this environment or to respond to it systematically. Akyuz and Gore (2001) demonstrated that African countries performed better than the Asian tigers in the export boom of the 1970s in terms of savings, investment, and export revenues. But whereas Asian countries saved and invested their modest funds to transform and diversify their economies, African counties remained dependent on primary exports beholden to an international system—whose terms of trade for primary products have declined consistently since the second oil shocks of 1978. This weakness is symptomatic of Africa's declining technical (policy-making), which is consistent with the logic of policy-making in patrimonial regimes (see Oslak, 1989; Mutahaba & Balogun, 1992).

- Africans' capacity to manage their physical environment has degenerated due to a blind reliance on specialists whose training made them derisive of local peoples' close knowledge of their environment (Davidson, 1993:216). In the meantime, much damage had been done by the rabid application of imported ideas, grains, and practices such as commercial deforestation, which has resulted in environmental degradation, and increased desertification, cyclical drought, and overall impoverishment (Salih, 1999). Western scholars such as Paul Richards (1985) now conclude from carefully collected and analyzed data that so-called backward methods of agriculture practiced by Africans are actually quite sophisticated systems of responding to a difficult environment—practices that are now attracting attention in temperate lands.

The root of this governance crisis is the poor articulation of new and modern governance structures (Dia, 1996; Mandami, 1996). Mabogunje (1995:6) notes that development requires nurturing two types of institutions. The first category, state or nation-wide institutions, includes educational, training, law-making at different levels, and central banks and other financial institutions to regulate a free enterprise economy. These higher-level institutions could become useless without a second category of community-based institutions that adapt traditional institutions to serve the needs of a wealth-creating society and a modern free-market economy. These include the traditional institutions for regulating land tenure, family formations, labor relations, inheritance laws, credit institutions, and traditional guild organizations. Unfortunately, most of the efforts at institutional renewal and reform seem to have focused on the first type of large-scale institutions, with the lower scale institutions ignored, distorted, or officially abolished. In contrast, most industrialized countries in the West and the newly industrializing countries of the East built their institutional infrastructure by combining both categories of institutions. It is difficult to see how Africa can be different. With these sets of institutions in place, state institutions can make policies that resonate throughout their territories. Without them, the state becomes a farce, its policy-making processes included.

The institutions described above are not only important for development but for a range of core or basic state roles. These include the maintenance of law and order, investment in basic infrastructure, social services and human resources, provision of an enabling macroeconomic policy environment, the protection of the environment, and international relations (World Bank, 1997). When a state develops fundamental rules that enable all institutions in the country (state, nonstate, central, regional and local, traditional and modern) to discharge these responsibilities, such a state is well governed. Bad governance is its obverse—the existence of rules that discourage human cooperation in solving problems—this was the condition of many African countries up to 1988 (Zolberg, 1995). A number of factors have pushed African countries in the direction of democratization (Bratton & van de Walle, 1997; Hyden et al., 2000) since 1989, a year regarded as a watershed in African governance (Hyden & Bratton, 1992).

Africa's Governance Changes of the 1990s and Institutional and Policy Reforms

Michael Bratton and Nicholas van de Walle (1997:3) highlight a pattern of major governance changes that swept through Africa in the 1990s: political protests, liberalization reforms often culminating in competitive elections, and the installation of new regimes. They were convinced that these changes "amounted to the most far-reaching shifts in African political life since political independence 30 years earlier."

These changes were aimed at tackling some of the worst forms of governance abuses and failures in Africa: the personalized nature of rule in which key political actors exercise unlimited power and are above the law, systemic clientelism, misuse of state resources and institutionalized corruption, opaque government, frequent violation of human rights, the breakdown of the public realm, the lack of delegation of power, and withdrawal of the masses from governance (Hyden, 1992 and 2000, Bratton & van de Walle, 1997). The institutional implications of change included constitutional and electoral reforms, civil liberties and political pluralism, power sharing, and decentralization (Bangura, 2000)—all elements of two forms of political liberalization and democratization.

First is a transformation from monocentricity to polycentricity, the development of institutions within and outside the state that are involved in governance and policy. Polycentric institutions are imbued with the capacity to exercise policy veto. Such veto powers are formalized with respect to legislatures and judiciaries but are informal with respect to other institutional actors such as civil service and local governments, autonomous entities such as research and policy centers, and civil society organs such as the media or trade unions (Ostrom, 1995).

Second is the increased number and quality of civil and political rights enjoyed by citizens. Democratization thus leads to greater autonomy for people as well as for institutions, which people create to advance causes important to them, both within the state and outside the state system. Increased rights are expected to boost the legitimacy of governments and the effectiveness of policies because it increases agreements between governors and the governed on the nature of the rules, the sanctity of those rules and the inputs of citizens and institutional actors into the policy process.

Freedom enjoyed by citizens, the state and societal institutions also implies that they can make inputs into the policy process in ways they could not before reform. So a larger number of institutional actors would be expected to be involved in the policy process, both from within and outside the state. New state organs emerge while old ones are reformed—the legislature, executive, judiciary, parastatals, and local governments—to become more effective players in the policy process. At the same time, key institutions outside the state—civil society groups including the media, academia, research groups, political parties, churches, and trade unions—are empowered to make inputs into the policy process.

The key empirical question is whether democratization has led to key policy-making institutions better processing information in ways that enable them to assist the policy process by making and implementing policies that are both responsive and fact-based. Table 4.1 highlights these institutions and provides a preliminary estimate of performance based on the available literature. Reading and review of Africa's post-liberalization experience gives much cause for hope, but also provides some grounds for worry.

The research on this subject in a number of developing countries identifies a paradox: the institutions that are expected to have the most impact on the policy processes—such as political parties, elections, civil society, legislatures, media and cabinet—have not played any great role in the policy process. On the other hand, some other organs—external actors, most notably international financial institutions, bilateral and multilateral donor organizations, and northern NGOs—have dominated the policy process. Other influential policy institutions have been the higher civil service (Jamaica, Sri Lanka) and regulatory agencies such as the Central Bank (Botswana). The explanation for this paradox is in the capacity of these institutions to process information and develop the required expertise in formulating alternative policy paths or scrutinizing policy options provided by the executive (Healey & Tordoff, 1995). The African case has followed this paradox (see Table 4.1).

Socialization Structures

African countries made great strides in educational attainments at all levels after independence. Enrollment at primary and secondary levels rose from 71% to 80% and 14% to 29% between 1975 and 1996 respectively, but problems still exist in terms of the quality and composition of the beneficiaries. Primary and secondary enrollments were 85% and 81% males in 1996, and in 1995, in nineteen of forty-eight countries more than one half of the adult population is illiterate (UNECA, 1999). Higher education has been the worst hit by economic crises, structural adjustment, and authoritarian governments. The latter perceived education as a threat to their continued rule, while international finance institutions analyzed them as not cost-effective for public investment compared to basic and secondary education. Higher education thus has enjoyed better governmental funding, donor support, and management in only a few cases—Makerere, Ibadan and some southern African universities (World Bank, 1997; Salih, 2001). The absence of an environment that enables these institutions to redefine their roles in society has aggravated the failure of higher education, which has cascaded down to the primary and secondary levels, in addition to hindering their ability to contribute directly to policy through research and the supply of top-level personnel.

Community organizations have been very active in many countries but they have not been effectively linked to either the system of local or central government. The failure of the latter has often meant that community organs become de facto local governance structures as documented for Zaire, Nigeria, and Chad (McGaffey, 1992; Olowu et al., 1991; Fass, 2002) while the formal local governments function more as field agencies of the state. In the 1990s, some countries began to redefine their decentralization policies (Olowu, 2001).

Interest Articulation

Civil society organizations were active in the transition to democracy and some of them have transformed from being oppositional movements to functioning as credible players in the policy process. Their resources are often slender, but some have been assisted by northern NGOs and have become quite effective in undertaking development projects. The religious institutions are the most advanced in many parts of the continent (Olowu, 1999c).

Civil societies are supposed to promote public participation in the policy process, but they are limited by their access to resources, their organizational ability, and the interest and financial abilities of their membership

(Bauer, 1999). Trade unions are reputed to be the most effective in these areas, although they tend in many countries to be limited to their membership's concerns after transition to democratic rule. Churches and religious groups and human rights groups in addition try to avoid being partisan.

The media has the potential role of providing information on government's public policy intentions as well as helping to establish public opinion on such policies. The problem is that the media, especially the press faces a series of problems in Africa: the readership is often limited to a small segment of the urban elite due to the cost of newspapers and the absence of newsprint. There is also the penchant of all governments for secrecy. Journalists are constantly detained for publishing facts that while true, may be embarrassing to governments or their key members. Some media houses have been closed and many journalists have been killed in suspicious circumstances. The training of media workers is often also quite deficient, as are the conditions of service by the owners of the private press, who may also want their own political agenda pursued by media professionals sworn to independence. The most effective media organs in Africa are radios and televisions—but these are mostly in the hands of the ruling government and are used lavishly to promote government propaganda. The structure of the media organs needs to change before there can be massive improvements in political communication (Olukotun, 2000). Ordinary people therefore have continued to rely on gossip shops in local bars and shops across the region (Monga, 1998).

Interest Aggregation

Political parties, expected to be crucial in presenting alternative policy choices to citizens during and after elections and promoting the accountability of ruling governments, have either sought to consolidate their hold on power through patronage politics when they are in power or else fragment into clientelist groups (the number of political parties is unusually high in Africa, the highest being Zaire with 230 political parties in 1991, although only a few of them win seats). Very few African political parties are effective in mobilizing the grassroots and almost all of them suffer from weak ideological differentiation. Where an ideological glue exists, however, ruling parties have been able to increase their hold on power with additional elections as seems to be the case in countries such as Côte d'Ivoire, RSA, and Namibia (Bratton & van de Walle, 1997). On the whole political parties have hardly been sources of major policy influence in many African countries.

All of the above are input or societal institutions. On the output side are the legislature, the executive (cabinet/president, civil service, parastatals, and local governments), and the judiciary. The legislature is expected to be an important policy making organ in many ways—in legislation, providing opportunity for greater public involvement in public policy debates and in ensuring public accountability through its oversight over the executive. Overall, the status of parliaments has improved as constitutionalism has grown. On the other hand, legislative assemblies are limited by internal as well as external constraints. Internal constraints include their lack of tolerance and restraint in relating to the opposition, lack of experience in taking the initiative on policy matters, and members' inability to reconcile their multiple loyalties to the party, constituency, nation, and their conscience. External constraints are those imposed by the constitution, such as limited time to scrutinize policy proposals, the executive branch's unwillingness to make available adequate resources for physical plant, equipment, supporting staff, and salaries—not to mention their own preoccupation with constituency and party concerns. These factors expose incumbents to "grave moral and institutional hazards" (Gyimah-Boadi, 1998:41). A number of donors—USAID, DFID, CIDA—have targeted the legislature for assistance in several areas in countries such as South Africa, Uganda, Ghana, and Nigeria.

Similarly, the judiciary's role in influencing policy is circumscribed by its limited financial and operational autonomy, lack of ordinary people's access to justice, and the culture of weak constitutionalism. Three successive surveys (1995, 1997, and 1999) of the Ghanaian judiciary found that 54% people believed court proceedings were always influenced by money (Institute of Economic Affairs, 2000). Language and culture remain serious problems of adjudication among the masses in Africa (Sa'ad, 1999). At the highest level, however, constitutional courts in South Africa and Benin as well as quasi-judicial institutions such as ombudsman have served to restrain the executive in many countries (Monga, 1998).

The main institutions for policy therefore remain the political executive, comprising the cabinet and the higher civil service. Many countries have sustained the Westminster tradition of neutral and well-motivated senior civil service even though they have suffered from wage erosion, decompression, and politicization (Adu, 1964, Hyden, 1984). Democratization halted these trends as multiparties were reinstated in many countries and has enhanced the demand for evidence-based policy. A study on the Zambian cabinet, in the wake of that country's liberalization, found that up to 75% of the policies enacted by the cabinet were never implemented. Also, cabinet meetings were dominated by wrangling among ministries that were never consulted about policies that would concern them (Garnet et al., 1997).

Many civil service reforms sponsored by multinational agencies have aggravated the damage with their preoccupation with retrenchment, when what was needed was to attract and create effective incentives for performance for senior civil servants to help manage the policy process (Olowu, 1999b; Grishanker, 1998; Haq & Aziz, 1999). With the wide differential between public and private sector wages, Africa has lost its top civil servants at a time when it needs them most. In many countries the prime role of the senior civil service in policy development has been taken over by foreign consultants and donors as economic and fiscal crises made countries more dependent on donors for capital and recurrent expenses as well as for policy advice (Doe, 1998; Mkandawire, 1999; Court et al., 1999). Policy management skills have therefore degraded as a result of the poor demand and supply in many countries. The negative effects on policies and institutions have slowed the prospects of economic recovery (UNECA, 1999).

A newcomer to the scene in many countries are policy centers (PCs), some of which are tied to universities with others based outside them but draw on resources of the university system. Some are also located within government. PCs have assisted many democratizing governments, which, under pressure from domestic and external actors, demanded analytical inputs into public policy. The role of organizations such as African Capacity Building Foundation (ACBF) has been considerable—they have generously provided funding for policy centers within and outside government throughout Africa since the organization was established in 1991, (ACBF, 2000).

The argument here is that good governance, viewed as outputs or outcomes of the governance system, depends on the state's ability to use available state and nonstate institutional capacities to make and implement effective policies. For African countries to strengthen their information-processing capacity, five existing institutions need to be further strengthened.

- Higher educational institutions as producers of high quality research and high-level personnel
- Local governments as delivery agents of basic services in collaboration with community organs (especially in mobilizing fiscal and institutional resources for basic services and local level development)
- Judiciary as institutions protecting the rule of law and property rights in the economy
- Higher civil service as institutions for strategizing and managing the policy process
- Parliaments for providing legitimate access to the policy process by nonstate actors (also critical for driving program evaluation and accountable management through their oversight functions over the executive).

Conclusion

Each country must research and choose exact combinations of institutions that will enhance its policy management potential. However, the African experience seems to suggest quite strongly that countries that have these critical institutions for connecting the people's will with policy-relevant information perform better than countries without these institutions— even though the latter might have more resources. The experiences of other countries in the developing world point in the same direction and underscore the case for identifying these five institutions that have suffered under autocracy and stabilization as strategic for research if not for immediate capacity building efforts in the continent.

References

Aberbach, J. R. D. Putnam, and B. A. Rockman. 1981. *Bureaucrats and Politicians in Western Bureaucracies.* Cambridge, Mass.: Harvard University Press.

African Capacity Building Foundation. 2000 *Annual Report.* Harare: ACBF.

Akyuz, Y. and C. Gore. 2001. "African Economic Development in a Comparative Perspective." *Cambridge Journal of Economics* 25: 265–88.

Adamolekun, L. 1986. *Politics and Administration in Nigeria.* London: Macmillan.

Adu, L. 1964. *The Civil Service in Commonwealth Africa.* London: Allen & Unwin.

Almond, G. and J. S. Coleman, eds. 1960. *The Politics of the Developing Areas.* Princeton: Princeton University Press.

Asiwaju, A. I. ed. 1985. *Partitioned Africans: Ethnic Relations across International Boundaries, 1884–1994.* London: Hurst Company.

Bangura, Y. 2000. "Democratization, Equity and Stability: African Politics and Societies in the 1990s." In D. Ghai, ed. *Renewing Social and Economic Progress in Africa.* London: Macmillan Press.

Bates, Robert. 1981. *Markets and States in Tropical Africa: The Political Basis of Agricultural Politics.* Berkeley, Calif.: University of California Press.

Bratton, M. and N. Van de Walle. 1997. *Democratic Experiments in Africa: Regime Transitions in Comparative Perspective.* Cambridge, Cambridge University Press.

Court, J. P. Kristen, and B. Weder. 1999. *Bureaucratic Structure and Performance: First Africa Survey Results.* Tokyo: United Nations University.

Davidson, B. 1992. *The Blackman's Burden: Africa and the Curse of the Nation-State.* London: James Currey.

Dia, M. 1996. *Africa's Management in the 1990s and Beyond.* Washington, D.C: World Bank.

Doe, L. 1998. "Civil Service Reform in the Countries of the West African Monetary Union" Special Issue on 'Governance': Journal of Social Sciences. Vol. 155, pp. 125–144.

Dornboos, Martin. 2001. "'Good Governance': The Rise and Decline of a Policy Metaphor?" Journal of Development Studies 37 (6): 93–108.

Easton, D. 1965. *A Framework for Political Analysis.* Englewood Cliffs, N.J.: Prentice Hall.

Ekeh, P. 1975. "Colonialism and the Two Publics in Africa: A Theoretical Statement." *Comparative Studies in History and Society* 19 (1): 91–112.

Fass, S. 2001. "Local Governance in Practice: The Case of Local Services in Chad," in D. Olowu and J.S. Wunsch, eds. *Democratic Decentralization and Local Governance in Africa.* Forthcoming.

Grindle, M. 1996. *Challenging the State: Crisis and Innovation in Latin America and Africa.* Cambridge: Cambridge University Press.

Grishanker, N. 1999. "Civil Service Reform: A Review of World Bank Experience." CSR Working Group Workshop Paper. The Hague: Ministry of Foreign Affairs and Development Cooperation.

Gyimah-Boadi, E. 1998. "The Rebirth of African Liberalism," Pp. 34–47 in L. Diamond and M. F. Plattner, eds. *Democratization in Africa.* Baltimore, Md.: Johns Hopkins University Press.

Haq, N. U., and J. Aziz. 1999. "The Quality of Governance: Second Generation Civil Service Reform in Africa." *Journal of African Economies* 8 (1): 68–106.

J. Healey, and W. Tordoff, eds. 1995. *Votes and Budgets: Comparative Studies in Accountable Governance in the South.* London: McMillan Press, pp. 237–52.

Hyden, G. 1984. 'Administration and Public Policy," Pp. 93–113 in J. Barkan & J. Okumu, eds. *Politics and Policy Making in Kenya and Tanzania.* New York: Praeger.

Hyden, G. D., and M. Bratton, eds. 1992. *Governance and African Politics.* Boulder, Colo.: Lynne Rienner Publishers.

Hyden, G. D. Olowu, and Okoth-Ogendo, ed. 2000. *African Perspectives on Governance.* North Trenton, N.J.: Red Sea Press.

Institute of Economic Affairs. 2000. *The State of Governance in Ghana in 1999.* Accra, Ghana: IEC.

Jackson, Robert and Carl Rosberg. 1982. *Personal Rule in Black Africa, Autocrat, Prophet, Tyrant.* Berkeley: University of California Press.

Kiser, Larry L., and Elinor. 1982. "Three Worlds of Action: A Metaphorical Synthesis of Institutional Approaches." In *Strategies of Political Inquiry*, ed. Elinor Ostrom, pp. 179–222. Beverly Hills, CA: Sage. Reprinted in McGinnis 1999a.

Mabogunje, A. L. 1995. "A Concept of Development," Working Paper 95.1. Development Policy Centre.

McGaffey, J. 1992. "Initiatives from Below: Zaire's Other Path to Social and Economic Restructuring" Pp. 243–262 in G. Hyden and M. Bratton, eds. *Governance and Politics in Africa.* Boulder, Colo.: Lynne Rienner.

Mandami, Mahood. 1996. *Citizen and Subject: Contemporary Africa and the Legacy of Late Colonialism.* Princeton, N.J.: Princeton University Press.

Mkandawire, T. 1999. "Crisis Management and African "Choiceless Democracies," Pp. 119–36 in R. Joseph Ed *State, Conflict and Democracy in Africa.* Boulder, Colo.: Lynne Rienner.

Monga, C. 1998. "Eight Problems of African Politics," Pp. 48–61 in L. Diamond and M. Plattner, eds. *Democratization in Africa.* Baltimore, Md.: Johns Hopkins University Press.

Mutahaba, G. and M. J. Balogun, eds. 1992. *Enhancing Policy Management Capacity in Africa.* West Hartford, Ct.: Kumarian Press.

Olowu, D., D. Ayo, and B. Akande. 1991. *Local Institutions and National Development.* Ile-Ife: Obafemi Awolowo University Press.

Olowu, D. 1999a. "Redesigning Civil Service Reform in Africa." *Journal of Modern African Studies* 37 (1): 1–23.

Olowu, D. 1999b. "Accountability and Transparency," Pp. 139–58 in L. Adamolekun, ed *Public Administration in Africa.* Boulder, Colo.: Westview Press.

Olowu, D. 1999c. "Building Strong Local Government through Networks between State and Non-governmental (religious) institutions in Africa." *Public Administration and Development* 19 (0): 409–12.

Olowu, D. 2001. *African Decentralization Policies and Practices in the 1980s and Beyond.* ISS Working Paper Series.

Olukotun, A. 2000. "Governance and the Media," Pp. 93–113 in G. Hyden, D. Olowu, and W.O. Okoth-Ogendo, eds. *African Perspectives on Governance.* Trenton, N.J.: Africa World Press.

Ostrom, E. 1990. *Governing The Commons: The Evolution of Institutions for Collective Action.*

Ostrom, V. 1997. *The Meaning of Democracy and the Vulnerability of Democracies.* Ann Arbor, Mich.: University of Michigan Press.

Ostrom, Vincent. 1990. "The Problem of Sovereignty In Human Affairs: In *The Failure of the Centralized State: Institutions of Self-Governance in Africa,*" ed. James S. Wunsch and Dele Olowu, pp. 228–244. Boulder, Colo.: Westview Press.

Oszlak, Oscar. 1989. "Public Policies and Institutional Development in Latin America," in Pp. 1–44 R. B. Jain, ed. *Bureaucratic Politics in the Third World.* New Delhi: Gitajali Publishing House.

Potter, D. D. Goldblatt, M. Kiloh, and P. Lewis, eds. 1997. *Democratization.* Cambridge, Mass.: Polity Press/Open University.

Price, Don K. 1967. *The Scientific Estate* Cambridge, Mass.: Harvard University Press.

Putnam, D. 1993. *Making Democracy Work.* Princeton, N.J.: Princeton University Press.

Richards, P. 1985. *The Indigenous Agricultural Revolution.* London: Hutchinson.

Saa'd, A. 1999. "Law and Justice on Gwoza Hills," in D. Olowu, A. Williams, and K. Soremekun, eds. *Governance and Democratization in West Africa.* Dakar, CODESRIA.

Salih, M, ed. 1999. *Local Environmental Change and Society in Africa.* Dodrecht: Kluwer Academic Publishers.

Salih, M. 2001. "A Breakaway African University." Mimeo, The Hague.

Shivakumar, S.J. 1999. 'The Constitutional Foundations of Development." Panel Paper, Workshop in Political Theory. Bloomington, Ill.: Indiana University.

Suleiman, Ezra. 1997. "Bureaucracy and Democratic Consolidation: Lessons from Eastern Europe" Pp. 141–58 in L. Anderson Ed. *Transitions to Democracy* New York: Columbia University Press.

de Tocqueville, Alexis. 1959. *Democracy in America.* New York: Anchor Books.

United Nations Development Programme. 1997. *Reconceptualising Governance* Discussion Paper No. 2. New York: Management Development and Governance Division.

United Nations Economic Commission for Africa. 1999. *Economic Report for Africa.* Addis Ababa: UNECA.

Wekwete Kadmiel, H. 1997. "Urban Management: The Recent Experience." In Carole Rakodi (ed) The Urban Challenge in Africa: Growth and Management of its Large Cities. Pp. 527–552.

World Bank. 1997. *Revitalizing Universities in Africa: Strategy and Guidelines.* Washington, D.C, The Partnership for Capacity Building in Africa.

Wunsch J. S. and D. Olowu, eds. 1990. *The Failure of the Centralized State: Institutions and Self-governance in Africa.* Boulder, Colo.: Westview Press.

Wuyts, M. et al. 1996. *Development Policy and Public Action.* Oxford: Oxford University Press.

Young, Crawford. 1999. "The Third Wave of Democratization in Africa: Ambiguities and Contradictions," Pp. 15–38 in R. Joseph Ed *State, Conflict and Democracy in Africa.* Boulder, Colo.: Lynne Rienner.

Zolberg, A. ed. 1995. *State Collapse.* London: Zed Books.

Part II

Capacity-Building Challenges

5

The Public-Private Sector Interface— The ACBF Perspective

SOUMANA SAKO

E fficient economic management, good governance, sustainable development, and poverty reduction are goals to which all development stakeholders have a contribution to make. The public sector, the private sector, and civil society are key stakeholders in a country or region's development process. Development experience across the world has clearly demonstrated that economic, social, and political progress cannot be sustained without complementary and constructive support from each of these stakeholders. Indeed, the process of sustainable growth and development is no longer characterized by the ideological cleavage between the dominance of the public or private sectors, as experienced during the 1960s, and 1970s. It is now increasingly evident that both sectors contribute to the process through the mutually reinforcing impact of increased economic growth and improved levels of human development. However, the links between economic growth and human development are not automatic, but when these links are properly identified and systematically forged with appropriate policies and strategic action plans, they can be mutually reinforcing for achieving sustainable development and poverty reduction.

The public and the private sectors need the capacity to perform their roles in the development process. Equally important are strategies and instruments for effective interface between the two sectors. The lack of capacity, a situation that constitutes the missing link in the development process in sub-Saharan Africa, has a significant impact on the effectiveness of the roles of both the public and private sectors, given the peculiarities and specificities of the needs within each sector. While addressing these sector-specific needs is important, it is also strategically prudent to address the capacity dimensions of the strategies for forging the links between the two sectors. This chapter draws on the experience of the African Capacity

Building Foundation (ACBF) in addressing this aspect of capacity needs in the development management process in sub-Saharan Africa, an important dimension of its expanded mandate, along with its focus on the core public sector.

The ACBF is Africa's premier capacity-building institution. Established in February 1991, ACBF was mandated to build capacity in macroeconomic policy analysis and development management. In June 1999, this mandate was significantly expanded with the integration of the Partnership for Capacity Building in Africa (PACT) into ACBF's mandate, but with the main focus retained in strengthening the effectiveness of the core public sector. Its mandate now includes capacity-building programs in other key areas of public policy involving the interface among the public sector, the private sector, and civil society. This expansion is to ensure that there is a significant and sustained intervention in key areas of capacity needs to enable sub-Saharan Africa to address the issues of good governance, poverty reduction, and sustainable development.

In meeting the challenge of effectively carrying out its extended mandate, the ACBF continuously explores ways and means of ensuring that its interventions make a visible and sustainable impact on good governance, development, and poverty reduction. One of the means is to ensure that the conceptual understanding and the application of public-private sector interface capacity-building strategies are consistent with the design and implementation of the capacity-building program.

This chapter is intended to make a modest contribution to the process, strategy, and instruments for public-private sector interface capacity building for good governance and development management. The intent is to provide some conceptual clarity and practical relevance to the approach based on the ACBF experience. The chapter is organized into five sections. Following this introductory section, the second section briefly examines the roles of the public and private sectors in development and the capacity needs in the process. The third section considers the implications for capacity-building efforts of the need to facilitate private sector development. The fourth section discusses the concept, significance, and strategy of public-private sector interface in capacity building. Section five provides concluding remarks.

The Roles and Capacity Needs of the Public and Private Sectors in the Development Process

In the development process, the public and private sectors play various roles, which are significant and complementary. The role of the public sector is manifested largely through the government in its exercise of power, authority, strategic vision, and the practice of sociopolitical and economic governance. This is achieved largely by formulating and implementing development policies designed to ensure a secure and stable social and macroeconomic environment conducive for private sector growth.

In this regard the public sector, through the appropriate government entity, is responsible for establishing a legal system that protects and enforces the constitution, laws, and regulations. This is necessary not only for enabling markets to effectively function, but also to build, strengthen, and sustain confidence in the investment climate and the management of the economy. The public sector is responsible for taking corrective measures for market failures, thereby ensuring that the appropriate interventions are put in place through its own mechanisms and those from civil society organizations. The public sector also has the responsibility of directly providing or facilitating the provision of essential public goods and services, including physical infrastructure, security of and access by the general public to health care, safe water and sanitation, affordable housing, education, and skills development. In addition, the public sector's role is to strategically guide the national development process from a short, medium and long-term perspective on the basis of the current realities and future outlook.

The role of the private sector, on the other hand, is manifested through private enterprise operations where markets, competition, and the profit motive determine the level and quality of production and distribution of goods and services. Its role is to create jobs, income, technological progress, and other economic opportunities through investment ventures and innovations that are vital to its own growth and as a contribution to wealth creation in general. This role is vital for economic growth and has enormous social and political impact on the sustainable development process.

From an economic perspective, jobs and income creation by the private sector can lead to a wider and more equitable distribution of national wealth. It can also lead to the diversification of goods and services production. This, in turn, can positively impact poverty reduction. The development of microenterprises can be particularly instrumental in this regard through their services to rural areas and poor urban centers. Furthermore, a vibrant private sector creates new stakeholders in the economy as more people become economically active and participate in decision-making that affects their welfare. In terms of the social and political benefits, it has been argued that private sector–led development contributes to a more pluralistic civil society, given its potential to engender accountability and transparency in the public sector.

To enable the public and private sectors to play the roles outlined above effectively, they require the requisite capacity. There is an acute shortage of this capacity in most African countries, which has been seen as a major cause of Africa's development constraints. A study on EU-ACP relations notes that the acute shortage of human and institutional capacity constitutes the most important obstacle to sustained economic growth in many ACP countries, particularly those in Africa. Many governments lack the capacity to design, implement, and monitor development policies and deliver programs (Sako, 2001, 2002). Inappropriate macroeconomic policies and poorly implemented economic reform programs stunt the private sector. These governments also lack an effective means for dialogue with the private sector. Civil society institutions are weak and not properly organized to contribute meaningfully to the development process. Facilities for training, research, and information technology remain grossly inadequate. Besides poor management, at the core of the obstacles to development in Africa are insufficient transparency and accountability in public decision-making processes and resource allocation.

Over the years, African governments and the donor community have made considerable efforts to address these capacity needs. While success has been recorded on a number of fronts, much still needs to be done. Indeed it is in response to the need to effectively address constraints in economic policy analysis and development management capacity in the core public sector that the ACBF was established. The broadening of its mandate in 1999, reflected the need to address capacity issue in the interface among the public sector, the private sector, and civil society.

Facilitating Private Sector Development— Some Implications for Capacity Building

Given the role of the private sector in development, countries throughout the world are working hard to enhance performance of the private sector because of its centrality to the poverty reduction process. The absence of a vibrant private sector implies that the public sector will have to take on a greater share of the responsibility for the production of goods and services, for which delivery capacity will be needed. Historically, and from abundant evidence, governments do not have the capacity to deliver efficiently in private sector domains due to the bureaucratic institutional environment of the public sector, lack of human and financial resources, and that monopolies through which the public sector provides services do not have the incentives to produce high quality goods and services. Restructuring the public sector is therefore fundamental for promoting the growth of a flourishing private sector.

Restructuring is often necessary to promote public sector efficiency, to privatize public enterprises, and to provide a conducive environment for private sector operation. Hence the growing consensus is that the public sector should be strong but small, and efficient. While a dynamic private sector is vital for economic growth, poverty reduction, and social development, it cannot function effectively without an efficient public sector. One of the major shortcomings of the public sector especially in sub-Saharan Africa has been too much concentration on regulation as opposed to the creation of an enabling environment. But the fact remains that sustained growth of the private sector depends on the availability of functional, efficient infrastructure and other key elements of an enabling environment such as:

- An effective and efficient regulatory framework
- Certainty of institutions
- A responsive macroeconomic environment

Regulatory Framework

Basic legislation is required to provide the framework for activities in the private sector. Such framework provides a legal basis for operations of the sector, defines conditions for entry and exit, performance, output quality, conduct, and social responsibility. Thus the public sector should not only have the authority to institute effective and credible regulatory mechanisms, it should have the capacity to do so. A strong regulatory framework without public sector responsibility and adequate resource backing for its implementation will be ineffective. However, regulatory frameworks are not without a cost; they require competent staff and resources to design, implement, enforce, and monitor them. As a result of these costs, resource-poor and weak public sectors find it extremely difficult to effectively manage regulatory mechanisms. A strengthened role of the public sector is therefore vital for instituting an effective regulatory framework.

In most sub-Saharan Africa countries, regulatory frameworks exist that are capable of supporting effective private sector development. Unfortunately, however, most of them were badly instituted, constituting a constraint to private-sector development and encouraging perverse behavior. Consequently, what is required in sub-Saharan Africa is a continuation of ongoing reform of regulatory systems. Such reforms should continue to target reduction in distortions, regulated incentive systems (with increased incentives through the market mechanism), legal reforms, administrative reforms, reduction of red tape and streamlining of regulations, revision of commercial codes, reform of investment and export rules and incentives, and removal of distortions in the labor market through revision of labor laws.

Thus, in terms of capacity building, the ACBF's target is support for legal and judicial reforms, public enterprise regulatory commissions, and standards organizations.

Certainty of Institutions

With respect to private sector development, simply put, institutions refer to the rules of the game in a development environment. Institutional uncertainty therefore arises from the malfunction of the rules of the game, which is due to the state's unlimited discretion to change rules at any time for any reason, a risk that arises from a highly volatile institutional environment. Thus, for private sector development, certainty of institutions is essential. Key elements of certainty are:

- Consistent enforcement of contracts
- A predictable judiciary
- Legal system continuity
- An environment free of corruption
- Selective and predictable controls

The growth and sustenance of institutional certainty requires effective capacity in the core public sector. Such capacity could be built and strengthened through:

- Reforms for the professionalization of the civil service
- Financial management and accountability
- Performance auditing and evaluation
- Improvement of the quality of national statistics
- Strengthening capacity of parliamentarians and parliamentary institutions

Responsive Macroeconomic Environment

A stable macroeconomic economic environment is critical for private sector development. Predictability of government interventions and the direction of movements in economic fundamentals as well as transparency and flexibility of incentive systems provide a strong basis for private sector investment and growth. The ability to design and maintain responsive economic policies relies on capacity within the core public sector, which is in short supply in many countries in sub-Saharan Africa. This explains why the ACBF has economic policy analysis and development management capacity building in the core public sector as the main focus of its mandate and interventions. In sub-Saharan Africa, there is a need to continue to pursue macroeconomic reforms to improve efficiency and competitiveness of the private sector and the economy as a whole.

Public-Private Sector Interface in Capacity Building

In the process of establishing the basis for and its approach to strengthening human and institutional capacities in Africa to meet development challenges, the ACBF is undertaking projects and programs to strengthen the public-private sector interface in sub-Saharan Africa. The concept and significance of this strategy are important to understanding of the rationale for some of ACBF's major capacity-building programs and activities, described in more detail in chapter six.

For the concept of public-private sector interface to have operational significance in the design and implementation of capacity building programs, it is important to clarify some of the issues involved, to appreciate the dimensions of ACBF's support and the scope of its intervention.

The concept is based on the principles underlying the roles of the private and public sectors and on bridging these roles through appropriate means to influence sustainable development. The private sector is the engine of modern economic growth, while the public sector is the overriding mechanism that enables the engine to function effectively. The public sector also serves as the organizing principle for achieving macroeconomic stability; providing incentives for efficient production and competition; and improving the legal, judiciary, and regulatory environment.

The public-private sector interface thus refers to the process by which the two sectors interact through dialogue, smart partnership, and constructive engagement to reach a common understanding on development strategies, policies, and programs as well as implementation mechanisms with the aim of maximizing growth, reducing poverty, and fulfilling social responsibility to society. Capacity is central to this process. The public-private interface capacity-building strategy involves identifying and assessing needs and then developing and implementing programs to meet these needs in the critical areas with mutually reinforcing potential to promote sustainable development. At the moment, ACBF intervention has been through support for:

- National consultative councils
- Special commissions/bureaus for cooperation

- National and regional economic summits
- National chambers of commerce, industries and agriculture
- National and regional business communities
- Applied policy research, policy analysis, and policy advocacy
- National and regional networks of civil society organizations
- Trade unions' capacity for tripartite negotiation
- Consumer protection policy and advocacy
- Corporate governance to enhance overall macroeconomic environment

The significance of this intervention lies in the recognition that sustainable development requires much more than good policies in either the public or private sectors. It also involves the requisite capacity for fostering understanding between the public and private sectors for consensus building and the strengthening of partnerships.

CONCLUSION

The dynamics and multidimensional characteristics of the sustainable development process require an integrated approach that involves the key stakeholders in both the private and public sectors. Capacity building is critical to the process. It is the view of the ACBF that, given the connections of in the roles of the public and private sectors in the development process, it is vital to provide a platform that will promote positive and constructive dialogue, smart partnership, and constructive engagement that could significantly contribute to improved development management, good governance, and poverty reduction. The ACBF is already implementing such programs. This chapter has attempted to illuminate the conceptual dimensions of the strategy and articulate its significance and relevance to the capacity building needs of sub-Saharan African countries. From its experience thus far, the ACBF is optimistic that its intervention in this area will significantly contribute to the development process in sub-Saharan Africa.

References

ACBF. 2001. Strategic *Medium Term Plan, 2002–2006.*
S. Sako. 2000. *Capacity Building Dimensions of Africa's Development Challenges in the 21st Century.* Presented at the Macroeconomic and Financial Management Institute's Forum on Economic Stabilization, Structural Reforms and Growth in the 21st Century: Which Way Forward for sub-Saharan Africa? Malta, September 16–17.

Sako, S. 2001. *Partnership for Capacity Building and Human Development in Africa: Some Issues for Reflection.* Presented at the African Development Bank Annual Symposium on Partnerships for Africa's Development. Valencia, Spain, June 28.

Sako, S. 2002. *Changing the Default Setting: Making Indigenous Capacity Matter.* Presented at the Accra Roundtable on Reforming Technical Cooperation and Capacity Building, Accra, Ghana, February 11–12.

World Bank. 1999. *The Partnership for Capacity Building in Africa: An Initiative of the African Governors of the World Bank.* Washington, D.C.: World Bank.

World Bank. 1999. *Giving Voice To Civil Society in Africa: A Framework for Capacity Building.* Capacity Building Unit, Africa Region. Washington, D.C.: World Bank.

6

The ACBF-PACT Model As a Best Practice Model for Capacity Building

GENE OGIOGIO AND GRACE ONGILE

Capacity building has been described as the missing link in Africa's development. There are perceptible efforts by countries and subregions to formulate and implement development strategies, policies, and programs; economic reform programs; civil service reforms; and numerous other activities to spur growth and development, but the requisite human and institutional capacity to support such endeavors is grossly inadequate. Sub-Saharan Africa continues to have a severe shortage of the capacity necessary for sustained growth and development. There is shortage of capacity in virtually every sector and in every country in sub-Saharan Africa. The situation was worsened by the deterioration of capacity-building institutions especially in the 1990s, which resulted in massive decline in the quality and standards of once top-flight tertiary educational institutions such as the Universities of Ibadan and Makerere; public sector ineffectiveness due to weak capacity, poor operational facilities, and lack of resources and capacity to implement civil service reforms. The capacity problem is not limited to the public sector. The stunted growth of the private sector in Africa and the relative ineffectiveness of civil society organizations are strong manifestations of weak and inadequate capacities. The private sector and civil society organizations need capacity for effective operation and dialogue with the government. All this is compounded by the problem of brain drain.

African countries and their development partners are very conscious of the state of Africa's capacity. However, the present intervention in the capacity problem is characterized by inadequate financial resources; ineffective coordination of capacity-building efforts, resulting in duplication of support; insufficient commitment by African governments, leading to weak ownership, leadership, and sustainability of the capacity-building process; continuing preference for traditional technical assistance by some donors and African governments; and inflexibility in donor policies and practices.

For sub-Saharan Africa to respond effectively to the development challenges it faces, it needs sustainable capacity for intervention in all sectors of its economies. In the absence of this capacity the missing link in Africa's development will not be restored. Sub-Saharan Africa's capacity problem requires a three-pronged approach. First, a reform of traditional technical assistance—about US$5 billion annually—is required to free resources for building indigenous capacity in Africa. Second, a best practice model for capacity building is needed to guide the process. Third, commitment to the capacity building process by African countries is fundamental. This chapter focuses on the role of a best practice model.

Country-Level Frameworks for Coordination of Capacity Building

To effectively build capacity, some fundamentals are necessary, such as stakeholders' participation in the determining core capacity needs to enhance ownership and leadership of, and commitment to, the process; prioritizating such needs; and coordinating intervention for efficient use of available resources in the capacity building process. This therefore calls for an institutional mechanism that can effectively support participation of all key stakeholders in country-level capacity building.

Beyond capacity building, the institutional framework should play a role in identifying strategic areas in which capacity is needed and supporting the implementation of the principles and elements of participatory development. Examples of such strategic areas include the strengthening of processes, strategies and programs geared towards poverty reduction; design and implementation of comprehensive development frameworks; and strengthening of institutional networks to support information and capacity exchange. The capacity building process should actively encourage countries to establish or strengthen existing institutional frameworks for coordinating capacity-building activities. The institutional framework will serve as a small, high-level body for government, private sector, and civil society participation in the capacity building process. It should have a mandate to plan, coordinate, synchronize, as well as monitor the implementation of capacity-building activities. In addition, it should provide information to support capacity building and play a key role in coordinating external technical assistance so that it can be appropriately channeled into the capacity development in the most pressing areas of need at the country level.

Towards a Capacity-Building Model: The ACBF-PACT Model

Basic Framework

In the 1980s, projects became the most common mechanism for delivering capacity-building interventions. These came in the form of training programs, institutional support, consultancies, and equipment, among others. Designed with duration of about five years, such projects provided a good basis for measuring impact against set targets and objectives. The approach has thus far proved effective, having led to a common methodology based on the project cycle with distinct phases of identification, design, appraisal, implementation, operation, and evaluation. The project cycle approach has therefore survived as an instrument for closely monitoring performance and provides donors with a mechanism for accountability of resources put into capacity building.

Over time, multilateral institutions such as the World Bank have introduced their own version of the project cycle. The aim has been to raise the level of participation of project beneficiaries in project development and management. Consequently, the World Bank, for instance, has replaced the various stages of the project cycle with the phases, "Listening, Piloting, Demonstrating and Mainstreaming." This essentially transforms the conventional project cycle into a learning cycle aimed at preventing the domination of supply-driven initiatives through listening more carefully to recipients' needs. The learning cycle also strongly supports the principle of starting small with pilot projects before scaling up and building commitment during the demonstration stage. Having secured the commitment of the main stakeholders, the stage of mainstreaming can then be embarked upon. As with the conventional cycle, the final phase of evaluation feeds back into the initial stage so that it supports a continuous learning process, which is vital for sustained future improvements.

The learning cycle therefore presents a significant starting point in articulating and specifying a project management model that is built on effective participation by all stakeholders.

A Model for Effective Capacity Development

To build sustainable capacity, a best practice model is needed. Its elements include:

Project cycle framework. A modified project cycle framework must draw on the conventional phases of the project cycle, while providing adequately for elements of a listening and learning cycle.

Capacity needs assessment. The project cycle must provide a comprehensive assessment of capacity needs. To this end, it must take stock of existing capacity, the effectiveness of its use, the absorptive capacity of project beneficiaries, the size of the capacity gap and constraints to the use and retention of capacity.

Participatory project development and management process. The project development process must facilitate mutual understanding between the donors and recipients so that the project commands a sense of ownership. Mutual understanding can only be built through participatory project development and implementation, which is a key factor in strengthening project ownership.

Ownership and sustainability. Ownership of the capacity-building process must be strengthened through maximum participation of beneficiaries in all phases of the project cycle. Long-run sustainability of and commitment by stakeholders and beneficiaries to the capacity-building process needs to be emphasized. Ownership requires effective participation of stakeholders both operationally and financially, while long-run sustainability hinges tenaciously on the development of indigenous human and institutional capacity, rather than reliance on external technical assistance for the delivery of capacity-building activities. Thus, stakeholders' participation needs to be maximized and systems and processes developed to sufficiently robust levels that can be sustained with minimal recourse to external technical assistance.

Partnering and coordination. A best practice model in capacity building should support a partnership and an integrated approach to capacity building. It must build on existing interventions and contribute to effective coordination of resources. Building partnerships is crucial for streamlining interventions, enhancing specialization among institutions, strengthening synergy across projects and programs, sharing information and best practices, and pooling financial and intellectual resources to support capacity building. Effective coordination is also vital in a best practice model to avoid duplication of efforts and enhance maximum impact of available resources.

Monitoring and evaluation of all stakeholders. Performance monitoring and evaluation are key elements of a project cycle. For effectiveness, monitoring and evaluation must be fully participatory and based on inputs by all stakeholders. A best practice model in capacity building must therefore encourage all stakeholders' participation in the monitoring and evaluation process. Such a model will also emphasize regular monitoring and evaluation of performance and continuous feedback of lessons learned into project implementation.

The ACBF-PACT Model

Geared towards building sustainable human and intuitional capacity for development management and poverty reduction in sub-Saharan Africa, the African Capacity Building Foundation/the Partnership for Capacity Building in Africa (ACBF-PACT) offers an integrated approach to capacity building that is based on a number of fundamental principles. These include centrality of capacity to the development process in Africa; a critical role of a partnership approach in addressing capacity problems; African ownership and leadership of the capacity-building process; and a systematic, sequenced, and coordinated approach to capacity building. These principles are effective guideposts for aligning the ACBF-PACT model to the key elements of a best practice model in capacity building or the use of traditional technical assistance for building sustainable capacity. For Africa, such a model is vital, if it is to address its development challenges.

The development challenges facing Africa in the twenty-first century are enormous, and one of the key constraining factors in Africa's development is the inadequacy of human and institutional capacity. To adequately address the key challenges there is need for a public sector that is highly competent, professional, objective and dedicated; a private sector that is not only innovative and growth oriented, but also efficient and competitive; civil society that is constructively responsive and capable of working in partnership with both the public and private sectors with a view to achieving development goals; an educational system that is relevant to the

African context and responsive to development needs; and a conducive socioeconomic and political environment. In order to effectively manage a development process that increasingly is being driven by the dynamics of reform and globalization, African countries need to step up considerably their investment in building human and institutional capacity and use technical assistance more productively.

Africa needs capacity for national and regional development as well as for effective participation in the global economy. Capacity is therefore needed to accelerate regional development in order to enhance Africa's presence globally as a respectable development partner. In spite of the somewhat generous flow of technical assistance to sub-Saharan Africa over the years, capacity is still direly needed in almost every sector in every country in Africa. However, in terms of priority, the most urgent need is to continue ongoing efforts aimed at strengthening the core public sector; giving voice to the private sector and civil society; rehabilitating educational institutions; and reforming systems, processes, procedures, and practices that affect the development process. Other important areas requiring strategic intervention are governance, poverty reduction strategies and programs, HIV/AIDS prevention and management programs, adaptation and application of science and technology, and environmental management. Building, retaining, and nurturing the required human and institutional capacity are necessary and vital for growth and development. Unless this challenge is addressed sustainably—rather than through traditional technical assistance—long-term growth and poverty reduction will remain an elusive goal. The ACBF was set up to address this task in partnership with other institutions with capacity-building mandates.

The ACBF was established in February 1991, through the collaborative efforts of the African Development Bank, the United Nations Development Programme (UNDP), and the World Bank as well as a number of bilateral donors and African governments. Its mandate was to build policy analysis and development management capacity in sub-Saharan Africa. The main aim was to ensure that every country in sub-Saharan Africa had its own core of top-flight economic policy analysts and development managers as well as the institutions necessary to sustain and nurture them. The strength of the ACBF lies in its capacity to provide systematic and sustained interventions geared to addressing core capacity needs of African development stakeholders in clearly defined areas of core competencies. During the first phase (1991–1999), ACBF focused on building and strengthening macroeconomic policy analysis and development management capacity in every country in sub-Saharan Africa.

In 1999, the ACBF 's mandate, objectives, and scope and scale of operation were broadened considerably as a result of the decision of the ACBF

Board of Governors to integrate a new initiative in capacity building—the Partnership for Capacity Building in Africa (PACT)—into the ACBF. PACT, like ACBF, grew from very extensive consultations between African governments and the donor community. The establishment of ACBF and the broadening of its mandate are therefore the direct result of new insights into and a better understanding by the development community of the need for innovative approaches and enhanced interventions on African capacity needs and thus of its development challenges. Acknowledgement of this need for a broader, more integrated approach has built partnerships among all major stakeholders, with the aim of bolstering capacity not only in the public sector but also in the private sector and for effective participation of civil society in the development process. The expansion of the ACBF's mandate recognizes the emergence of new players and stakeholders on Africa's sociopolitical and economic scene. The expanded mandate thus aims at providing new opportunities for partnerships among donors, resource mobilization, and acceleration of capacity-building interventions in Africa.

The ACBF has afforded African countries a significant opportunity to rethink the effectiveness of external technical assistance vis-à-vis the building of indigenous capacity and has also provided sub-Saharan Africa an opportunity to step up investment and appropriately channel external funding support into building and sustaining indigenous capacity. As the new millennium progresses, Africa's efforts to achieve reasonably stable levels of growth and development, reduce poverty, improve the quality of governance, tackle the HIV/AIDS pandemic, and participate effectively in the rapid pace of globalization will be stunted without a strong, sustained program for capacity building. At this stage of Africa's development, support by African governments and their development partners will need to go far beyond simply creating enclaves of technical assistance projects and programs to commitments that will make a visible, meaningful, and sustained change through an effective approach to capacity building. Today, ACBF-PACT has become Africa's premier institution in capacity building for development policy analysis and management for sustained growth and has made significant contributions to strengthening Africa's human and institutional capacity.

Vision and Mission of ACBF-PACT

Over the years, and more vigorously since 2000, the ACBF has pursued relentlessly a clear vision in capacity building with a valued niche in core public sector interventions. Its mission is to build sustainable human and institutional capacity for good governance and poverty reduction in Africa.

Objectives. The main objective of ACBF-PACT is to build sustainable human and institutional capacity for growth, poverty reduction, and good governance in Africa. Under the expanded mandate, the Foundation seeks to achieve three main objectives:

1. to provide an integrated framework for a holistic approach to capacity building in Africa;
2. to build a partnership between African governments and their development partners that allows for effective coordination of interventions in capacity building and the strengthening of Africa's ownership, leadership, and responsibility in the capacity-building process; and
3. to provide a forum for discussing issues and processes, and sharing experiences, ideas, and best practices related to capacity building, as well as mobilizing higher levels of consciousness and resources for capacity building in Africa.

ACBF approach to capacity building. For Africa, the capacity-building agenda is still very extensive, but its core elements are focus, contents, and features. In terms of focus, the agenda should aim to influence development policies and programs by addressing sustained growth, poverty reduction and improvement of living standards. With regard to contents, capacity-building activities will need to be geared towards strengthening human skills and knowledge as well as institutions. This will involve the development of new skills and structures, reorganization of existing institutional structures or processes for more efficient performance, and reordering of incentive systems for more intensive and efficient use of existing skills and institutions. The institutional dimension should continue to emphasize reform or the enhancement of development norms, behaviors, practices, systems, processes and procedures. The key features of this agenda should continue to emphasize indigenous capacity and less reliance on external technical assistance or effective reform of traditional technical assistance for building sustainable capacity; African ownership and leadership of the capacity-building process; African ownership of institutions, development policies, and programs; systematic, coordinated, and sustained intervention; and skills retention, use, and sustenance.

Effective implementation of this agenda requires a capacity-building approach that can sustainably support the development process beyond the dispensing of external technical assistance. In this regard the approach that guides ACBF-PACT's interventions becomes very relevant, as its approach to capacity building is largely demand-driven with emphasis on carefully assessed capacity needs, ownership, sustainability, and complementarity and synergy across interventions. The ACBF places considerable premium on needs-specific and appropriately targeted projects and programs as well as a process approach to capacity-building. Experience has shown that to generate optimal results in capacity building interventions, dialogue and partnership are vital. Equally important is the need to build a participatory and transparent policy environment through good governance. And, of course, it is vital that visible efforts be made, as a matter of policy, to address systemic obstacles to women's participation in decision-making and development management processes. Most technical assistance programs are grossly lacking in these elements.

Operations. Due to the extensive nature of capacity needs in Africa compared to the dwindling available resources, interventions under the ACBF-PACT expanded mandate require that strategic choices be made with respect to focus, sectors, and activities. These choices are guided by the need to design interventions that will strengthen the core public sector; its interface with the private sector and civil society; regional institutions for specialized training, applied policy research, negotiation and policy advocacy; and the emergence of suitable institutional frameworks that support an inclusive, participatory process in capacity building and development management.

The expanded mandate has broadened the scope and the level of the ACBF's capacity-building interventions. In specific terms, it is now strategically positioned to take capacity building in Africa to new heights and emerge as a learning and knowledge-based institution. To guide this evolution and growth over the next five years, a Strategic Medium Term Plan has been drawn up for 2002–2006, and provides a strategic medium-term framework for vigorous implementation of the ACBF-PACT expanded mandate.

This plan will strengthen ACBF-PACT niches in:

- economic policy analysis and development management
- financial management and accountability
- enhancement and monitoring of national statistics
- public administration and management
- strengthening of policy analysis capacity of National Parliament
- professionalization of the voices of the private sector and civil society

The core competence areas are based on core projects and programs as well as knowledge-based programs. The strategic priorities and programs presented in the plan will vigorously address capacity needs through:

- projects and programs in the core public sector, in interfaces with the private sector and civil society, and in regional organizations;
- knowledge management programs that strengthen the ACBF's orientation and emergence as a knowledge-based institution; and
- support for the emergence of institutional frameworks for country ownership and coordination of capacity-building activities as well as for participatory development.

Towards A Learning and Knowledge-Based Institution

As an emergent best practice model in capacity building, ACBF-PACT must effectively combine its primary task of project development with knowledge management. It has to document and share knowledge on best practices both in capacity building and development policy management in the areas of its core competence. When contrasted with technical assistance programs that are largely implemented offshore or through institutions that are transplanted to Africa, this emerging orientation places ACBF-PACT one huge step ahead.

To address the challenge of the transition to a learning and knowledge-based institution, ACBF-PACT is continually enhancing its internal capacity, operational modalities and strategies, research capacity, and information sharing and dissemination mechanisms and is therefore poised over the medium term to make direct contributions to the creation, acquisition, dissemination, and effective use of knowledge in capacity building for growth, development management, good governance, and poverty reduction.

Some of the activities that will be undertaken in this connection will include the strengthening of institutional networking, partnering and experience sharing mechanisms especially in best-practice capacity-building strategies and instruments, poverty reduction programs, policy and program development and management, public sector reforms, and the provision of professional advice to development stakeholders on issues in policy analysis and development management capacity building.

ACBF-PACT Governance Structure

One of the fundamentals for the effective implementation of a capacity-building model is the effectiveness of its underlying governance structure. This structure must allow for effective leadership of the process, institutional structures, and practices that support effective policy decision-making and oversight of management, finances, and general administration.

The ACBF-PACT model offers a three-tier governance structure: a Secretariat that carries out day-to-day operations; an Executive Board that is responsible for operational policies and guidelines; and at the apex of the governance structure, a Board of Governors responsible for broad policy matters relating to the operations.

The World Bank serves as the administrator of ACBF-PACT trust funds and administers all funds for ACBF-PACT that are committed by African governments and bilateral and multilateral donors through the trust fund mechanism.

Operational Performance

ACBF completed its pilot phase in December 1996, after five years of operation. During this period, it supported twenty-six projects in twenty African countries. In 1997, it planned its transition into a second phase, which was launched in 1998. By the end of 1999, the total portfolio had grown to thirty-one active projects in twenty-one countries. However, with the integration of PACT, this portfolio has grown significantly, from thirty-one active projects in 1999, to fifty-seven projects and programs and twenty national focal points by the end of 2000.

At the end of 2001, the ACBF-PACT had a total portfolio of sixty-seven projects and programs and twenty-six national focal points. The projects and programs are classified into Core Public Sector Interventions, Interface Projects, Support for Regional Institutions, and Special Intervention. The core public sector projects and programs consist of interventions in economic policy analysis and management (twenty-seven projects), economic and financial management training (eleven projects), financial management and accountability (four projects), public administration and management (one project), and policy analysis capacity of national parliament (three interventions). The interface projects and programs consist of national economic consultative councils for tripartite negotiations (two projects), networks of nongovernmental organizations for dialogue and policy advocacy (three projects), public-private sector interface (two projects), support for corporate governance in the private sector (one project) and a project to reform the public sector to support the emergence of a growth-oriented private sector.

Beside the eleven economic and financial management programs (which support master's level and specialized training institutions) at the regional level, the portfolio also had eleven projects supporting regional organizations—nine interventions in core public sector areas and two interface interventions. The public sector projects support capacity-building activities largely through training, policy analysis and research, exchange programs, internships in economic and financial management, policy analysis, trade and international negotiations, as well as issues in regional integration. One special intervention strengthens capacity for managing and administering community-level AIDS programs in order to share experience and best practices, as well as raise awareness.

Thus far, ACBF-PACT's intervention has made some contributions to sub-Saharan Africa's capacity needs. Achievements, however, are not limited to direct operations-related activities alone. Other areas of significant achievement include:

Institutional Growth

Reorganization of the Secretariat for enhanced effectiveness and creation of new departments enabled the ACBF-PACT to foster smart partnerships and strategic networking, document and disseminate best practices in capacity building, provide backup services to operations, and take vital preliminary steps towards making ACBF a knowledge-based institution able to participate actively in the global knowledge economy. Streamlining of budgetary, financial and administrative management systems raised internal operations efficiency.

Broadening of Consultation, Collaboration, Outreach, and Institutional Networking

Development, through extensive dialogue with stakeholders, of a robust pipeline of project ideas guide the ACBF 's intervention in capacity building and enable it to track changes in capacity needs, which is vital for the implementation of its Strategic Medium Term Plan. Networking arrangements with partner institutions within and outside Africa have also been strengthened, as have frameworks for consultation and stakeholders' participation in the capacity-building process through the national focal points.

The ACBF has expanded national and regional coverage of projects, providing progressive outreach to new countries and regions, which has made possible by stepping up consultation and collaboration with partner, bilateral, regional, and multilateral institutions to implement the expanded mandate. For example, mutually beneficial collaborative arrangements have been developed with the World Bank, IMF, UNDESA, AFRISTAT, UEMOA, Club du Sahel, the Municipal Development Program, IDS, ECDPM, and the Rockefeller Foundation.

Table 6.1 Summary of ACBF-PACT Operational Performance

Phase I and Period Since Integration of PACT
1991–1999

Cumulative Grants Approved	42
Number of Active Projects *(Dec. 1999)*	31
Active Policy Units	*21*
Active Training Programs	*10*
Country Coverage	21
Cumulative Commitments to Projects	US$86.5 million

2000–2002

Cumulative Grants Approved	88
Total Active Project Portfolio	67
National Focal Points (established)	26
Country Coverage	33
Commitment to Projects	US$162.2 million

Experience Sharing and Strengthening of Commitment to Capacity Building

The ACBF-PACT organized the first Pan African Capacity Building Forum at which heads of state, prime ministers, senior cabinet ministers, heads of multilateral and bilateral donor organizations, and country teams participated and addressed issues in capacity building in Africa. It also organized a series of regional capacity-building workshops to strengthen commitment to the capacity-building process in sub-Saharan Africa, including:

- operational approaches to institutional and capacity development, which shared experiences in approaches to the design and implementation of capacity-building programs;
- communication strategies for development networks, which examined issues of knowledge management and the potential of new information technology in promoting information exchange and partnership; the framework of National Focal Points in capacity building, which offered participating countries and organizations an opportunity to discuss the concept, objectives, functions, role, and funding of National Focal Points in the capacity building process;
- for Directors of Economic Policy Management Programs, to share program management experiences and streamline training curricula and harmonize course contents;

- the African Policy Institute Forum, which brought together directors of policy institutes in Africa to share information and strengthen institutional networking; and
- the Strengthening of African Civil Society, which provided an opportunity to reflect on strategies and programs for building capacity in African civil society.

Strengthening Support for
Poverty Reduction Strategies and Programs

ACBF-PACT has continued to encourage institutions in its portfolio to support the design, implementation, and review of poverty reduction strategies and programs in their respective countries. Thus far, the Directorate for Macroeconomic Policy Analysis, Zambia; the Economic and Social Research Foundation, Tanzania; the Namibian Economic Policy Research Unit, Namibia; the Kenya Institute of Public Policy Research and Analysis, Kenya; and Cellule d'Appui à l Analyse de Politique Economique, Benin have continued to play visible and effective support roles. The ACBF-PACT Secretariat, in collaboration with UNDP and IDS-DFID, UK, commissioned a mapping study on programs and institutions supporting poverty reduction strategies and programs in sub-Saharan Africa. The study will be an important guide for streamlining, coordinating, and targeting support to this process and for ACBF-PACT to revisit the design of its initiative and the type of support it can provide directly to Poverty Reduction Programs and strategies at national and regional levels.

Utility of Output

Institutions supported by ACBF-PACT undertake research, policy analysis, training, linkage and exchange programs, institutional reform programs, and numerous other capacity building activities, which contribute improved development management at the national and regional levels. These institutions have also begun contributing to a stronger voice of civil society and the private sector in the articulation, design, and management of development policies and programs. Many research and policy analysis works are commissioned: by governments to enhance understanding of the behavioral functions of fundamentals in the development process and provide necessary inputs into policy and program design and implementation; by donor agencies to facilitate reforms in development assistance policies and programs and their management; and by the private sector to provide informed analysis for investment planning and foster effective dialogue with the public sector.

Training provided by the institutions strengthens skills in the core public sector. On average, beneficiaries from the core public sector account for about 80% of participants, and the retention rate for beneficiaries of postgraduate training has remained very high as demonstrated by the collaborative Master's Program of the African Economic Research Consortium and Programme de Troisième Cycle Interuniversitaire.

The general level of output utility produced by institutions supported by ACBF-PACT is summarized below.

- Macroeconomic and sectoral policy analysis and research continue to provide a strong basis for policy reforms, design, implementation, and monitoring. These analyses contribute to improvements in:
  - Rural development and agricultural policy reforms (e.g., Tanzania, Kenya)
  - Public expenditure review and reform of tax policy and budgetary processes (e.g., Benin, Ghana, Senegal, and Tanzania)
  - Efficacy of economic forecasting and enhancement of macro and sectoral policy analysis and planning models in areas such as agriculture, industry, education, infrastructure, heath, small and micro-enterprises, and tourism (e.g., Côte d'Ivoire, Kenya, Nigeria, and South Africa)
  - Preparation of national development plans and development of national vision documents (e.g., Botswana, Kenya, Namibia, and Zambia)
  - Country Development Assistance Strategy (Tanzania)
  - Research and consultative support, drafting and review of poverty reduction strategies and programs and the consultative process involved (e.g., Kenya, Tanzania, Namibia, Benin, Mali, and Zambia)
  - Understanding the dimensions and implications of the new EU-ACP Cotonou Agreement and challenges for African countries (e.g., Benin, Côte d'Ivoire).
- Secondment of core professionals to economic ministries and agencies to help strengthen capacity for policy analysis and to assist in implementing specific development policies and programs (e.g., Botswana, Kenya, Senegal and Zambia)
- Participation of the professional staff of the institutions supported in national delegations to regional and international meetings and conferences, including World Trade Organization conferences to help inform policy dialogue and assist countries to stand sensibly on policy issues (e.g. Botswana, Kenya and Zambia)

- Institutional participation in interministerial task forces and committees for policy analysis, review, reform and monitoring to contribute vital inputs in the design and implementation of policy and institutional reforms as well as the effectiveness of development policies and programs (e.g., Kenya, Namibia, and Zambia)
- Portfolio project contributions to reform of policy institutions, including prepared briefing papers for government on development policy issues (e.g. review of the President's Economic Advisory Council and Land Reform Program in Namibia, briefing papers in Namibia, Senegal and Zambia)
- Institutional contribution to the flow of economic information through book series, research report series, working papers, occasional papers, economic reviews, policy briefs, policy analyses journals, monthly macroeconomic indicators, and economic reports helps heighten awareness of development issues and enhance understanding of policy options. This is playing a vital role in dialogue among stakeholders in national development
- Platform for broadening consultation and dialogue among development stakeholders at the national level, especially through the activities of the interface projects such as NGOCC, Zambia; NGO Council, Kenya; PRIESP, Mali; PSCGT, Kenya; SANGOCO, South Africa; CSD-PSF, Tanzania
- At the regional level, institutions undertake activities geared towards the design of convergence criteria for harmonizing economic policies in UEMOA countries, strengthening of the capacity of highly indebted poor countries on issues relating to debt relief and poverty reduction, as part of regional delegations to conferences, roundtables, and negotiations addressing issues of interregional relations (e.g., PASU, Africa Union).

THE ACBF-PACT MODEL:
SOME CONSTRAINTS AND LESSONS OF EXPERIENCE

Despite its strong performance record, the ACBF-PACT model has had to contend with a number of constraints to project development and implementation. The environment for capacity-building activities, which is largely outside ACBF's control, continuing conflict in some African countries has made it difficult to commence project development activities, explore further potential interventions for pipeline development or effectively monitor project implementation. Recent examples include an attempted coup in the Comoros, gunfire and heightened tension in Central African Republic, separatist insurgence in Cameroon, and ethnic and religious violence in Nigeria. The eight-year civil war in Burundi was brought under control by the transitional government that provided for power sharing in November 2001, but the environment is still characterized by uneasy calm. Sierra Leone, Liberia, Angola, Mozambique, Eritrea, and the Democratic Republic of Congo, among others, are to varying degrees still politically volatile, rendering systematic intervention through the ACBF-PACT model difficult at times.

On the operations end, for a few projects management instability, low remuneration to staff, and inability to mobilize cofinancing constitute some of the constraints to effective project implementation. Lessons in project management include the need for greater attention to project location to strike a reasonable balance between visibility and effectiveness, as amply demonstrated by the relocation of some projects from offices of presidents to those of the prime ministers. Inadequate funding and lack of strong political commitment to National Focal Points suggest that the prospects of having these points serve as an effective institutional support for upstream project development activities will be a long term expectation. It has also become evident that more attention needs to be paid to tracking project impacts and broadening policy dialogue at the country level so as to strengthen support for participatory development and the role of the private sector and civil society in the design, implementation, and monitoring of development programs. Some of the lessons that need highlighting include the following:

Location of policy unit in government. Increasingly obvious to ACBF-PACT is that the high profile office of the president, vice president or prime minister while good for visibility, is not often the most suitable location for a policy unit in government. The distraction suffered by such units more than offsets the benefits of its locational advantage.

Cofinancing. Projects face increasing difficulty in their efforts to raise cofinancing. Official development assistance is currently on a declining trend, which implies that fewer absolute and relative resources will be available for development financing in the years ahead. This has implications for bilateral donor cofinancing support to ACBF-PACT–funded institutions. This means there will be pressure for ACBF-PACT to moderate its cofinancing policy and take on an increasing share of project financing responsibility. Yet the case for full financing, as tempting as it may seem, poses a potential moral hazard that ACBF-PACT would prefer to avoid. Cofinancing by project promoters, especially beneficiary governments, is key to growing commitment to a project and enabling long-run sustainability as donor support terminates.

Institutional sustainability. For a good number of ACBF-PACT projects, long-run sustainability will remain a threat. And yet, there has to be a limit to the number of times an institution can be refinanced. While it would be most appropriate for the ACBF-PACT to look at individual project cases on their own merit, it will not be out of place to begin to contemplate guidelines for the maximum refinancing an institution can receive. A policy guideline in this direction is desirable, but all its ramifications will need to be examined.

Staff retention. A few institutions in ACBF-PACT portfolio have recently suffered staff retention problems due to the noncompetitiveness of compensation packages, constraining project environment and the short-term nature of employment contracts. Institutions without a stable source of funding for their operations are usually regarded as high-risk employers. Consequently they experience difficulty in attracting the best professionals in the labor market. This partly explains why in countries such as Botswana and Namibia where highly skilled nationals are easily absorbed by well-established institutions, including the government, donor-funded institutions find it difficult to implement indigenous staffing. The situation is exacerbated further if such institutions decide to offer contracts with durations of no more than one year. Thus, generally, grant-financed institutions are perceived as insecure and consequently need premium remunerations to enable them to offset the risk. Without enhanced remuneration, ACBF-PACT–supported institutions will find it difficult to attract the best employees.

Staffing of policy units in government. An open and competitive recruitment policy remains a cornerstone for staffing institutions that benefit from ACBF-PACT support, and this has been pursued relentlessly in the supervision of project implementation. Vacancies filled by ACBF-PACT–supported institutions adhere strictly to the guidelines. However, what seems to be emerging is that sometimes officers drawn from the civil service to staff a policy unit located within government are not easily acceptable.

The reason is either that the rule of transparency and competitiveness may have been compromised in the recruitment process, or the sudden change in the status of the newly-appointed officers creates tension, leading to lack of cooperation among departments that are supposed to work with and benefit from policy unit activities. Some of the policy units in government, typified by an experience in Zambia, have had to grapple with this tension. The impact is that the project becomes underused and less effective.

Role and responsibilities of institutions' board and management. ACBF-PACT is still grappling with the issue of the tenure of project board members, within the context of institutionalized membership and entrenched interest of project founders or promoters who have a vision to actualize. Meanwhile, it has been able to deal with the issue of dual membership of board and management, when such cases did arise, although there is strong concern about projects in which board members double as members of management staff, despite the perceived effectiveness. Experience with a project case in Nigeria showed that when board members also are responsible for implementing project activities as members of management, operational ineffectiveness tends to set in. One reason for this is that the governing board finds it difficult to guide, or it becomes complacent in issuing directives to the management. ACBF-PACT must therefore continue to pay considerable attention to the nature of the governance structure that guides the operation of its institutions.

In spite of the constraints and shortcomings identified above, what is emerging is that the ACBF, since its establishment and particularly since the integration of PACT, has demonstrated visible potentials to respond effectively to some of the core human and institutional capacity needs associated with the development challenges facing Africa. Its achievements are, however, modest compared to the magnitude of the needs still remaining.

Expansion of ACBF-PACT's mandate has generated strong momentum in capacity building, with Africa and its development partners showing a strong sense of commitment to the capacity-building process. This development, if sustained, will contribute immensely to a significant reorientation of traditional technical assistance in the direction in which it needs to be reformed over time. Given this model, it is tempting to consider the possibility of bilateral and multilateral donors, over time, folding into ACBF-PACT their traditional technical assistance programs. A few donors have expressed positive disposition to this possibility as a potential long-term outcome of traditional technical assistance reform. The development community must build on this optimism; it is a challenge that the development community must meet in the true spirit of partnership for Africa's development.

The demand-driven approach that underpins the implementation of ACBF-PACT expanded mandate, and the intensive consultation that has given rise to the process by which it is building capacity, hold tremendous prospects for future interventions and the effective targeting of some of the capacity needs required to address Africa's development challenges. Indeed, the launching of the national focal point (NFP) program, which has seen the establishment of NFPs in twenty-six countries, represents a good start for African countries striving to launch participatory development frameworks and for the preparation of poverty reduction strategies and programs.

Given the growing pipeline of requests for support from African countries, ACBF-PACT will need to play an even more visible and significant role in helping countries implement principles of participatory development and, very importantly, enhance their capacity to design, implement, monitor, and evaluate poverty reduction strategies and programs given the pressing capacity needs being expressed.

Finally, the expansion of the mandate has caused the ACBF-PACT model to emerge as an institutional framework with a clear orientation, strategies, and instruments for building and strengthening sustainable indigenous capacity rather than relying on external technical assistance. The ACBF-PACT model should constitute one of the cornerstones of the new vision that guides capacity building in Africa in twenty-first century. The growing strength and performance of the model calls for far-reaching reforms in traditional technical assistance programs so that well-established institutional frameworks can manage the declining flow of resources for capacity building in sub-Saharan Africa.

Conclusion

Policymakers in Africa and in the development community agree that capacity building, use, and retention are the greatest challenges facing the region in its quest for sustained growth and development. Declining development financing from domestic and external sources points to the need for new approaches to how technical assistance is used, to ensure its effectiveness, particularly in Africa. Failure of most technical assistance projects and programs has arisen from the fact that many of them lack the fundamentals for successful capacity building. Poor design and inefficient implementation have been major pitfalls. Worse still, the ultimate effect on capacity building and institutional development is very minimal.

The ACBF-PACT model offers an opportunity for the development community to effectively use resources for capacity building. As an emerging best practice model, ACBF-PACT embraces a number of the fundamentals for a successful approach to capacity building and institutional development. Built on a listening and learning project cycle framework, the ACBF-PACT model supports capacity needs assessments as the basis for the design of capacity-building interventions; a participatory project development and management process; governance structures for ownership and accountability; partnering and coordination in the capacity-building process, all stakeholders monitoring and evaluation system; and strategies for long-run sustainability. The model has been tested over ten years with demonstrable results.

The ACBF-PACT model could constitute one of the cornerstones of the new vision that should guide capacity building in Africa in the twenty-first century. It ventures to suggest that donors consider the possibility of folding into the framework offered by the model, over time, their traditional technical assistance programs. A few donors are sanguine about this possibility as a potential outcome of the reform of traditional technical assistance. The development community must build on this optimism—it is a challenge that all should meet to in a true spirit of partnership for Africa's development.

References

ACBF. 2001. *Strategic Medium Term Plan*, 2002–2006.

ACBF. 2001. *Status Report on Project Implementation*, 2001.

Ogiogio, G. 1999. *ACBF-PACT: Implications of Changing Mandate on Networking and Communication Strategy*. Paper presented at the ACBF-ECDPM Workshop on Communications Strategies for Development Networks: Lessons and Potentials, December 15–17.

———. 2000. *Economic Renewal for Africa: Some Fundamentals*. Discussion presented at the Rockefeller Africa Renewal Colloquium, January 17–18.

———. 2002. *Donors-Funders Expectation in Program Management*. Discussion presented at the First Regional Members' Strategic Meeting of Consumers International, January 29.

Ongile, G. 2000. Gender and Development in sub-Saharan Africa. *ACBF Newsletter*, November–December.

Botchwey, K. 2002. *Traditional Technical Assistance Practice in sub-Saharan Africa: A Preliminary Assessment*. Cambridge, Mass.: Center for International Development.

World Bank. 1991. *The African Capacity Building Initiative: Toward Improved Policy Analysis and Development Management Capacity in sub-Saharan Africa*. Africa Region. Washington, D.C.: World Bank.

———. 1999. *Giving Voice To Civil Society in Africa: A Framework for Capacity Building.* Capacity Building Unit, Africa Region. Washington, D.C.: World Bank.
———. 1999. *The Partnership for Capacity Building in Africa: An Initiative of the African Governors of the World Bank.* Washington, D.C.: World Bank.

7

Governance and Policy Analysis

VASANT MOHARIR

Importance and Antecedents of Governance

The issue of governance has attracted considerable attention from political leaders, international development agencies, and social scientists in the last decade. Governance has become the cornerstone of much of the recent development cooperation and "has emerged from virtual obscurity to take a central place in contemporary debates in social sciences" (Pierre & Peters, 2000:1). The motives behind donor agencies' interest in the governance phenomenon may be different, ranging from genuine interest in giving more attention to the neglected political dimension in development cooperation, to finding a scapegoat for the failure of the economically oriented structural adjustment programs especially in Africa. Such scapegoating allows them to blame this failure on the African political environment characterized by authoritarian regimes, lack of accountability and transparency, corruption, civil wars and ethnic conflict, and violation of human rights (World Bank, 1992; Abrahmson, 2000:65) or to provide "an acceptable face for spending cuts" (Rhodes, 2000:55). At any rate, this resumed interest in political and administrative development issues is to be welcomed.

In fact, the issue of governance is not new in development debates. In the 1960s and 1970s, a number of prominent social scientists tried to conceptualize and operationalize the concept of political development and its stages, and to delineate its important attributes of democracy, representative government and administration, accountability and transparency, equitable access, and legitimacy of rule (Lipset, 1960; Almond & Coleman, 1960; Almond & Powell, 1962; Almond & Verba, 1963; Riggs, 1964; Apter, 1965; Pye, 1966; Braibanti, 1969). Also, international organizations such as the United Nations tried to develop indicators of political development, corresponding to considerable work done by the economists in measuring economic growth and experimented with competing Western pluralistic and socialist mobilization models in some African countries, with mixed results but with little impact on governance performance (Tordoff, 1993). In the last few years both local political leaders in less developed countries (LDCs) and the international development community have shown interest in rehabilitating many aspects of governance (political development) including promoting multiparty democracy, periodic and free elections, better observance of human rights, and better access for women and minorities to public services. This is an opportune time to make the ideas of governance concrete and extend them to major government decision-making processes such as policy planning, public budgeting, public service recruitment, and location and criteria for service delivery mechanisms.

This chapter concentrates on the redesign of the public policymaking process in LDCs, which is one of the main instruments that gives shape to the constitutional provisions, rhetoric, and vague, ambitious policy statements of political leaders. This is also an area that has not yet received priority in donor-assisted projects on governance, which on the one hand support improvement of more visible political institutions such as elections, legislature, and political parties, and on the other hand concentrate on narrow efficiency oriented administrative reforms based on the New Public Management (NPM), which in their home country England has led to a shift of emphasis from policy to management (Harrison & Gretton, 1987).

There is a very close link between the concept of governance and the process of public policy-making (Rhodes, 2000). Unfortunately, in most developing countries, as yet there is no explicit process for policy analysts or policy makers to follow or specific governance related criteria to be used to compare policy options or assess past policy performance. In the last decade, awareness for improving the process of public policy-making has been stimulated through the World Bank initiated African Capacity Building Fund, located in Harare (Moharir, 1991). At the national level some initiatives have been taken to set up training programs in policy analysis. Think Tanks to stimulate research and new ideas in policy-making have been set up inside or outside the government machinery in Botswana, Mauritius, Namibia, and Nigeria, and African organizations such as the African Centre for Training and Research in Development Administration (CAFRAD) have also conducted some short-term training programs in policy analysis for senior administrators (Moharir, 1992; CAFRAD, 1997). The ECA has also organized a few workshops on developing indicators of governance for African countries. However, the impact of these measures is still limited, particularly with reference to linking the ideas of governance with public policy-making (IDS, 1995).

Governance and Public Policy Literature

Despite its close relationship with governance, theoretical and empirical literature on public policy provides few insights, especially about developing countries. Much of this literature originated in the United States and recently in western Europe, which often discusses issues in the context of political and social institutions, environment, and political culture of these countries, which are characterized by political pluralism, strong institutionalization of interest groups, participative political culture, well settled notions of nationhood, relative abundance of resources, and a generally acceptable level of governance performance. In these countries there was no need to look at the policy process from the governance perspective, as the governance issues were settled and effective constitutional and other mechanisms for ensuring compliance with various attributes of governance were already in place. Hence, in these countries policy change could be incremental and criteria for assessing policy performance could be limited. In the absence of these attributes of political development and political culture, the countries of the developing world need a more explicit, comprehensive, multicriteria approach to policy process and policy analysis, to partly compensate for their late start on political and economic development.

From our perspective in this study, most of the generic literature on public policy can be categorized into process oriented and criteria oriented. It can also be grouped into normative approaches (how the policy process should be structured or designed) and behavioral (how the process actually takes place or what the policy really is). Many analytical models of policy-making enumerate stages and steps in policy formulation, implementation and evaluation (Anderson, 1975; Hogwood & Gun, 1984) and some normative models of the process also exist (Dror, 1968; Etzioni, 1988; Dunn, 1981). Although these models provide interesting insights for simplifying the complexity of the process, they do not provide any comprehensive set of criteria, comparable to the concept of good governance, except partial criteria of cost and benefits, or the criteria of policy change to be incremental, comprehensive or mixed. The assumption behind many of these models is that the proof of the pudding is not in eating but the way it is made. The only guarantee of a successful policy is to have a decision-making process based on steps and stages indicated in their respective models. In actual practice, a policymaker may go through the steps suggested in the models, but the outcome may still not be optimum.

In ensuring a successful outcome of the policy process in terms of solving or minimizing particular social problems, we need, in addition to the normative ideas of the process, normative criteria to compare different policy options, appraise existing policy designs, and assess past policy performance. This is what the criteria approach to policy analysis aims to provide and refers to the contents of the policy, its objectives, alternatives chosen, consequences considered, and mechanisms provided for compliance. In the literature on public policy, this approach is still not as prominent as the process approach, despite its relevance to real life policymakers. In real life, when a particular policy is criticized by someone, he or she has in mind a particular criterion that the policy does not fulfill or its realization is very limited. Most of the policy debates in legislature, media, political campaigning, and discussions of ordinary citizens take place around criteria of a "good" or "successful" policy that different stakeholders have in mind. The problem for the policy makers is how many and which criteria should they use in designing public policies?

Another issue is the source of these criteria. There are many recipes for good policies derived from political philosophies, ideologies, and social sciences. Dror mentions twenty-two disciplines/fields of studies that have contributed to public policy literature (1968:223–24) but it is difficult to use insights derived from all of them. It is practical and desirable to concentrate on the most important ones, such as political science, economics, sociology, public administration and management, law, logic, and ethics. Central to all these approaches is the emphasis on equity, evidence, cause and effect relationship, exception and universality, thesis and antithesis, and manner of argumentation. Some of them also provide specific formats and checklists for appraising or assessing policy design or impact such as that provided by Dunn, which is used at many training institutes (Gasper, 1996) but their use in actual government decision-making is still very limited. In this regard we need to pay attention to Etzioni's comment: "From the perspective of policy sciences, the quality of a decision is assessed not on the degree to which it conforms to or uses theory or specific methodologies, but on the degree to which it actually helps citizens or meets specific goals" (1988:67). Peter deLeon, the former editor of *Policy Sciences*, also reminds us about the characterization of policy sciences by its pioneer, Harold Lasswell, as a "problem oriented, contextual, multi-method enquiry in the service of human dignity for all" (2000:165). Similarly, Lynn advises us not to rely on centrality of any one discipline and only quantified evidence in assessing policy performance (2000:165). To be useful, policy analysis has to be based on a minimum set of commonly acceptable normative criteria of a good policy, which are usable in actual practice.

The literature does not clarify what constitutes this minimum set of criteria for a good policy. Each of the social sciences has an implicit notion of a good policy that covers the ambit of that discipline. However, policymaking is a multidisciplinary phenomenon. Policy sciences and policy studies as two main multidisciplinary fields have this challenge of integrating the criteria derived from different disciplines in an operational framework that can be used by policy analysts and policymakers. However, not much work has been done in this direction so far. Some of the attempts to enquire why policies fail or succeed and to develop a set of criteria are discussed below.

In the public policy literature, the criteria for a good or successful policy can be derived from (a) empirical studies of public policy-making and (b) from normative treatises and models of public policy-making, referred to earlier. There are many empirical studies of policy implementation, including those commenting on the political dimension, but very few generic or comparative studies like the ground-breaking study in business management by Peters and Waterman *In Search of Excellence* (1982), from which a set of criteria can be distilled. Most public policy studies are of failures, rather than success. An exception is Samuel Paul's *Managing Development Projects: Lessons of Success* (1982), which suggests a process model derived from successful project interventions in developing countries. Important contributions in public policy are Ingram and Mann (1980) *Why policies succeed or fail?* and T. B. Smith's 1989 article, "Analysis of Policy Failure: A Three Dimensional Framework." While the former provided many insights to causes of failure, there was no systematic attempt to come up with a set of operational criteria for future policy analysis. Smith's contribution suggested appropriate perspective, consensus and agreement, implementability, sustainability, effectiveness, adequacy, and sufficiency, especially in the context of developing countries.

On the normative side, in the social science literature in general, there are many treatises on a single criterion, such as equity, justice, efficiency, participation, transparency, or accountability, which are put forward by individual scholars as guides for public action and also empirical studies showing their presence or absence, but (a) their operational implications for policy-making have not been drawn out, and (b) in reality the policymaker cannot decide only on a single criterion. Dunn (1981), one of the early contributors to policy analysis literature suggested the criteria of effectiveness, efficiency, adequacy, equity, responsiveness, and appropriateness. Stuart Nagel, based on his model of Super Optimum Solutions or "win-win" approach, which claims to make both conservatives and liberals happy with policy choice, and which has been tested in training situations in many developing countries, suggests criteria of a successful policy as inexpensive, visible and accessible, politically feasible, specialized competence and aggressive representation (1998:52–53, 2000:27–29). In the recent literature on the New Public Management (NPM), there has also been considerable discussion on the significance and adequacy of the three

Es criteria—effectiveness, efficiency, and economy—derived mainly from economics and management literature, as evaluation criteria justifying new policy options and overall public sector reform. In response, the political scientists and public administrators have come up with their own 3Ps: participation, predictability, and procedure and adding their own fourth E, electability (Nagel, 1998:101). Christopher Hood suggests selection among many alternatives, matching the policy instrument with the task at hand, satisfying ethical values (without specifying which), effectiveness and efficiency (Hood, 1983:133). From the point of view of linking governance and policy studies, Rhodes points out that "much of the previously dominant literature on policy networks has been reformulated and reinterpreted into a governance framework" (1997:50.). Further, in his treatise *Understanding Governance: Policy Networks, Governance, Reflexivity and Accountability* (1997), he pleads for using governance as a framework for comparing policy performance of different types of governments. In this context the study of power and policy in four liberal democracies of the United States, England, France, and Japan using criteria of efficiency and responsiveness is also relevant (Harrop, 1992). To this can also be added the criteria emphasized by international development agencies such as environmental sustainability, equal access to men and women, and observance of human rights.

The literature in project planning and management has also tried to come up with a multicriteria approach to project decision-making based on analysis of technical, economic, financial, institutional, environmental, project design feasibility and project impact, and some checklists were also suggested (Rondinelli, 1976, 1979). But this approach was criticized as narrowly conceived in relation to reality, minimizing the impact of social, political, and cultural dimensions. However, adding these missing links a multicriteria framework can also be suggested for policy design (Rondinelli, 1983).

From a practical perspective of actually using some of the above criteria in governmental decision-making three questions arise: (1) how many and which criteria should be used, (2) what should be the source of these criteria, and (3) how to make them operational for actual use? Too many criteria will confuse and delay decision-making, while too few will continue present inertia and lead to dysfunctional policy results. Based on the insights from the literature reviewed above and based on author's experience of teaching public policy for developing counties for the last three decades, he has developed a framework of policy analysis using the following criteria, which many participants over the years have found relevant and usable in practical analysis of public policies.

Minimum Criteria a
Successful Public Policy Must Fulfill

The following six criteria are fairly well known, can be made operational for application, and their presence is found in many successful public policy interventions:

> *Effectiveness* (Achievement of goals and objectives of policy). Indicated by the contribution policy outputs make to realization of policy objectives.
> *Efficiency* (Realization of policy objectives in less time and with less cost). Indicated by the ratio of outputs to inputs.
> *Responsiveness* (Degree to which policy design is responsive to the legitimate interests of different groups affected by policy. Can be seen in all aspects of the policy design and the process.
> *Innovation* (Creativity and innovation in policy design mainly to realize the first three criteria, in practice difficult in bureaucratic environments).
> *Political feasibility* (Degree of acceptance of policy by proximate policy makers, political executives, legislature, and interest groups).
> *Administrative feasibility* (Willingness, capacity, and ability of implementing agencies and target groups to realize policy objectives within stated time and cost parameters).

Other criteria such as equity, adequacy, efficacy, transparency, and accountability can be subsumed under one or the other of the above mentioned criteria for example equity is part of responsiveness, adequacy and efficacy are covered under effectiveness and efficiency, and accountability is covered both by political feasibility and responsiveness. Also, the various other aspects of governance discussed earlier, such as the concern with ethnicity, corruption, and so forth are also implicit in the above six criteria.

Effectiveness

This concept has been discussed in different disciplines but has been developed well in management and planning studies. It can be applied both at the policy and organizational level. Management studies particularly have developed methodologies for clear statement of objectives, their prioritization and categorization into short and long term, their operationalization through selection of indicators, and relating policy options to the realization of selected objectives. The concept of effectiveness is at the heart of methodologies such as strategic planning, organizational audit, value for money analysis, and program evaluation.

Application of the concept at the policy level is still comparatively underdeveloped, partly because in most developing countries, including Africa, there is no metapolicy, or policy on policy-making (Dror, 1971: 74–79) and no explicit process or procedure for public policy-making. In the absence of this the bureaucratic routine and orientation of particular political leaders influence the actual process. Often the policy statements of political leaders are vague and ambiguous without prioritization among objectives, partly as a matter of habit or to gain consensus. The lack of specification and clarity in the policy design leads to distortion of intended objectives during implementation by the bureaucrats or local level political decision-makers. Incorporation of effectiveness in policy design will make visible the concept of accountability of political and administrative leadership, and individuals and organizations can be rewarded or sanctioned more objectively on the basis of their contribution to effectiveness of public policies. Much of the recent public outrage against governments and the trend towards curtailing rather than improving the scope of government intervention indicate lack of effectiveness in public policies. Hence, the criterion of effectiveness is at the core of public policy performance.

Efficiency

There is comparatively more awareness of efficiency criterion in government decision-making, and concerns about efficiency are often expressed in government manuals, audit reports, and in general discussion of government activities in legislatures and the media. However, the actual practice of governance in most LDCs does not pay much attention to defining, monitoring and rewarding, or sanctioning good or bad efficiency performance. Much of the attention paid in many LDCs to efficiency has been in terms of internal bureaucratic performance, rather than the performance of government as a whole. Also, whatever intermittent appraisals of efficiency take place relate to financial and management efficiency of organizations, rather than policy efficiency. The whole design of the policy and particularly the choice of policy instruments have to be subjected to this criterion. In the context of an ambitious policy agenda, acute scarcity of resources in most developing countries, and the need to narrow the gap between the rich countries and themselves, critical attention to efficiency is essential.

In the last two decades, considerable progress has been made in measurement and assessment of government efficiency through development of statistical information and of direct and indirect indicators. Application of the efficiency criterion at the policy level is more difficult than at the organizational level, and it may be difficult to have one indicator of efficiency for a policy incorporating all objectives. Nevertheless, with a set of direct and indirect indicators and quantifiable and nonquantifiable outputs and inputs of policy, at least the direction of policy efficiency can be determined, if not the exact magnitude. However, in application of efficiency criterion, it is important to ensure that its enhancement is not at the cost of policy effectiveness.

Responsiveness

In Africa, for instance, responsiveness to clients and the population at large has been the hallmark of public accountability (Olowu, Soremolekun, Williams, 1999). The governance issues relating to ethnicity and equal access are covered by this criterion. A modern democratic state is expected to deal with all citizens equitably and to provide equitable access to public services. Rhetoric of governmental decision-making often calls upon political and administrative leadership to be responsive to all sections of the population and often the principle is also enshrined in the constitution. To the extent political executives, legislature, media, and interest groups are alert and carefully monitor policy formulation and policy implementation to safeguard their interests, policy designs may incorporate responsiveness. In the context of many developing countries, however, these institutions are still weak and policy pluralism is limited (Olowu, 2000:155). Thus, there is a need to make responsiveness an integral criterion of policy analysis in developing countries. In other words policy designs, policy objectives, policy options, and their consequences, and policy impact, need to be appraised on the extent to which the policy is responsive to all groups affected by public policies.

Sometimes responsiveness is narrowly conceived in terms of satisfaction of the immediate beneficiaries, which explains popularity of most distributive policies such as subsidies, extension of educational facilities to different groups and regions, or free health services. Often policies are responsive to politically strong and organized, urban interest groups but not to unorganized, disadvantaged, rural groups. Even a representatively elected legislature is not able to ensure this, as not all policy proposals come to the legislature for approval and, even when they do, their design does not facilitate analyzing their impact on different groups. Unless responsiveness becomes part of the standard procedure of policy-making, its realization in actual practice in most developing countries will be intermittent, uneven, and opportunistic. To the extent government decision-making is open and consultative and participation mechanisms proliferate, responsiveness is enhanced. In the absence of these, training of senior civil servants and incorporation of this criterion in performance evaluation of individuals and organizations are the main avenues for ensuring responsiveness.

Innovation

Innovation refers to creativity in policy design. Creativity, according to Jane Henry, is "about the quality of originality that leads to new ways of seeing and novel ideas" (1991:3). Creativity is associated more with lateral than with horizontal thinking (de Bono, 1991:3–23) and with the activity of the right side of the brain (Henry, 1991:58–71). The leading gurus in business administration are also emphasizing this as the "soft side" of management, which is the main function of chief executive officers in leading multinational business organizations. Peters and Waterman in their celebrated contribution *In Search of Excellence* observe that "soft is hard" and that "innovative companies not only are unusually good at producing commercially viable new widgets; innovative companies are especially adroit at continually responding to change of any sort in their environments" (1982, 12) Creativity according to Dror is "dreaming realistic dreams" and to Geoffrey Vickers it involves "change in the appreciative system" which constitutes the art of judgment (1965, 1991:177–92). Creativity in policy-making requires more synthesizing and integrative skills and the ability to look at the problems from a broader, more holistic perspective, visualizing the proverbial whole elephant, rather than its trunk, ears, or tail alone (Dror, 1968:179). Forces of globalization, and the world economy becoming one, do not allow smaller nations to rely on the safe boundaries of the policy space of the nation state (Drucker, 1991:294–97). In the context of a heavy and complex agenda for public policy-making, limited policy consensus and unsatisfactory past performance in most African countries, the importance of innovation cannot be overexaggerated.

Political Feasibility

Despite the obvious significance of political factors in public policy-making, in the literature on politics and public policy, there have been very few attempts to operationalize this concept for practical use in policy analysis, some considering it Machiavellian, or too slippery to be caught neatly in any analytical framework and others considering it the prerogative of the politicians. In practice all political leaders and some senior administrators do think intuitively about the political feasibility of their policy ideas, but as yet there is no systematic tool or training for it. The politics-administration dichotomy also prevents many senior administrators from actively and systematically indulging in it. Response to this situation has been the rise of appointed political advisers by prime ministers and ministers. Unfortunately, their main purpose is to look at policy initiatives mostly from the perspective of party political agenda, rather than looking at political feasibility from the perspective of policy consequences on different political groups and making policy options acceptable to stakeholders.

Scholars such as Dror (1971:83–98), Meltsner (1972:859–66), Weimer and Vining (1989:292–22) have conceptualized political feasibility and provided formats to appraise political feasibility of policy options. In business administration and public management literature formats for doing stakeholders analysis are also to be found. Of these formats, the one provided by Dror is the most comprehensive, factoring the concept of political feasibility into various components and even providing some indirect quantification of probable political feasibility of different options (1971:83–92). The format provided by Weimer and Vining is too specific to the American local government scene. The format provided by Meltsner, derived from the literature on community power studies, is simpler and makes fewer demands on information and training of the analyst. It requires the analyst to identify the policy problem at issue; the relevant stakeholders, their orientation to different possible options, their resources, power base, and possible reactions; and their bargaining, negotiating, and coalition with other actors in the policy process. The end result of the exercise is to draw a scenario of political feasibility based on which existing alternatives can be adjusted, and strategies for overcoming resistance can be adopted by the policy-makers. In training situations, the format has been found useful by senior administrators from developing countries. This criterion of a successful policy is the most crucial one in terms of links with governance agenda.

Administrative Feasibility

In the context of the rediscovery of institutional development, (Lane & Ersson, 2000), considerable attention is now being paid to institutional prerequisites of externally stimulated policy interventions. Many past policies in developing countries have floundered on the bedrock of administrative inability to implement policies according to their designs and priorities, leading to a limited or negative impact. At the level of national governments in LDCs, there is increasing awareness of this, but there is not yet much substantive change in the way administrative feasibility of policies is tested. If it is done at all, it is being done intuitively, on the basis of past experience or rule of thumb. In many developing countries, however, at the project level the project design often contains an implementation plan, schedule of implementation, milestones of achievements, and indication of financial and manpower requirements for implementation, partly as a result of donor requirements, but similar specifications do not exist in policy designs and policy proposals. Even in industrialized countries the implementation phase of public policies has been found to be very difficult (Pressman and Wildavsky, 1973). The literature on project planning and implementation documents, many failures due to lack of administrative feasibility, and even though some checklists used by bilateral and multilateral donors exist for appraising project proposals, there have been few attempts to conceptualize the criterion of administrative feasibility to be used in policy analysis.

Conceptually, administrative feasibility means that the policy proposal that fulfills other criteria is also feasible on administrative grounds (Whang, 1978). When a proposal is administratively feasible, either required administrative capacity exists in implementing agencies (public, private, and voluntary) entrusted with the whole or part of public policy implementation, or this can be created and appropriate resources are available. However, implementation of many public policies requires certain responses not only from public, private, and voluntary organizations but also from social groups and individuals. A set of incentives and sanctions may be needed to get the desired behavioral changes from recipients of public policy; thus resources, legislation, and political persuasion may be required. Explicit, analytical attention paid to such aspects at policy design stage, enhances their administrative feasibility; and policy analysts need to be trained to do administrative feasibility analysis, using case studies of policy implementation, available checklists in the literature, and experience of successful policy implementers.

Priority Among the Criteria

For greater consistency and coherence, these six criteria need to be used simultaneously—a successful policy will in the long run display conformity with all of the criteria. If because of resource or time constraints, priority or different weight has to be given to different criteria, this has to be done with the consent of the policy-maker, depending upon the degree of novelty and uncertainty in realizing policy objectives within the time and cost span, present status of policy performance, and degree of support of or opposition to the policy in the environment. Other things being equal, the most important criterion for most developing countries is effectiveness. If the objectives of the policy are not the desirable ones and if the desirable objectives are not being realized, there is little use improving performance on other criteria, particularly improving the efficiency of implementing a wrong policy (Nagel, 1998:101). If policy performance is satisfactory on the effectiveness criterion, paying more attention to efficiency will be useful in improving policy performance. But for many complex redistributive policies in developing countries such as income distribution; poverty alleviation; low-income housing; agricultural subsidies; employment; AIDS; and language, ethnic, and population control policies, higher weight needs to be given to the effectiveness criterion.

Hierarchy of Successful Policies

A better policy or a policy option hierarchically is one that:

- scores high on all six criteria
- scores high on one criterion without adversely affecting existing performance on other criteria
- scores high on one criterion but low on another criterion and the trade off is acceptable to the policy-maker; trade-off can be defended and made politically and administratively feasible.

In the long run, all criteria should have equal weight. There will be criticism of the policy whenever performance falls below the acceptable level on any of criteria. However, at a particular point of time, policy-makers' attention may be focused more on one particular criterion such as efficiency or responsiveness because of a strong deterioration of performance on that criterion requiring special attention. For example, improving financial efficiency of public policies became a very high priority for most governments in Africa in the last decade, partly as a result of external and internal pressures. But care needs to be taken to ensure that improving performance on that one criterion is not at the cost of deterioration of performance on other criteria. This is where the innovation criterion becomes very relevant. Also if the present monitoring of policies, only of financial and physical inputs and outputs, is replaced by monitoring based on the six criteria, problems can be detected earlier.

Quantifying policy performance on each of the criteria using a set of indicators will add to objectivity and explicitness in policy analysis, but, if that is not possible, performance against each criterion can be assessed using a subjective five-point scale of Excellent, Very Good, Good, Average, and Unsatisfactory. This may be done by the policy analyst based on available performance data, or a group may be asked to this, as is done in many cases using the score-card or Delphi method. At the present stage priority in developing countries needs to be given to qualitative assessment of policy performance using multiple criteria to ascertain the direction of policy change, rather than its exact quantum. In the final analysis, the criteria approach to policy analysis is expected to assist the exercise of intuition and judgment by the political decision-maker. The purpose is not to supplant the prerogative of the political decision-maker to exercise judgment but to supplement and help in informed and responsible exercise of it.

The above framework can be used for appraising ex-ante and ex-post-facto performance of a particular policy, or for comparing different policy alternatives, for comparative studies of similar public policies in different countries, or policy performance of total political systems. Based on his comparative study of power and policy in four liberal democracies of England, France, Japan and the United States, using some of the criteria suggested above, Martin Harrop concludes, "If the balance in Japan is tilted towards effective rather than responsive government, emphasis in the more liberal democracies of the West is for responsiveness" (Harrop, 1992:279).

Conclusion

Bringing together the concepts of governance and public policy-making will be mutually beneficial by providing substantive operationalization to the concept of governance and affording a usable, relevant set of norms for assessing public policy performance, specific policy alternatives, or comparing total policy systems. Further work on these lines promises fruitful results. Even in business administration, with its comparatively more limited parameters of success, Peters and Waterman suggest a set of eight criteria, giving prominence to innovation and management of values for achieving excellence in business (1982:8–16). Similarly, Stephen R. Covey, in his international best-seller, *The Seven Habits of Highly Effective People*, included, among others, "be proactive, "think win/win" and "synergize," all emphasizing creativity and innovation essential for public success (1989:45–62).

References

Abrahmson, Rita. 2000. *Disciplining Democracy: Development Discourse and Good Governance in Africa*. London: Zed Books.

Adamolekun, L. and C. Bryant. 1994. *Governance Progress Report: The African Region Experience*. Washington, D.C.: World Bank.

African Training and Research Centre in Administration for Development. (CAFRAD). 1997. CAHIERS—African Administrative Studies, No. 49. Tangier, Morocco: CAFRAD.

Almond, G. A., and J. S. Coleman, eds. 1960. *The Politics of Developing Areas.* Princeton, N.J.: Princeton University Press.

Almond, G. A., and G. B. Powell. 1962. *Comparative Politics: A Developmental Approach.* Boston: Little Brown and Co.

Almond, G. A., and S. Verba. 1963. *Civic Culture: Political attitudes and Democracy in Five Nations.* Princeton, N.J.: Princeton University Press.

Anderson, James E. 1975. *Public Policy-Making.* London: Thomas Nelson.

Apter, D. E. 1965. *Politics of Modernization.* Chicago: University of Chicago Press.

Braibanti, Ralph, ed. 1969. *Political and Administrative Development.* Durham, N.C.: Duke University Press.

Covey, Stephen R. 1989. *Seven Habits of Highly Effective People: Powerful Lessons in Personal Change.* New York: Simon and Schuster.

De Bono, Edward. 1991. "Lateral and Vertical Thinking," Pp. 3–23 in *Creative Management,* ed. Jane Henry. London: Sage Publications.

De Leon, Peter and Todd A. Stedeman. 2000. "Making Public Policy Programmes Effective and Relevant: The Role of Policy Sciences: Curriculum and Case Notes." *Journal of Policy and Management* 20(1): 163–71

Dror, Y. 1968. *Public Policy-Making Reexamined.* San Francisco: Chandler Publishing.

———. 1971. "Prediction of Political Feasibility." Pp. 83–92 in *Ventures in Policy Sciences,* ed. Y. Dror. New York: American Elsevier.

Drucker, Peter. 1991. "Transnational Economy—Transnational Ecology." Pp. 294–97 in *Creative Management,* ed. Jane Henry. London: Sage Publications.

Dunn, W. N. 1981. *Public Policy Analysis: An Introduction.* London: Prentice Hall.

Etzioni, A. 1988. *Moral Dimension.* New York: Free Press.

Gasper, D. 1996. "Analyzing Policy Arguments." Pp. 36–62 in R. Apthorpe and D. Gasper, eds. *Arguing Development Policy: Frames and Discourses.* London: Frank Cass.

Harrison, P. and John Gretton, eds. 1987. *Reshaping Central Government.* Oxford: Transaction Books.

Harrop, Martin, ed., 1992. *Power and Policy in Liberal Democracies.* New York: Cambridge University Press.

Henry, Jane, ed. 1991. *Creative Management.* London: Sage Publications.

Hogwood B., and L. Gunn. 1984. *Policy Analysis for the Real World.* Oxford: Oxford University Press.

Hood, Christopher. 1983. *Tools of Government* (Public Policy and Politics Series). London: Macmillan.

Ingram, Helen, and Dean Mann, eds. 1980. *Why Policies Succeed or Fail?* Beverly Hills, Calif.: Sage.

Institute of Development Studies. 1995. "Towards Democratic Governance." *IDS Bulletin* 26(2).

Lane, Jan Erik, and Svante Ersson. 2000. *The New Institutional Politics: Performance and Outcomes.* New York: Routledge.

Lipset, S. M. 1960. *Political Man: The Social Basis of Politics.* London: Heineman.

Lynn, Laurence E., Jr. 2001. "The Changing Public Policy Curriculum : Introduction." *Journal of Policy Analysis and Management* 20(1): 161–62.

Meltsner, Arnold. 1972. "Political Feasibility and Policy Analysis." *Public Administration Review* 32(6): 859–66.

Moharir, V. 1991. "Capacity Building Initiative for Sub-Saharan Africa." *Public Enterprise* 11(4) 1991: 235–44.

———. 1992. "Institutionalization of Policy Analysis in Developing Countries: An Exploratory Approach." Pp. 253–74 in Asmerom, H. K., R. Hoppe, R. B. Jain, eds., *Bureaucracy and Development Politics in the Third World.* Amsterdam: VU University Press.

Nagel, Stuart. 1998. *Public Policy Evaluation: Making Super Optimum Decisions.* Aldershot, England: Ashgate.

———. "Win-Win Development Cycle for Africa and Developing Regions." *Development Policy Management in Africa* 7(2): 27–9.

Olowu, Dele. 2000. "Bureaucracy and Democratic Reform." Pp. 153–80 in *African Perspectives on Governance.* Goran Hyden, et al. eds. Africa World Press, Inc.

Olowu, Dele, Kayode Soremolekun, and Adebayo Williams, eds. 1999. *Governance and Democratization in West Africa.* Dakar, Senegal: CODESERIA Press.

Paul, Samuel. 1982. *Managing Development Projects: Lessons of Success.* Boulder, Colo.: Westview.

Peters, Thomas, and Robert H. Waterman, Jr. 1982. *In Search of Excellence: Lessons from America's Best Run Companies.* New York: Warner Books.

Pierre, Jon, ed. 2000. *Debating Governance.* Oxford: Oxford University Press.

Pierre, Jon and B. Guy Peters. 2000. Governance, Politics and the State, Political Analysis Series, Macmillan Press, London.

Pressman, J., and A. Wildavsky. 1973. *Implementation.* San Francisco: University of California Press.

Pye, L.. 1966. *Aspects of Political Development.* Boston: Little Brown.

Rhodes, R. A. V. 1997. *Understanding Governance: Policy Networks, Governance, Reflexivity and Accountability.* Birmingham: Open University Press.

Rhodes, R. A. V. 2000. *Governance and Public Administration.* Oxford: Oxford University Press.

Riggs, F. W. 1964. *Administration in Developing Countries: The Theory of Prismatic Society.* Boston: Houghton Mifflin Co.

Rondinelli, D. A. 1976. "Why Development Projects Fail: Problems of Project Management in Developing Countries." *Project Management Quarterly* VII (1976): 10–16.

———. 1979. "Designing International Development Projects for Implementation." In G. Honadle and R. Klauss, eds. *International Development Administration-Implementation Analysis for Development Projects.* New York: Praeger.

———. 1983. *Development Projects as Policy Experiments—An Adaptive Approach to Development Administration.* London: Methuen.

Smith, T. B. 1989. "Analysis of Policy Failure: A Three Dimensional Framework." *Indian Journal of Public Administration* 35(1) 1989: 1–15.

Tordoff, W. 1993. *Government and Politics in Africa.* London: Macmillan.

Transparency International. 1997. *TI Newsletter,* June 4.

Vickers, Geoffrey. 1965. *The Art of Judgement: A Theory of Policymaking.* London: Chapman and Hull.

———. 1991. "Judgement." Pp. 177–92 in *Creative Management,* ed. Jane Henry. London: Sage.

Weimer, David L. and Aidan R. Vining. 1989. "Thinking Strategically about Adoption and Implementation." Pp. 299–322 in Weimer and Vining Policy Analysis: Concepts and Practice. New York: Prentice Hall International.

Whang, I. J. 1978. "Administrative Feasibility Analysis for Development Projects: Concept and Approach." *Philippine Journal of Public Administration* 12(2): 155–68.

World Bank. 1992. *Governance and Development.* Washington, D.C.: World Bank.

8

European Union Environmental Regulations and Their Potential Impact on Market Access for Africa's Exports

PASCHAL B. MIHYO

The Setting

Africa's participation in the Uruguay Round negotiations was constrained by economic, institutional, information, and capacity problems. The economic constraints emanated from Africa's severe economic crisis as many countries were sinking under a heavy debt burden. Most traditional sectors were undergoing restructuring, especially industry and agriculture. Even so, these countries were restructuring and still did not have adequate capacity for new issues and problems such as climate change, environmental management, and world trade.

In terms of information, wide information gaps reduced the capacity of many African governments from adequately formulating common positions on key issues or even supporting their missions in Geneva to make informed decisions. Successful participation in the negotiations required— organized management information systems, requiring information technology and resources not available to many African governments.

In spite of these capacity problems African governments undertook and still are undertaking serious reforms and establishing the necessary institutions to enable their countries to participate in the emerging world trade regime. They have done this at a very high cost and against many odds. But in spite of the reforms traditional obstacles to market access for Africa's products continue (van Dijk et al., 1994:55–69). These include import restrictions, rigid quotas, unreliable commodity agreements, subsidies, pricing mechanisms, and rigid regional trade arrangements.

In addition new barriers have emerged and may have a longer and deeper impact on Africa's trade. These barriers, which emerged during the same period of the Uruguay Round negotiations and early period of implementation, include technical barriers to market access contained in the new environmental regulations and are based on international conventions on the use of natural resources (FAO, 1995; FAO, 1998a; ITTO, 1996) as well as international environmental agreements on the protection of human and animal health. Some arise from mandatory and some from nonmandatory treaties and recommendations. Although the majority are regional such as those of the EU or the OECD, their impact is global because they emanate from the world's biggest trade partners. Once these standard setters implement mandates within their own national borders, those seeking to trade with them either have to comply with them or adopt them in their own countries.

During the preparations for the Uruguay Round, the OAU, UNCTAD, and UNDP worked to mobilize regional economic communities and the African missions in Geneva to take a proactive approach, prepare positions on key issues and be ready to spend time and resources in the new round. In 1996, the UNDP launched a US$10 million project to support African negotiators in hopes of removing some of the problems of marginalization and passive participation that characterized Africa in the last round. This chapter seeks to evaluate the traditional and new obstacles to Africa's trade with the EU.

Traditional Barriers to Market Access for Africa's Products

Africa's share of the world's export market dropped from 0.8% in 1970 to 0.3% in 1995 (Njinkeu, 1998). Blackhurst and Lyakurwa (1996:4) have observed that tariff cuts instituted during the implementation of the Uruguay Round Agreements are not likely to increase market access for African products significantly because of the nature of Africa's products and export policies and the import policies of Africa's trade partners.

Africa's exports are characterized by a single commodity dependency, for example Angola (94.5% on minerals), Gabon (99% on oil), Nigeria (94.5% on oil), and Zambia (99% on minerals) (Njinkeu, 1998:2). In Zambia most of these minerals have fixed quotas and unstable prices and are exported, unprocessed, to traditional importers. Control of demand and destination by multinational corporations is very well established, and suppliers have very little say on the conditions that shape market access for their products.

The composition of export products has remained static for a long time. Ghana for example has always exported cocoa, cocoa butter, gold, and wood products. Kenya and Uganda have always relied on tea, cotton, and coffee and to that list Tanzania adds sisal, diamonds and pyrethrum. Botswana exports beef and diamonds. Due to this static composition, efforts have traditionally been made to step up production without delivering accompanying strategies for increasing processing capacity. Increased production without diversification has led to overproduction in some cases, resulting into stagnant market access and in most cases reduced prices (Brown and Tiffen, 1992). This has led in turn to the decline in the contribution of traditional exports to GDP, for example Kenya, from 70% 1980 to 47.6% in 1996 (Mwega and Muga, 1998:1).

Tariffs remain a major obstacle. Although on the EU market tariffs were already low and have been slashed in most of the traditional African product destinations after the Uruguay Round, some nontraditional markets have retained very high tariffs. Coffee, cotton and rubber exports still attract high tariffs in China and several other Asian countries. Cotton, cotton yarn, and textiles encounter stiff tariffs on the North American market. Exports of cocoa, cocoa butter, garments, and tinned fish are also subjected to high tariffs in Latin America, especially Brazil and Argentina, the biggest markets in that region (Njinkeu and Monkam, 1998:9; Oussu and Diomande, 1998:4). Furthermore, tariff reductions have been marginal on products of interest to Africa such as fish and fish products, textiles, clothing, and processed or semiprocessed goods. According to Njikeu (1998), in the EU, U.S. and Japanese reductions of tariffs on textiles and clothing were less than one percent.

Tariff peaks, nuisance tariffs, and tariff escalations on processed products have become a powerful instrument in the hands of the OECD countries to maintain a primary commodity export syndrome in developing countries. They are used as a mechanism of protectionism and serve to perpetuate the current world division of labor. It has been predicted (Njinkeu and Monkam, 1998:38) that while the average ordinary tariffs facing imports from the developing to developed countries will be as low as 12% in the post-Uruguay period, tariff peaks for important products will rise to an average of 350%. The most devastating tariff peaks and escalations will be in processed foods and textiles. Mwega and Muga (1998:33–6) have argued that developed countries are using these as instruments for establishing trade enclosures. Kenya, Mauritius, South Africa, and Zimbabwe are already beginning to absorb the impact.

Direct import bans and regular quarantines or restrictions also affect market access for developing country products. In some cases, the reasons for the restrictions are not convincing. For example, in 1998 the United States imposed restrictions on textiles from Kenya on the claim that Kenya was importing and reexporting them. Rules of origin were used but there was no substantiation and, due to power relations and lack of resources, Kenya did not avail itself of the dispute settlement procedures. Similarly regular bans of imports of fish from East Africa are imposed by the EU and the United States either on grounds of health or other sanitary standards.

Rigid quotas have been used in the Lomé Convention and under the various commodity agreements to restrict imports of commodities such as sugar and bananas. The quotas for sugar remained predictably static for a long time. This has suppressed the expansion of the sugar industry in Africa and other sugar producers. The United States was equally protective and limited the import of sugar, thereby almost stagnating the sugar industry in the Caribbean (IDRC, 1992:16–17).

While developed countries were enforcing these rigid quotas the World Bank and the EU continued supporting African countries for crop improvement, even for crops whose quotas were already stagnant. Crop improvement programs raised the level and quality of production while demand stagnated or decreased. Without a supportive increase in demand, prices crumbled, which coincided with the crumbling of the commodity agreements.

The combination of rigid and static quotas, funding of overproduction thus depressing prices, and the collapse of the commodity agreements is going to affect market access for a very long time. Many African countries have not had a chance to examine the potential opportunity presented by the Uruguay Round against the established historical barriers to trade that may not be removed by the new trade agreements.

Policy Reforms by African Countries

To increase their competitiveness African countries have undertaken deep and serious institutional and policy reforms. Exchange rate, import policy, and tax reforms have been effected in almost all the countries (Collier and Gunning, 1998). Some countries have even introduced deeper policy and institutional reforms to prepare themselves to participate in the world trade system. Ghana for example has introduced commodity-specific export promotion policies. Through these reforms institutions have been formed, incentive packages introduced, quality standards established, and notification made to the WTO about these policy reforms and institutions (Oduro and Yahya, 1998).

Trade liberalization has entailed the disbanding of crop marketing boards, deregulation of prices, and abolition of subsidies (Clapp, 1996). Regional economic communities are working on common policies in agriculture, industry, trade and intellectual property, aiming at a zero tariff regime by the end of 2002. For most countries, however, the reforms have meant lost revenues and job, income and welfare losses (Simon, 1994).

Although some researchers feel Africa's reforms haven't been rapid enough, given the available resources, African countries have done their best in restructuring their economies (see Shirley, 1999 and Ramamurti, 1999, for contrasting views). However, more reforms are needed in transport, tourism, and telecommunications.

Product and Process Environmental Regulations

These regulations cover products and processes deemed to be potentially hazardous. In the area of foodstuffs, for example, they are designed to prevent illness and death caused by food-borne diseases. Another example is the processing of wood products, which restricts use of certain chemicals harmful to humans and animals.

European companies have taken measures to comply with process-oriented environmental standards such as environmental management systems IS0 9000 certification standards. In April 1995, the European Commission established an environmental management audit scheme (EMAS) in which certified companies receive a special logo that they use for marketing purposes. The EU has also introduced the annual environmental report system on implementation of environmental standards. Such companies, if involved in importing products, will always want to import from countries applying similar standards.

Another significant process policy is waste management policy. For most products there are regulations on standards for disposal of packaging materials, and standards set within the EU are very high.

As a result, EU importers are increasingly going for packaging that can be recycled. The 2001 EU packaging regulations (European Commission, 1994) require that:

- Manufacturers and importers must recover 50% to 65% of the packaging materials brought into the market
- The packaging and weight are limited to the minimum for safety, hygiene, and consumer interest and acceptance
- Packaging must be designed so as to permit its reuse or recovery as in recycling
- Packaging must be manufactured to minimize the environmental impact of its disposal
- Packaging must minimize the use of noxious or hazardous substances.

From the outset most of these regulations were developed and put into force during the Uruguay Round negotiations. By establishing them at the same time free trade was being strengthened, the European nations were creating new technical barriers that would ensure they retained an upper hand in world trade. Together with this they were already setting the pace of environmentalism as a legitimate mechanism for defining the new rules of trade. They have used environmentalism to develop a new set of scientific and technical standards that will be transferred, copied, and applied by all countries that hope to trade with them.

Product and process environmental regulations have other, more significant, implications. One is that they create joint responsibility between importers and exporters because processes in the exporter country have a bearing on the liability of the importers. Due to this joint responsibility some obvious choices emerge. Either the exporters can form joint ventures with importers to be able to acquire the necessary technology to comply with the standards or get the necessary legitimacy and acceptance on the European market. The other alternative is for African countries to invite European companies to invest and operate from Africa because their acceptability on the European markets is almost guaranteed.

There are broader policy implications of this phenomenon. To comply with strict standards about fish products, for example, aquaculture has to be more and more privatized. In order to control levels of toxicity or pollution, communities may have to be closed out of commercial agriculture, forestry, or aquaculture. As is already happening in horticulture, farms have to be fenced and kept out of reach, calling for further intensification of private property and trespass laws. It also calls for a new culture that involves the exclusion of local communities from commercial farming areas. The political implications of this are social exclusion, concentration of land in the hands of a few, and garrison economies.

EU Legislative Measures and Products of Interest to Africa

Fresh Fruits and Vegetables

Africa's competitiveness is in horticulture, and the main destination of Africa's fruits and vegetables is Europe. Benin, Cameroon, Côte d'Ivoire, Ghana, Guinea, Kenya, Madagascar, Mali, Reunion, South Africa, and Zimbabwe are major exporters of passion fruits, pineapples, chilies, avocados, beans and mangoes to the EU, contributing to about 10% of EU imports in vegetables and fruits (Profound, 1997:29–30). Environmental regulations passed by the EU will affect Africa's access to this market:

maximum residue levels an example is the set of regulations defining and regulating the maximum concentration of pesticides in food products, and good agricultural practices based on European agricultural and ecological conditions.

Until 1995, implementing international standards on tolerable levels of pesticides in foodstuffs was voluntary and set jointly by the FAO, WHO, and Codex Alimentarius. Since 1995, the principle of voluntary enforcement has been set aside. The regulation provides that exporters who cannot meet the Codex standards can, with the help of the importer, take legal action to be exempted from such standards. However, most less developed countries will find it difficult to fund and sustain legal proceedings.

Another EU directive prescribes maximum levels of food additives and lists additives that are acceptable within the EU, and exporters must ascertain that these acceptable levels are not exceeded. High technical skills are required for scanning the products, which, in turn requires advanced and reliable technologies at the same level as those in importing countries. In some cases the maximum levels are not specified. Instead, vague clauses set the standard as "not more than necessary" and can be used to impose multiple standards and discriminate against least favored exporters. Such clauses encourage discretion, which can be abused.

A third area regulated by the EU is the presence of heavy metals such as cadmium, lead, and mercury, which are potentially hazardous to human health. These requirements cover tubers, yams, beet roots, mushrooms, fruit, vegetables, root vegetables, legumes, and fresh vegetables, most of which come from Africa and are produced by poor farmers with limited knowledge about such metals.

The control of mouldy foods is another area that will strain Africa's technical and technological capabilities. Tropical conditions are naturally conducive to the growth of moulds, which produce toxins that can affect the environmental quality of tropical foods. Although moulds such as fungus are easily detectable, their toxins are not. Small-scale producers, from whom most of the export foodstuffs are purchased, do not have the necessary resources to detect and control toxic substances in the foods they produce. These regulations pressure exporters to the European market to equip themselves with the means to control the quality of food exports.

The EU directive requires that exporters use techniques such as crop rotation, use of fungi-resistant techniques, use of fungicides, and the cleaning of fruits and vegetables with fungicides or hot water after harvest. These practices introduce new and rigid standards about best practices in farming and ignore traditional or indigenous systems of fungal control that vary from region to region. As a result they favor exports from large-scale, modern, and perhaps private commercial farmers. In addition, the regulations require drying facilities and climate control to reduce moisture in storage and transport facilities. All these require technologies and techniques recognized by and respected in the European countries, but such resources are not available to the poor farmers who form the bulk of suppliers to exporters.

Finally, standards for grading food products regulate their assortment, size, uniformity, color, marking, packaging, and presentation. These regulations are not known to many African exporters and reflect the cultural gaps between the two continents. European and African perceptions of measures and size are determined by cultural values, geographical and ecological conditions, family size, and other factors.

Regulatory Measures for Wood Products

Wood products constitute a significant component of African exports to the EU. Cameroon, Côte d'Ivoire, Gabon, and Nigeria together supply more than 50% of EU timber and wood product imports (Njinkeu, 1998). Four major types of EU regulations relate to timber and wood products.

One EU directive sets standards for the maximum levels of cadmium by weight in wood paints. At national level the maximum levels allowed in such paints are even much lower. Second, EU regulations restrict the use of pentachlorophenol, or PCP salts, which preserve wood (controlling fungi and insects) intended for indoor purposes. The use of creosote oils in treating wood or the sale of creosote-treated wood is prohibited if such wood is intended for use in public buildings, product, packaging or the production of breeding trays. A survey of twelve wood-exporting companies from Ghana, Nigeria, Cameroon, and Tanzania indicates that only 20% of them were aware of the European limitations on preservatives. But 60% indicated that some preservatives were unavoidable because of the climatic conditions. All of them indicated that, even if aware of the restrictions, they were unable to actually ascertain the levels due to the lack of relevant technologies.

Environmental Regulations for Fish Products

Developed countries are significant exporters of fish. Over 80% of the world fish exports are still from developed countries, with Japan alone accounting for over 30% of the world total fish exports. To protect their own interest and to regulate health standards, developed countries are introducing various quality control measures, which will affect developing countries.

The most effective set of standards, enacted in 1997, requires that all fish intended to be sold to markets must come from plants that comply with the standards.

To comply with these principles an exporter must acquire new technologies and start completely new production processes. The resources required to install new equipment are enormous and cannot be afforded by small or poor producers.

The EU countries have adopted sanitary additional guidelines on:

- Means of production (physical installation, construction and equipment water quality, disposal of refuse).
- Public health and hygiene of processing staff, maintenance, cleaning and disinfection of fishing boats, landing sites, and processing plants.
- Product standards on freshness, cleanliness, microbial contaminants, chemicals, toxic substances, and parasites.
- Standards on self-monitoring, official monitoring by national agencies, and EU monitoring and inspection (FAO, 1998b:7).

In March 1998, an outbreak of cholera in Mozambique led the EU to ban fish from all the East African countries. Three months later, the ban was lifted after the WHO declared that the disease-causing bacteria could not be transmitted through hygienically prepared fish or fish products. In March 1999, the EU imposed a new ban of fish from Lake Victoria after it was alleged that some fisher people were using pesticides to increase their catches.

Three East African countries invited EU experts to visit fishing sites. Several visits were made and a selective lifting of the ban followed. Tanzania and Uganda were then exempted while Kenya continued to be covered. Many fishing companies moved from Kenya to Uganda and Tanzania forcing Kenya to reduce its fishing operations by 80%. Until the ban was lifted in November 2000, Kenya was losing annual earnings worth US$50 million.

Many African countries are trying to introduce quality control measures, but few will manage to satisfy the high standards laid down by the EU. One easy option for them to comply is to go into joint ventures with European fishing companies. A second option is for African countries—through regional economic communities forming quality control, information, and standards units—to support fish exporters. In May 1999, the FAO gave the East African Cooperation about US$2.5 million to help the East African countries to improve quality standards of their fish for export to the European market. During the same period another US$2.5 million was donated by the EU to support improved quality of fish exports.

Consumer and Market Oriented
Environmental Standards

The EU has developed two types of regulatory mechanisms to strengthen their producers by stimulating a culture of environmental consciousness. In addition, international codes of conduct developed under the stewardship of OECD countries lay the basic standards for resource development and management. These two sets of environmental regulations have enabled the importers and producers in developed countries to dictate the pace, rhythm, and conduct of international trade in key areas globally.

Stimulation Policies to Create Environmental Competitiveness

The EU leads on importer incentives aimed at stimulating competitiveness and institutionalizing environmental values and standards at a global level. The three major instruments in this area are financial incentives, eco-information systems, and eco-labeling procedures and standards. Financial incentives include eco-taxes and the new Green General System of Preferences. Eco-taxes operate by sanctions and penalties, targeting environmentally unsound products and production processes through higher taxes. A pollution tax has been on the EU table for half a decade but no general policy has emerged. However, lead-treated fuel has higher prices in some European countries, while low energy products attract low tax rates.

In 1998, the EU introduced the concept of an encouragement regime based on 20% to 30% additional import tariff preferences for ecologically friendly and humanly sound products (child labor, social protection, and trade union rights). Human rights have crept into the EU trade regulations despite the social clause still being resisted by developing countries as part of the world trade standards. By introducing an encouragement policy of this type, the EU has introduced new trade conditionality in the world trade regime.

Eco-information systems are another set of EU instruments to enhance competitiveness among European companies on the EU market. European companies are encouraged to keep detailed information on product components, environmental characteristics, consumer preferences, and their eco-label records. This comprehensive product cycle information system aims to make the market more accountable to consumers. The effect, however, is to preserve the superiority of European products and to compel EU trade partners to comply with EU standards.

The third mechanism is the eco-labeling system, also developed as a marketing tool. Manufacturers and traders, who have used eco-information systems, have been allowed to develop their own private eco-labels, which are given to or allowed to be used by companies with a strong track record on environmental standards. Private companies have been quick to establish themselves as leaders on environmental quality, including garments manufacturers and wholesalers such as Esprit and Steilman (CBI and SIDA, 1996:51). In addition to private eco-labels there are a number of national eco-label systems.

In spite of the new agreement on textiles, eco-labeling seems to present a barrage of nontariff barriers that will keep textiles from developing countries out of the European markets. The new eco-labeling regulations have been popularized through an aggressive environmental consciousness campaign. There are about six EU ecolabels, but Germany alone has more than twenty-five eco-labels systems, The Netherlands and the Scandinavian countries about eight each. In addition to general product and process labels, organic labels are emerging both as a marketing tool and as instruments of screening imports and where they do not meet European standards, excluding them from the market or taxing them highly, thereby making them more expensive.

Codes of Conduct for Responsible Management of Environmental Resources

Most of the legislative and administrative regulations discussed above can be enforced through nonmarket mechanisms such as customs inspection and procedures. But market mechanisms are not enforced through administrative procedures—most although administratively engineered, are voluntary and have been popularized by the media, forming part of consumer culture. Two examples are discussed below. The EU has become a frontrunner in enforcing these policies.

The FAO Code of Conduct for Responsible Fisheries, drafted at the request of UNCED member countries and adopted in 1995, addresses the environmental, social, and economic impact of shrimp aquaculture, such as siting of ponds, benefits accruing to local communities arising from ponds in mangrove areas, ensuring shrimp aquaculture does not exhaust creek capacity, preservation of lagoons and coastal waters, and the nutritional and socioeconomic impact of conversion from agriculture to aquaculture.

The code also outlines the basic standards for responsible fishing beyond shrimp aquaculture, covering fisheries management, fishing operations, aquaculture development, integration of fisheries into coastal area management, post-harvest practices, and trade and fisheries research. Some of the problems of the code are inherent in the process through which it was developed. Berg and others (FAO, 1998:7) have noted the lack of institutional and legal support for carrying out the obligations prescribed by the code. Lack of adequate information by FAO member countries on the code and the Eurocentric bias of its provisions have been noted even by the FAO itself (FAO, 1996). It should be noted, however, that the code tries to address these limitations.

The last set of consumer oriented international codes is the Code on Sustainable Forest Management. The EU has taken the lead in developing a policy that allows trade only in wood products made out of sustainably managed forests. For a long time it has operated a system of voluntary certification. Following the EU, the ITTO also has established standards for sustainably managed forests. The standards require, among other things, that information is kept on the felling of trees in forests in which social and ecological aspects are important. They also call for action to ensure sufficient growth of trees, and they allow timber to be harvested from natural or primary forests if the quality of forests is not damaged. Such criteria are skill and information intensive and require good information systems and effective enforcement mechanisms.

Conclusion

Environmental standards are necessary to preserve health and quality of life, but they need to be developed jointly by all trade partners as they affect the livelihoods of millions living outside the OECD countries. Furthermore, they should not only target areas where protectionism is deemed essential but all areas relevant to public health.

Second, the introduction of environmental standards based on cultural norms and practices in the North may have disruptive effects in the South. Laws may need to be passed that require large-scale commercial agriculture, aquaculture, and civiculture. These policy shifts can seriously alter the entitlement systems of poor and indigenous communities. Controls may be introduced that limit the freedoms of communities to share resources. Violations of human rights may arise out of such policies. Many African countries are already caught up in environmental and resource conflicts and wars (Mohamed Salih, 1999).

Enforcement capacity is another issue. Montague (1998:46) has shown that after a quarter of a century of environmental regulation, health standards have been deteriorating in nine industrialized nations in spite of the superiority of their scientific infrastructure. The new environmental regulations add to an already long list of substances that need testing for toxic levels. The EU directive on permissible compounds for coloring paper for example, has six lists of compounds covering about 146 substances on coloring paper and another 153 for the treatment of writing materials—a huge task even for developed countries. According to Montague, the U.S. National Toxicology Program can study only twenty-five chemicals per year. For pesticides, it has not managed to cover more than 50% of those in use. If that is true, LDCs cannot be expected to do better.

It can therefore be concluded that such regulations can only perform three major functions. One, they can become instruments for integrating the economies of the South into those of the North by choice or necessity. Second, they can be used as instruments of protectionism.

But third, they can be gainfully used to raise global environmental awareness, including raising awareness of developing countries to the need to upgrade their systems, which can lead to partnerships beneficial to all involved. If adequate resources and time for transition were set aside for a gradual process, these regulations would go a long way to promote competitive cooperation and cooperative competition in world trade.

References

Blackhurst, R., and W. L. Lyakurwa. 1996. "Markets and Market Access for African Exports: Past, Present and Future Directions." Nairobi: African Economic Research Consortium.

Brown, M. B., and P. Tiffen. 1992. *Short-Changed: Africa in the World Trade.* London: Pluto Press.

CBI and SIDA. 1996. "Environmental Quick Scan Textiles: A Trade Related Environmental Orientation for the EU Market." Rotterdam: CBI.

CBI. 1996. "Environmental Quick Scan. Building Materials: Wood Products." Rotterdam: CBI.

Clapp, J. 1996. *Adjustment and Agriculture in Africa: Farmers, the State and the World Bank.* New York: St Martin's Press.

Collier, P., and J. W. Gunning, L. 1998. "Policy Commitment Arrangements for Africa: Implications for Aid, Trade and Investment Flows." Mimeo. Centre for the Study of African Economies, University of Oxford and Free University, Amsterdam.

European Commission. 1994. EC Directive 94/62/EG, in Official Journal of the European communities, No. L 365 of 20/12/1994, Brussels.

FAO. 1995. FAO Code of Conduct for Responsible Fisheries. Available at http://www.fao.org/fi/agreem/codecond/ficondc.asp.

———. 1996. "Integration of Fisheries into Coastal Areas Management. FAO Technical Guidelines for Responsible Fisheries." Rome: FAO.

———. 1998a. FAO Code on Integrated Coastal Areas Management." Rome: FAO.

———. 1998b. Committee on Fisheries, Sub-Committee on Fish Trade. "Report on Important Events Concerning Trade in Fisheries Products." June 3–6, 1998. Rome: FAO.

IDRC. 1992. *Our Common Bowl: Global Food Interdependence.* Ottawa: IDRC.

ITTO. 1996. "Multilateral Framework Agreement on Tropical Timber." ITTO.

Mohamed Salih, M. A. 1999. *Environmental Politics and Liberation in Contemporary Africa*. Dordrecht: Kluwer Academic Publishers.

Montague, P. 1998. "Lots of Regulations, Little Effect." In *Small Is Beautiful, Big is Subsidized. How Our Taxes Contribute to Environmental Breakdown*, ed. S. Gorelick, Hardwick, Vt.: International Society for Ecology and Culture.

Mwega, F,. and Muga, K. L. 1998. "Africa and the World Trade System: The Case Study of Kenya." Nairobi: African Economic Research Consortium.

Njinkeu, D., and A. Monkam, 1998. "Africa and the World Trade System: The Case of Cameroon." Nairobi: African Economic Research Consortium.

Njinkeu, D. 1998. "Pre and Post Uruguay Round African Market Access Conditions. (Executive Summary)." Nairobi: African Economic Research Consortium.

Oduro, A. D., and K. Yahya. 1998. "The Uruguay Round and Ghana." Nairobi: African Economic Research Consortium.

Oussu, D. A., and K. Diomande. 1998. "Africa and the World Trade System: The Case of Côte d'Ivoire." Nairobi: African Economic Research Consortium.

Profound. 1997. "Exporting Fresh Fruits and Vegetables. A Survey and Marketing Guide on Major Markets in the European Union." CBI, CLOACP, and Protrade.

Ramamurti, R. 1999. "Why Haven't Developing Countries Privatized Deeper And Faster?" In *World Development* 27, No. 1, pp. 137–155.

Shirley, Mary. 1999. "Bureaucrats in Business: The Role of Privatization versus Corporatization in State-Owned Enterprise Reforms." *World Development* 27.

van Dijk, Meine P., et al. 1994. *Privatisation Experiences in African and Asian Countries*. Amsterdam: SWISWO.

Part III

Case Studies

9

Environmental Governance, Policies, and Politics in Eastern and Southern Africa

M. A. MOHAMED SALIH

Environmental governance, an inseparable part of the multi-faceted economic, political, and social dimensions of governance, is about how societies organize themselves to manage their environment and deal with fundamental environmental problems. Environmental governance is concerned with the interaction between governmental and civil institutions and actors that influence how the environment is managed while constraints and negative impacts are reduced or eliminated. In short, environmental governance is how environmental problems are framed and identified and how relevant policies and acts are developed and implemented. In common with other areas of governance, environmental governance could be defined as the exercise of political, economic, and administrative authority to manage a nation's environmental affairs. Another conceptualization could be the way power is exercised in managing a country's economic, social, and environmental resources for development. In this sense environmental governance encompasses a wide range of government actions from exchange rate management to corruption in awarding public contracts.

No domain demonstrates the links between public policy and the environment more comprehensively than the current concerns with the role of governance in usurping accountability, transparency and participatory public policy formulation, implementation, monitoring, and evaluation. Because of the role environment plays in integrating socioeconomic, political, and economic processes expressed in direct and indirect environmental management, environmental policy transverses several public policy domains. Some of these domains are obvious (health, food, water, air, and their direct relationship to the environmental life support system) and others,

141

which can be labeled as impact domains (industry, transport, the living environment, and workplace to mention but a few). Furthermore, these public environmental policy concerns are multilayered, often operating at four levels simultaneously—local, national, regional, and global—and it is difficult to conceive discernible success or failure in one or more of these layers without inflicting some level of degradation on the other levels. This integrative nature of the environment poses complex policy issues and debates that require humility, the capacity to integrate rather than fragment efforts, and a continuous dialogue between local, national, regional, and global environmental governance.

The upsurge of research and studies on the causes and consequences of environmental degradation in Africa and elsewhere is not accidental (Mohamed Salih, 1999). It is part of a growing global awareness of the dire consequences of unchecked environmental degradation for the well-being of humans and nonhumans alike. This chapter expands earlier discussion (Salih & Tedla, 1999a) by looking specifically into the environmental governance concerns.

Most studies on environment policy and planning contributions have been concerned with whether African National Conservation Strategies and National Environmental Action Plans (NEAPs) have worked. What constraints and impediments have they confronted and are these constraints and impediments surmountable? This chapter attempts to synthesize these issues while exploring the mutual influence of global, regional, and subregional governance institutions and instruments such as conventions, treaties, and laws on African environmental management policies.

Africa and Global Environmental Governance

The relationship between Africa and international environmental institutions date back to the colonial era. The Convention for the Preservation of Wild Animals, Birds and Fish in Africa, signed by the colonial powers in London in 1900, bound its signatories to control and protect wildlife in their respective African colonies. In 1933, the United Kingdom convened the second London Conference for the Protection of African Fauna and Flora to establish national parks, game and forest reserves, and various other measures for the conservation of wildlife and its habitat in Africa (Anderson and Grove, 1987).

Colonial concerns with the environment have left their mark in postcolonial African states policies, particularly their nonparticipatory character and neglect of the interest of the surrounding communities vis-à-vis the interests of the expanding tourism industry (see UNESCO, 1963).

Africans' awareness of transboundary environmental resources and the need to control pests and epidemics was galvanized during the early years of independence. Several conventions, either between individual countries or countries that belong to the same regional groups, were convened to ratify environmental conventions (see UNEP, 1991), for example:

- Convention on the African Migratory Locust, Kano, 1962.
- Convention and statue relating to the Development of the Chad Basin, Fort-Lamy (N'djamena, 1964).
- African Convention on the Conservation of Nature and Natural Resources, Algiers, 1968.
- Agreement for the establishment of a Commission for Controlling the Desert Locust in Northwest Africa, Rome, 1970.
- Convention concerning the status of the Senegal River and Convention establishing the Senegal River Development, Orgasatton, 1972.

These followed by a number conventions resulting from the multilateral environmental movement during the 1980s and the African countries' efforts to avoid disputes over river basin water resources:

- The convention creating the Niger Basin Authority and protocol relating to the Development Fund of the Niger Basin, Faraah, 1980.
- The agreement on the Action Plan for the Environmentally Sound Management of the Zambezi River System, Harare, 1989.

Two political/economic subregional groupings such as the Inter-Governmental Authority for Drought and Development (IGADD), and Southern African Development Coordination Conference (SADCC), now the Southern African Development Community (SADC), have clear mandates to promote environmentally sensitive development, IGADD (now Intergovermental Authority on Development IGAD) was established in 1988 as a response to the recurrence of drought and famine in the Horn of Africa (Djibouti, Ethiopia, Kenya, Somalia, Sudan, and Uganda). Eritrea joined after independence from Ethiopia in 1993.

SADC countries (Botswana, Lesotho, Malawi, South Africa, Tanzania, Zambia, Zimbabwe) stated in the Lusaka Declaration (1980) that the livelihood of the majority of the people of Southern Africa is threatened by environmental degradation, which undermines both crop and animal husbandry, the mainstay of rural livelihoods in the region. The declaration considered Lesotho to be the country most seriously affected by ecological imbalance. Thus in November 1981, the SADCC Council of Ministers assigned to Lesotho the role of coordinating regional soil and water conservation projects within the SADCC.

Realizing the severity of environmental degradation, chronic food shortages in some countries, as well as the socioeconomic benefits that could accrue to them by being integrated into the global environmental movement, the African Ministerial Conference on the Environment (AMCEN) was convened in Cairo, in December 1985, to develop a concerted effort to meet the challenge posed by environmental degradation. This was the first all-African regional conference concerned with the environment and as such it symbolized the continent's commitment to conservation and sustainable development. AMCEN adopted a program of action for regional cooperation on the environment. Its main objective was battling the degradation of the natural resource and ensuring environmental rehabilitation, with the fundamental aim of securing self-sufficiency in food and energy by mobilizing Africa's human, scientific, and technical resources as well as through the application of environmentally sound, economically feasible, and socially acceptable environmental management methods.

In addition to these initiatives, the Organization for African Unity (OAU), at its 21st Ordinary Session of the Assembly of Heads of State and government, adopted Africa's Priority Programme for Economic Recovery 1986–90 (APPER). The African heads of state themselves deplored the fact that little progress had been made in environmental conservation measures. The assembly nevertheless recommended intensifying the struggle against drought and desertification, implementing measures for improved food security, and rehabilitating agriculture and the environment.

However, Africans' experience with national environmental planning is a result of the growing global environmental awareness marked by: 1) the Stockholm Conference on Human Settlement (1972); 2) The establishment, in 1977, of the United Nations Environmental Programme (UNEP) and its location in Nairobi, Kenya; 3) The World Conservation Strategy (WCS, 1980) and the call for the establishment of national conservation strategies (IUCN, 1984), which subsequently laid the foundations for the National Environmental Action Plans (NEAPs). According to Garew-Reid et al. (1994:36), "National Conservation Strategies are closely associated with the World Conservation Strategy and they were meant to identify the country's most urgent environmental needs, stimulate national debate and raise public consciousness, help decision makers set priorities and allocate human and financial resources, and build institutional capacity to handle complex environmental issues; 4) The United Nations Commission on Environment and Development process (UNCED, 1987–92), which culminated in *Environmental Perspective for the Year 2000* (1990),

Agenda 21 (1992), and more than 100 or so environmental conventions, treaties, and declarations.

National Conservation Strategies (NCSs) and National Environmental Action Plans (NEAPs) have been prominent in informing African environmental planning, and as such have influenced African environmental policy process. These plans have often been undertaken by national governments, coordinated by a ministry or ministries, with technical and financial support from the World Bank and other international organizations, including bilateral donors. NCSs and NEAPs were originally designed to transcend conventional development planning and to usher in an interactive policy process that involves not only national governments and donors, but also national and transnational environmental NGOs, civic associations, and corporate and business interests.

With a few exceptions, most African countries are members of the major conventions dealing with global environmental issues. However, relatively very few African countries are signatories to the Tropical Timber Agreement, the Hazardous Waste Convention, and the Desertification Convention (see Table 9.1). Due to the nature of the African physical environment and its endowment with rich biological diversity and endangered species, the African states are less hesitant to sign these conventions. The politics of using specific conventions to gain advantage over other countries in conventions closely associated with their socioeconomic development and pollution rates, is a familiar phenomenon in international environmental politics (see Thomas, 1992; Sjostedt, Svedin, & Aniansson, 1993). The countries that have been in the forefront in signing global environmental conventions are highlighted in bold.

By and large, African countries subsequently reflected the sentiment of the global environmental conventions and agreements that they have signed in their NCSs and NAEPs. In fact, the environmental policies of most African countries are essentially informed by the strategic imperative of sustainable development as espoused by *Our Common Future* (1987) and *Agenda 21* (1992).

At least four observations can be made: 1) The similarity of the environmental problems and the link between environmental degradation and poverty. These include soil erosion and degradation, which contributes to low farm productivity and is linked with high population growth rate, food shortages, malnutrition and undernutrition; subsequent drought and desertification; deforestation and biodiversity loss; infectious and parasitic diseases; air pollution in major cities, and the erosion and pollution of coastal; and shortage of adequate drinking water and sanitation facilities. 2) The African continent has long been integrated into the global environmental movement, with a long history of regional and subregional

Table 9.1 African Signatories and Parties to Conventions (as of July 1997)

Convention	Signatories
Biodiversity	Algeria, Benin, **Botswana,** Burkina Faso, Burundi, Cameroon, Cape Verde, Cent. Africa Rep., Chad, Rep. of Congo, Côte d'Ivoire, Djibouti, Egypt, Eritrea, **Ethiopia,** Gambia, Ghana, Guinea, Guinea Bissau, **Kenya, Lesotho, Malawi,** Mali, Mauritania, Mauritius, Morocco, Namibia, Niger, Nigeria, Senegal, Seychelles, **Sudan, Tanzania,** Togo, Tunisia, **Uganda, Zambia,** and Zimbabwe.
Desertification	Algeria, Benin, Botswana, Burkina Faso, Burundi, Cameroon, Cape Verde, Côte d'Ivoire, Djibouti, Egypt, Eritrea, **Ethiopia,** Gabon, Gambia, Ghana, Guinea, Guinea Bissau, **Kenya,** Mali, Mauritania, Mauritius, Morocco, Namibia, Niger, Nigeria, Senegal, Seychelles, **Sudan, Tanzania,** Togo, Tunisia, **Uganda,** and **Zambia.**
Climate Change	Algeria, Benin, **Botswana,** Burkina Faso, Burundi, Cameroon, Cape Verde, Cent. Africa Rep., Chad, Rep. of Congo, Côte d'Ivoire, Djibouti, Egypt, Eritrea, **Ethiopia,** Ghana, Guinea, Guinea Bissau, **Kenya, Lesotho, Malawi,** Mali, Mauritania, Mauritius, Morocco, Namibia, Niger, Nigeria, Senegal, Seychelles, Somalia, South Africa, **Sudan, Tanzania,** Togo, Tunisia, **Uganda, Zambia,** and Zimbabwe.
Hazardous Waste	Burundi, Rep., of Congo, Côte d'Ivoire, Egypt, **Malawi,** Mali, Morocco, Namibia, Nigeria, Senegal, Seychelles, South Africa, **Tanzania,** Tunisia, and Zambia.
Endangered Species	Algeria, Benin, **Botswana,** Burkina Faso, Burundi, Cameroon, Cent. Africa Rep., Chad, Côte d'Ivoire, Rep. of Congo, Djibouti, Egypt, Eritrea, **Ethiopia,** Ghana, Guinea, Guinea Bissau, **Kenya,** Liberia, **Malawi,** Mali, Mauritius, Morocco, Mozambique, Namibia, Niger, Nigeria, Rwanda, Senegal, Seychelles, Somalia, South Africa, **Sudan,** Swaziland, **Tanzania,** Togo, Tunisia, **Uganda, Zambia,** and Zimbabwe.

Source: World Bank 1997: 5th Conference on Environmentally and Socially Sustainable Development.

institutions concerned with the environment. 3) The continent is not short of plans, policies, or concern for the environment as has been demonstrated by its long history of sectoral environmental policy proclamations. 4) Due to its specific historical experience of four centuries of colonial domination and underdevelopment, its regional and subregional environmental policy thrusts are still externally driven and reactive rather than proactive.

These observations repeat themselves at the national environmental management level, particularly when countries, after signing subregional,

regional, or global environmental conventions, find themselves economically, technologically, and socially ill-equipped to deliver what they have promised. The problem is not that Africans lack policies or knowledge about the environmental imperative, but that they lack the financial and skilled human resources required to implement these global conventions and agreements.

Since the 1970s, the environmental governance structure of Africa has changed with the introduction of more legal policy instruments, the creation of new institutions, and an active civil society engagement. The width and breadth of actors have also signaled a shift in some countries from customary law and communal environmental management institutions to state or state-sponsored and private institutions. The multitude of actors and governance institutions means that environment takes center stage in socioeconomic planning as well as integrating environmental policy principles and development. As the following section illustrates, the gulf between environmental policy principles adopted by most African countries and the practice of these policy principles leaves much to be desired.

Environmental Policy: Principles and Practice

Five main principles of environmental policy, as described by Turner and Opschoor (1994:4) can be used to examine whether African environmental policies satisfy these requirements. They are:

1. The polluters pay principle: polluters pay the cost of meeting socially acceptable environmental quality standards;
2. The prevention or precautionary principle: recognizes the existence of environmental and social uncertainty and seeks to avoid irreversible damages from the imposition of a safety margin into policy; it also seeks to prevent waste generation at the source, as well as retaining some end-of-pipe measures;
3. The economic efficiency–cost effectiveness principle: applies both to setting standards and designing policy instruments to attain them;
4. The subsiderity principle: assigns environmental decisions and enforcement to the lowest level of government capable of handling it without significant residuals;
5. The legal efficiency principle: precludes the passage of regulations that cannot be realistically enforced.

The environmental policies that the case studies dealt with hardly satisfy all the requirements of common environmental policy principles, particularly when judged against implementation record. How from the vantage point of an ideal world situation, could environmental policy principles realistically be implemented through fiscal and legal instruments, socioeconomic incentives, and institutions?

Strategically, the main objective of legal and economic instruments and institutions is to ensure environmental quality control through policy windows pertaining to regulation, incentives, and internalization of environmental costs. Environmental governance without instruments is hopelessly inept to deliver results. First, environmental laws are concerned with regulating activities that have potential to cause environmental hazards, including the authorization of discharges to the environment, containment of toxic substances, setting standards, and licensing emission levels and manufactured products. Legal instruments, including customary laws, are the oldest instruments used by humankind to manage their environments. However, even modern legal instruments are dated and link back to the colonial legacy, as mentioned earlier.

Second, economic instruments and socioeconomic incentives fall within the anticipatory/preventive polluter pays principle and economic efficiency/cost effectiveness. Although these have been recognized by governments and multilateral environmental institutions as enforcement instruments fiscal instruments (for example, aggregate abatement costs, user charges levied on emissions; financing emission charges, tradeable permits, and environmental taxes), these instruments seem to be designed to operate better in industrially advanced OECD market economies where they can be an effective means for high-level environmental quality control. However, African countries, with their underdeveloped economies, have yet to use stringent fiscal instruments within the framework of cost-effectiveness, administrative costs, distribution impacts, and policy-making contexts as described by authors for the industrially advanced economies (Folmer, Gabel, & Opschoor, 1995: 1–17; Lohman, 1994:58–62; Weizsacker & Jesinghaus, 1992:41–2).

Furthermore it implies that different policy instruments or instrument choice can be used in different contexts, and that they also depend on the social, political, and economic context (developing or industrialized) within which financial instruments and socioeconomic incentives (such as subsidies, affordable and efficient public transport, incentive charges on low emissions, and demarcated bicycle tracks and walk paths) are implemented.

Third, environmental institutions are authority levels for decision-making such as specialized ministries for the environment, backed up by environmental training, information and research institutions, environmental regulation, and quality control institutions. Some of these institutions operate as coordinating bodies working with the public and private sectors through environmental action plans and conservation strategies, as not earlier.

However, although Eastern and Southern African states are aware of the environmental policy principles and their instruments for implementation, these are seldom implemented. The case studies reveal at least six common tendencies in Eastern and Southern African environmental policies:

1. Since the late 1970s, regional and national environmental policies have been increasingly influenced by the resolutions of global environmental forums, negotiations, conventions, treaties, and declarations and by the emergence of the concept of global environmental governance (Commission for Global Governance, 1995).
2. The existence of governmental and nongovernmental institutions involved in environmental policy process, implementation, and monitoring. Most countries involve such institutions in public debate about key environmental issues and concerns. However, these institutions operate on a sectoral basis, with inadequate coordination, and knowledge base, limited information, and overlapping responsibilities.
3. The integration of environmental impact assessment as an anticipatory-preventative environmental policy instrument. This relates particularly to the insistence of international finance institutions such as the World Bank and bilateral development agencies for better cost-effectiveness and distributional impacts.
4. Owing to underdevelopment and market weakness (inadequate pricing, lack of trained human resources, and institutional constraints), the use of fiscal and socioeconomic incentives as environmental policy instruments is almost absent. This is an area where human resources development is desperately needed if African environmental policies are to be translated into powerful resource management tools.
5. The absence of economic instruments has been compensated for by the use of legal instruments, some of which dates back to the colonial period. However, regional and national environmental laws are increasingly influenced by the international environmental law as espoused by global environmental forums, negotiations, conventions, treaties, agreements, and declarations and the emergence of the concept of global environmental governance (Commission for Global Governance, 1995).
6. Even legal environmental policy instruments are promulgated within a dysfunctional regulatory framework, with insufficient and inadequately trained human resources.

However, it would be grossly misleading not to recognize and appreciate the limited achievements attained by NEAPs and the NCSs in the

African context. One of the main achievements is that they have succeeded in raising environmental awareness and placed Africans environmental concerns high on the national development agenda. Poverty and lack of resources, rather than the lack of political will or knowledge about the environment/sustainable development imperative, beset the commitment of these countries to sustainable environmental management.

Second, African countries' environmental policies are sectoral or single-issue driven (for example, water policy in isolation from industrial policies or mineral policy in isolation from forestry policy). Paradoxically, these policies represent a step forward in environmental management efforts as well as awareness. Third, the attempts to integrate environmental concerns as part of the constitutions of Malawi, Uganda, and Tanzania have evaluated the right to a healthy environment to a human right. For example, the revised Constitution of Malawi, following the collapse of Banda's autocratic regime, calls upon the state "to manage the environment responsibly in order to prevent the degradation of the environment; provide a healthy living and working environment for the people of Malawi; accord full recognition to the rights of future generations by means of environmental protection and sustainable development of natural resources; and conserve and enhance biological diversity of Malawi" (Malawi Constitution, May, 1994).

Fourth, serious attempts have been made by some states (Uganda, Malwai, Ethiopia, Zambia, Lesotho, and Kenya) to develop a new generation of investment plans that integrate environmental concerns in individual investment projects, based on clear guidelines, with a wide array of projects in capacity building in environment management, enhancing resource (land and water) productivity, conservation and use of biological resources, environmental education and public awareness, and environmental health and pollution management. These projects will be implemented in phases depending on availability of funds. Fifth, Due to the democratization process, which has swept throughout these countries, except Sudan, popular participation in environmental planning and development have become more acceptable than ever before. Citizen organizations and development and environment NGOs are organizing for change, taking conservation into their own hands.

Environmental Governance:
An Engagement with the Possible

This section discusses the main findings of the Organization for Social Science Research in Eastern and Southern Africa (OSSREA) research project, analyzed by Africans with long experience in teaching and research on environmental issues.

A major theme of the study is what Wamicha and Mwanje (1999) call, in the Kenya case, "the politics within," or institutional politics, which engulf state and nonstate actors. In other words, the concern is the politics of the state actors and institutions, rather than with state/civil society conflicts over environmental resources, the subject of many recent publications. The research is particularly concerned with the competing and at times overlapping interests inherent in sectoral environmental management policies and governance institutions. Contradictions in sectoral environmental policies have become more apparent due to the increasing awareness of environmental policy institutions of the significance of popular participation in policy formulation. Because environment cuts across development and environment management policy issues, it becomes a battlefield in which social and political interests clash. These views are vindicated by a number of recent publications on the relationship between environmental degradation, poverty and land grabbing in Kenya (see Wamicha and Mwanje, 1999).

In the case of Ethiopia, Tedla and Lemma (1999) argue that sectoral contradiction and overlap is a major source of weakness in the body of Ethiopian environmental law in relation to land tenure and administration, land use, fisheries, environmental health—particularly solid and liquid waste disposal—as well as toxic and hazardous waste management. The strong urban-based industrial sector does not lend itself to champion any call for environmental quality standards for air, water and land pollution, which are indeed very serious in certain localities having industries and large farms with high chemical input. On the other hand, peasant communities are weary of environmental management plans thrown at them by the central government without proper consultation. Telda and Lemma see the creation of a people's space as a prerequisite to sustainable resource management and better implementation of the national conservation plans.

According to Wamicha and Mwanje (1999), Kenya's state authority on the environment has not been clearly defined in public law. So the Kenyan Constitution falls in that portion of the state's law, which, on account of its prominence, is made following special legislative procedures and can only be mended in the same manner. To this end other legal norms and bylaws are subordinate to the constitution, while local authorities using bylaws currently manage substantial portions of Kenya's natural resources. A more somber analysis (NCCK, 1992) was conducted earlier, showing that little has been done during the seven years preceding Wamicha and Mwanje's research. With the increase in violence over land ownership, environmental management governance and institutions have lost much of their assumed potential of protecting the public good. As the final section of this chapter shows, like other public policy issues, environmental policy is overly political, sometimes leading to insurgency and bloody conflicts.

Until recently, Lesotho's concern with environmental education and awareness mostly remained in the limited context of agriculture and targeted farming communities (Marake and Molumeli, 1999). The failure to provide skills and knowledge to other sectors involved in environmental programs (grazing, mining) has cost Lesotho dearly. The current vicious cycle of population pressure, poverty, food deficit, and degradation of the environment can only be seen as an indictment of the county's conservation planning and implementation. This is partly due to the fact that Lesotho's conservation approach and strategy were not set to accommodate people's immediate needs, which has rendered conservation unaffordable both to urban and rural communities. Neither can Lesotho invest in technological solutions for long-term conservation measures. According Marake and Molumeli, the legal framework of Lesotho's environmental and conservation policy has failed to inspire the protection of natural resources.

Uganda has been praised for its high GDP growth rate (eight percent in 1996), since the implementation of structural adjustment programs (SAPs) in the late 1980s. Sengendo and Musali (1999) argue that Uganda's investment plan (IP) includes a calculated effort to stem environmental degradation through careful handling of the underlying causes of identified problems. Given its varied natural resource base, however, Uganda fell prey to the conflict posed by how to achieve sustainable economic development while meeting the formidable challenge of nature conservation. In fact, Sengendo and Musali argue that the impulse to develop rapidly has resulted in serious environmental degradation that is threatens the productivity of the natural resource base on which development depends. Poverty has created a vicious spiral of environmental degradation and has exacerbated the problem.

Uganda Environmental Management Authority (NEMA, 1999), the institution entrusted by the state to oversee the state of the environment, concurs with Sengendo and Musali's findings, i.e., the need for action rather than words. Also see Mohamed Salih (2001) for more on Uganda's energy and food security policies. The Uganda case illustrates imperative that economic and environmental strategies are reconciled and that a proper balance between economic development and environmental conservation is ensured. Another serious problem according to Sengendo and Musali is that some colonial environmental laws are still being enforced even though they are not in touch with today's reality. These laws are not only obsolete but are also scattered in different statues that have been drawn up by different sectoral environmental management institutions. This again renders current environmental conservation efforts difficult, if not impossible. As a result, Uganda natural resource management institutions lack clear understanding of stakeholder attitudes towards these resources; thus Ugandan environmental policies and laws hardly reflect the aspirations of society. In fact the managing institutions continue to rely on authority derived from the law rather than from people's acceptance.

The Sudan, situation according to Abdel Atti and Awad (1999) is the result of technical weaknesses of the environmental plans and various contextual constraints. As a result, plan performance and impact have been insignificant. With the exception of DECARP efforts, monitoring of environmental changes and follow-up are hampered by the problems of accuracy and information coverage. Further, despite the long history and immense body of sectoral legislation to protect the environment and manage resource use, logistical problems, administrative weakness, and corruption greatly reduce government institutions' ability to apply the law. These technical and contextual weaknesses severely hamper the effectiveness of environmental planning in monitoring changes and follow-up in applying legislation (see, for example, Pearce et al., 1990:147). The Sudan environmental crisis has worsened since the discovery of oil and subsequent oil exports of 250,000 barrels a day. Although oil has provided the government of the Sudan with revenue that could be used to improve the environmental conditions, it seems only to have wetted its appetite for more destructive development (Mohamed Salih, 1995:1997).

In Tanzania, in addition to similar patterns of sectoral environmental planning contradictions, as Mwalyosi and Sosovele (1999) note, that almost all the strategic plans and policies in Tanzania were motivated by the government's desire to exploit international or bilateral funds. Donor conditionality attached to such funds included secondment of consultants or experts, usually from the funding agencies. The result has been hurriedly produced reports and policies without adequate local consultation. In the end such policies are difficult if not impossible to implement. A study conducted by Mwandosya et al. (1998) on climate change policies and their potential impacts of in Tanzania exposed the same pattern of policy aloofness from citizens, policy fragmentation, and lack of coordination between line ministries concerned with environmental protection. That the governance structures are donor driven purports that Tanzania is increasingly dependent on foreign support to protect the very agricultural exports that engendered environmental degradation in the first place.

According to Darkoh (1999) one of Africa's richest countries, Botswana, an ill-planned livestock sector development and inappropriate use of the country's grazing resources has created a complex relationship between people and environment, giving rise to severe dryland degradation or desertification. In Darkoh's view, the greatest environmental policy constraint in this mineral-rich country is the void and confusion created by the breakdown of traditional structures and the lack of adequate institutional capacity and mechanisms for implementing community-based natural resource management projects. However, given the strength of Botswana's economy, the political will as well as the democratic gover- nance and environmental consciousness among the political leadership and educated elite alike, signal good prospects for sustained effort and possible environmental policy success. However, other literature (Carew-Reid et al., 1994, 28) illustrates that, "Establishment of a National Conservation Strategy Advisory Board and Coordination Agency resulted in the intro- duction of Environmental Impact Assessment (EIA) procedure as part of national planning and development control system. This has resulted in cost savings from the selection of dam sites, and a reversal of a decision to implement the Southern Okavango Integrated Water Development Pro- ject." Also see Pearce et al. (1990) for a long-term view on sustainable development policy in Botswana.

Mwafongo and Kapila (1999) deal with Malawi and the role of market and related policy failures as crucial elements in resource degradation, including insecure property rights, limited information on resource con- servation, labor market weaknesses, and limited access to credit. They argue that, even in densely populated Malawi, property rights regarding environmental resources are ill defined and insecure, with the resultant easy access for excessive exploitation. The contradiction between modern and traditional resource management authorities is exemplified by the fact that a chief's powers to allocate land do not extend to enforcing sustainable use of the land. Property rights have not promoted the adoption of sus- tainable land use practices in Malawi, even where titled land had been granted. Larger synthesis could be deceptive. Wood (1997:89) argues, "One of the factors favouring Malawi's NEAP is the involvement of key individuals within various line ministries and agencies, NGOs, the univer- sity and other parastatals and the private sector and the full participation of the local communities at the district level." The establishment of the Environmental Support Programme supports this optimistic view, although little has been done on the ground. However, the question often asked is how much sound environmental management would satisfy the researcher, the government agencies, and local communities with their diverse policy options and interests.

Despite its noble endeavor, the commonly idealized perspective on global sustainable development policies has been contested by some con- tributors to the debate. For instance, Theo and Chabwela (1999) argue that in Zambia, the World Bank–driven NCSs and NEAPs were established as preconditions to releasing national economic mobilization funds. Zambia's access to external loans has, to some extent, depended on NEAP status. Usually such plans fail to be integrated into national socioeconomic priori- ties, as was the case with NCS. According to Theo and Chabwela, Zambia's

NCS and NEAP are driven by external forces from conception and preparation to implementation, monitoring, and evaluation.

So is there any trace of life in Zambia's NEAPs? Surprisingly, commendable level of national expertise, well trained and capable of conducting environmental impact assessment, auditing, and accounting has emerged and begun to replace foreign expatriates (Mohamed Salih, 2000). The message is not to underestimate the capacity of national institutions to overcome constraints that some present as insurmountable.

The constructive criticisms and policy proposals made here are meant to contribute to the ongoing debate on the need for devising sustainable development policies and introducing those that can be implemented. This section has also emphasized the following policy points:

1. A major problem is the continued separation between environment as a policy domain and conventional public policy. The duality of policy in which some policies are called environmental and dealt with in institutions often isolated and designated as such, also means separation of obviously interconnected policy domains;
2. The weakness of environmental governance institutions and their inability to implement environmental policies, due to internal and external rivalries and problems in these institutions;
3. The incapacity of environmental policy institutions, particularly at the national level, to implement national and regional environmental policies because, in most cases, these institutions do not own the environmental policy initiative and thrust. Even when the environmental institutions own the environmental policies, they often lack the human and financial resources to make these policies happen;
4. The restrictive nature of conventional public policy has constrained and thus undermines the possibility of participatory policy implementation and assessment at the national and regional levels, significantly restricting the opportunity to engage a wider spectrum of governance—including business, NGOs and communities.

Implicit in the constraints confronting Africa's environmental governance institutions is the absence of integrative policy mechanisms to bring together the pervasive nature of environmental policies and the public policy imperative. Because African national environmental policies are, in most cases, externally driven, the governance structures tend to be reactive rather than proactive. This point is better illustrated in the domain of environmental politics where proactive governance structures are inseparable, particularly in relation to accountability, participation, and environmental and other conflict resolution.

Conclusion

Even though Africa's socioeconomic, political, administrative, and environmental governance restructuring has gone hand in hand, environmental governance has not been accorded the attention it deserves. The positive attributes of efficient, responsible, democratic, and transparent environmental governance, particularly when judged from a perspective of universal good, are not different from those expected in the most dominant paradigm of good governance. Here we can see a fundamental link between open, democratic, and accountable governance and the ability to achieve sustainable economic and social development. Indeed, sustainable socioeconomic development in Africa and most developing countries is impossible without the maintenance of their natural environment for development.

Further, if governance is about self-governance, local environmental governance accountability should be accorded equal weight to that of official accountability. The current level of violence and conflict over environmental resources questions the capacity of the prevailing environmental governance institutions to contribute to ensuing peace efforts. If environmental degradation, underdevelopment, and political conflicts are mutually reinforcing, the prospects of working on the three fronts simultaneously is potentially more rewarding. Obviously, the unity of governance can be disentangled into environmental, economic, administrative, and political strands for methodological imperative, but not from a life and real-world perspective. Embedded environmental governance can potentially be used as an instrument for political transformation, including people-centered environmental democracy and struggle for the respect of citizen's environmental rights. The political space created by environmental politics transcends environment and development to other equally important aspects of political life where governance seems to be more pronounced.

Evidently, positive national governance values and norms are often mirrored in local patterns and structures of local governance and vice versa. Such recognition may contribute to questioning whether elite-dominated centralized governance institutions could ever establish roots among citizens whose participation in environmental management is constrained by poverty, exclusion, and political illiteracy. Managing environmental democracy in these situations is surely more complex, even more difficult, than managing dictatorship.

References

AMCEN. 1993. *Workshop Documents of the 5th AMCEN Session.* Addis Ababa. November 22–27, 1993.

———. 1995. *African Ministerial Conference on the Environment, 6th Session. Report of the Expert Group Meeting.* Nairobi. December 11–13, 1995.

Anderson, D. M., and R. H. Grove. 1987. *Conservation in Africa: People, Policies, and Practices.* Cambridge: Cambridge University Press.

Commission on Global Governance. 1995. *Our Global Neighbourhood: Report of the Commission on Global Governance.* Oxford: Oxford University Press.

Doe, L. 1998. "Civil Service Reform in the Countries of the West African Monetary Union" Special Issue on 'Governance': *Journal of Social Sciences.* Vol. 155, pp. 125–144.

Engoff, M. 1990. "Wildlife Conservation, Ecological Strategies and Pastoral Communities: A Contribution in Understanding Parks and Peoples in East Africa." In Mohamed Salih, M. A. 1990; "Pastoralism and The State in Africa"; *Journal of Anthropological and Ethnological Sciences,* Nos. 25–27, pp. 3–18.

Folmer, H. Gabel, and J. B. Opschoor. 1995. *Principles of Environmental and Resource Economics: A Guide for Students and Decision Makers.* Aldershot, U.K.: Edward Elgar.

Garew-Reid, J., R. Prescott, S. Bass, and B. Dalal-Clayton. 1994. *Strategies for National Sustainable Development: A Handbook for Their Planning and Implementation.* London: The World Conservation Union (IUCN), International Institute for Environment and Development, and Earthscan Publications Ltd.

Golden, Ian, and L. Allan Winters. 1995. *The Economics of Sustainable Development.* Cambridge: Cambridge University Press.

Hanley Nick, Shogren, F. Janson, and Ben White. 1997. *Environmental Economics in Theory and Practice.* London: Macmillan Press.

IUCN. 1980. *World Conservation Strategy.* Geneva: International Union for Conservation of Nature, United Nation Environmental Programme, and World Wildlife Fund.

Lohman, Lex de Savorinin. 1994. "Economic Incentives in Environmental Policy: Why Are They White Ravens?" In *Economic Incentives and Environmental Policies: Principles and Practice,* ed. J. P. Opschoor and R. K. Turner. Dordrecht: Kluwer Academic Publishers.

Mohamed Salih, M. A. 1997a. "Global Ecologism and Its Critics." In *Globalisation and the South,* ed. C. Thomas, and Peter Wilkin. New York and London: St. Martin's; Macmillan Press.

———. 1997b. "Natural Capital." In *Encyclopedia of Political Economy* ed. P. O'Hara. London: Routledge.

———. 1999b. *Environmental Politics and Liberation in Contemporary Africa.* Dordrecht: Kluwer Academic Publishers.

———. 2000. *Local Environmental Change and Society in Africa.* Dordrecht: Kluwer Academic Publishers.

Mohamed Salih, M. A. and S. Tedla, eds. 1999a. *Environmental Planning, Policies and Politics in Eastern and Southern Africa.* New York and London: St. Martin's; Macmillan Press.

Mwandosya, M. J., B. S. Nyenzi and M.L. Luhanga. 1998. *The Assessment of Vulnerability and Adaptation to Climate Change Impacts in Tanzania.* Dar es Salaam: Centre for Energy, Environment, Science, and Technology.

NCCK. 1992. *Perspectives of Environmental Degradation in Kenya Today: Findings of NCCK Research and Study*. Nairobi: NCCK.

NEMA. 1999. *State of the Environment Report for Uganda*. 3rd edition. Kampala: National Environment Management Authority.

OAU. 1993. *21st Ordinary Session of the Assembly of Heads of State*. Addis Ababa: Organization for African Unity.

Odegi-Awuondo, G., Haggai W. Namai, and Beneah M. Mutsotso. 1994. *Masters of Survival*. Nairobi: Basic Books (Kenya) Ltd.

Ogot, B. A., ed. 1979. *Ecology and History in East Africa*. Nairobi: Kenya Literature Bureau.

Opschoor, J. B., and R. K. Turner. 1994. "Environmental Economics and Environmental Policy Incentives: Introduction and Overview." In *Economic Incentives and Environmental Policies: Principles and Practice*, ed. J. P. Opschoor and R. K. Turner. Dordrecht: Kluwer Academic Publishers.

Spink, P. "Possibilties and Political Imperatives: Seventy Years of Administrative Reform in Latin America." In Spink, P. and Luiz Carlos Bresser Pereira (eds.) *Reforming the State: Managerial Public Administration in Latin America*. 1999; pp. 91–114. Lynne Rienner Publishers.

Sjostedt, G., U. Svedin, and B. H. Aniansson, eds. 1993. *International Environmental Negotiations: Processes, Issues and Contexts*. Stockholm: Swedish Council for Planning and Coordination of Research.

Thomas, C. 1992. *The Environment in International Relations*. Energy and Environment Programme. London: Royal Institute of International Affairs.

Tolba, M. K., and El Kholy. 1992. *The World Environment 1972–1992: Two Decades for Challenge*. London: Chapman and Hall, for United Nations Environmental Programme.

UNEP. 1991. *Register of International Treaties and Other Agreements in the Field of Environment*. Nairobi: United Nations Environment Programme.

UNESCO. 1963. *A Review of the Natural Resources of the African Continent*. Paris: United Nations Education Scientific and Culture Organization.

United Nations. 1990. *Global Outlook 2000: Economic, Social and Environmental*. New York: United Nations Publications.

Wamicha, W. N. and Justus Inonda Mwanje. 1999. "National Resource in Kenya: The Politics of," in M. A. Mohamed Salih and Shibru Telda (eds.), *Environmental Planning, Policies and Politics in Eastern and Southern Africa*. Basingstoke: Macmillan and New York Press: St. Martins Press.

WCED. 1987. *Our Common Future, World Commission on Environment and Development*. Oxford: Oxford University Press.

Wekwete Kadmiel, H. "Urban Management: The Recent Experience." In Carole Rakodi (ed.) *The Urban Challenge in Africa: Growth and Management of its Large Cities*. 1997. Pp. 527–552.

von Weizsacker, E. U., and J. Jestinghaus. 1992. *Ecological Tax Reform: A Policy Proposal for Sustainable Development*. London: Zed Books Ltd.

World Bank. 1996. *Toward Sustainable Development in Sub-Saharan Africa*. Washington, D.C.: World Bank.

———. 1997. *5th Annual Conference on Environmentally and Socially Sustainable Development*. Washington, D.C.: World Bank.

10

Policy Process in a Democratic Context: A Glimpse at Nigeria's Privatization Program

EJEVIOME ELOHO OTOBO

D emocratic civil rule was restored in Nigeria in May 1999, after a second military regime that lasted for sixteen years (1984–1999). The first military incursion into politics had lasted nearly as long, from 1966 to 1979. Since Nigeria gained independence in 1960, the military has ruled the country for twenty-nine years. One area where the transition from the military regimes to democratic civil rule can be felt is in the policy process. Now in its third year, the current democratic civil rule in Nigeria is very much a fledgling one. Nonetheless, the essential outlines of the public policy process are emerging.

This chapter describes the main features of the policy process, with a focus on one aspect, namely, the privatization program. The government has repeatedly stated that economic recovery and growth are high priorities on its policy agenda. This reflects recognition of the need to move the country from the current path of slow growth to more robust and sustainable growth. Privatization is crucial to the government's economic reform agenda and is viewed as essential to its objectives of fostering economic competitiveness and strengthening a private sector–led economy. Moreover, because of the diversity of actors involved, the privatization program offers a glimpse at the policy process under the new civilian government.

The author acknowledges, with thanks, the assistance of Mr. Adeyemi Dipeolu and Mr. Sola Enikanolaiye for their comments and of Mr. Nasir Ahmad El-Rufai for his clarifications on the sale of public enterprises during the different periods of the privatization program. The views expressed here are his alone and do not reflect those of the United Nations Economic Commission for Africa.

Two essential points need to be emphasized in this regard. First, the focus will be on the central tier of government—commonly referred to as the federal government, one of the three tiers of government in Nigeria. The other two tiers are the states and local governments. Second, the public policy process encompasses policymaking, policy implementation, and policy evaluation. These various components of policy process are closely interrelated and policy outcomes depend on careful management of each of the components.

The Political Framework for the Economic Policy Process

A distinguishing feature of the current democratic rule is that the economic policy process is being conducted in a constitutional context. Democratic constitutionalism imbues the policy process with several attributes that were lacking during military rule. Three are particularly outstanding in this regard. The first is the rule of law. This means that the policy process must be conducted within the law, and it opens the possibility for any government policy to be challenged in the courts. This in turn potentially gives a greater role to courts in the policy process. During the military regime, the combination of retroactive decrees and ouster clauses significantly undermined the rule of law and diminished the role of the courts in the policy process. Ouster clauses are the practice of preventing courts from challenging the validity of some of the decrees enacted by the military government.

The second effect of constitutionalism is that it allows for freedom of association and expression. As a result, civil society organizations and professional bodies interested in particular policies become important stakeholders whose views can influence public policy. This is not to suggest that civil society has a role only under civil rule. Civil society organizations were fairly active during the military rule in Nigeria and, indeed, mitigated the harsh political environment (Otobo, 1999).

Third, constitutionalism also impacts policy process through its emphasis on representative democracy. The abolition of the legislature was a hallmark of military rule in Nigeria. By contrast, under democratic civil rule, the existence of the legislature—alongside the other arms of government (executive and judiciary)—provides a vehicle for the legislative arm to have an input into the policy process. Indeed, the constitution assigns a significant role to the legislature in the economic policy process.

The 1999 Constitution provides the legal and institutional framework for the economic policy process, explicit provisions for the establishment of certain institutional structures pertaining to the economic policy process. For example, the constitution creates a National Economic Council with responsibility for advising the president on economic matters, in particular, measures for coordinating economic planning efforts or economic programs of the various governments of the federation. The constitution also provides means to monitor accruals and disbursements of revenue from the federation account, review the revenue allocation formulas and principles, and advise federal and state governments on fiscal efficiency and ways revenue can be increased. The constitution also delineates the economic areas in which only the federal government can legislate, such as banking, borrowing money from outside Nigeria, commercial and industrial monopolies, customs, insurance, labor, trade and commerce, and taxation on income and profits. It also sets out the role of the legislature in the control of public funds. These provisions give the legislature a significant role in the economic policy making process. The constitution further requires the president to meet regularly with the vice president and all ministers of the federation to determine the general direction of domestic and foreign policies. This meeting, popularly referred to as the Cabinet, plays a pivotal role in economic policy-making.

Yet the constitution is only one source. Several institutional structures that are not provided for in the constitution will increasingly contribute to the economic policy process. These include, for example, the newly established Poverty Eradication Council, chaired by the president; the National Council on Privatization, chaired by the vice president; Economic Policy Coordinating Committee, chaired by the Vice President; and the Presidential Advisory Committee.

The economic policy process is mediated by formal structures as well as by ad hoc institutional structures and by interactions between the government and other stakeholders, such as private sector groups, nongovernmental organizations, labor unions, professional associations, research institutions, political parties, bilateral and multilateral development partners, and state and local governments. How these stakeholders contribute to the economic policy process is discussed in the following section.

The Privatization Program

Historical Background

The effort to reform the public enterprise sector in Nigeria dates back to 1981, when the Onosode Presidential Commission on parastatals was established by the then civilian federal government. The military government that came to power in 1984, established another committee, the Al-Hakim Committee, to review the performance of public enterprises. The effort towards privatization gathered momentum when yet another military government adopted the structural adjustment Program (SAP) in 1986, which had privatization as a key objective.

The inclusion of privatization as a major component of the SAP reflected the liberalizing intention of the SAP, in particular the need to reduce the role of government in the economy. Other reasons included the desire to reduce dependence on government funding of public enterprises (PEs) and stem the losses incurred by government. The share of public enterprise in the gross domestic product of Nigeria from the 1970s to the early 1990s has been estimated at 35% to 50% (Okigbo, 1981; El-Rufai, 1999), between 30% and 40% of fixed capital investment, and nearly 50% of formal sector employment. Total investment by the federal government in PEs as of 1985, was about US$35 billion (Kuye, 1990). The financial transfers and subsidies amounted to US$3 billion in 1998 and US$800 million by 2000 (El Rufai, 2001:8).

The period from the adoption of the SAP in 1986, to the promulgation of the privatization and Commercialization decree in July 1988, set the stage for the privatization program. An implementation committee was established which advised on initial arrangements for privatization. A series of executive decisions rather than a coherent legal framework governed the program. By contrast, the subsequent periods were governed by a legal framework.

Periods of Privatization

There are three identifiable periods in which privatization has taken place in Nigeria (see Table 10.1). The Technical Committee on Privatization and Commercialization (TCPC) managed the implementation of the privatization from 1989, until it was dissolved in June 1993. This period focused mainly on public enterprises in the financial, commercial, and industrial sectors. The revenue yield from privatization of the fifty-five enterprises undertaken by TCPC has been put at N3.7 bn, the equivalent of US$400 million (El-Rufai 2001:9).

From August 1993, to May 1999, there were three governments: The outgoing military government that signed the privatization decree handed over power to an unelected civilian administration known as the Interim National Government (ING), which ruled for less than ninety days before being replaced by a military regime that ruled from November 1993, to June 1998. This military government exhibited policy somersaults over the privatization program, most graphically illustrated in the attempt to reacquire

Table 10.1 Evolution of the Privatization Program in Nigeria

Period	Legal framework for privatization	Organizational vehicle for privatization	Stock of public enterprises at beginning of period	Privatization completed during the period	Remarks
1989–1993	Technical Committee on Privatization and Commercialization Decree No. 25/1988 of 6 July 1998	Technical Committee on Privatization and Commercialization (TCPC)	600*	82 PEs were partially or fully privatized by the end of 1993.+ (includes 55 of 145 public enterprises listed in Decree 25 of July 1988; 18 enterprises privatized before TCPC was established, and 9 others privatized)	The 145 public enterprises listed in Decree 25 of 6 July 1988 were classified into four categories: to be fully privatized (67), partially privatized (43), full commercialization (11), partial commercialization (24)
1993–April 1999	The Bureau of Public Enterprise Decree No. 78/1993 of 25 August 1993	Bureau of Public Enterprises + Management Board	518**	No privatization during this period.+	The 123 public enterprises listed in Decree 78 of 25 August 1993 were classified into four categories: To be privatized fully (66), partially privatized (19), full commercialization (14), and partial commercialization (23).
					This period was marked by policy changes reflected in the stalling and attempted reversal of the privatization process. The government in 1998 said that it was pursuing a strategy of "guided privatization towards the existing state-owned enterprises."

(continues)

Table 10.1 Cont.

Period	Legal framework for privatization	Organizational vehicle for privatization	Stock of public enterprises at beginning of period	Privatization completed during the period	Remarks
May 1999–Present	Public Enterprises (Privatization and Commercialization) Decree No. 28/1999 of 10 May 1999	National Council on Privatization (NCP) + Bureau of Public Enterprises (as secretariat of the NCP) There are also five standing committees and ten sector steering committees, chaired by the relevant ministers. Membership includes stakeholders from public and private sectors, unions, academia, and NGOs.	588***	Since December 1999, 12 have been sold, 2 transactions are coming to closure, and 30 are at various stages.++	The 95 public enterprises listed in Decree 28 of 10 May 1999 were classified into four categories: to be fully privatized (25), partially privatized (37), full commercial-ization (9), and partial commercialization (24). On 6 July 1999, the new civilian government announced that the privatization program envisages full or partial divestiture of its interests in over 60 of the 95 public enterprises in three phases: **First phase:** Divestiture of federal government shares in the cement, banking, and oil marketing industries. **Second phase:** Divestiture of assets in paper manufacturing, sugar, and vehicle assembly plants. **Third phase:** Divestiture of govern-ment holdings in the utilities.

Sources: Privatization and Commercialization Decree No. 25, 6 July 1988: Bureau of Public Enterprises Decree No. 78, 25 August 1993; 1998 Budget Address by the Head of State, 4 January 1998; Public Enterprises Decree No. 28, 10 May 1999, National Council on Privatization–Privatization Handbook 2000; Zayyad (1992); and BPE (2001).

*According to a 1991 survey by the Technical Committee on Privatization and Commercialization, an estimated 1,800 public enterprises in Nigeria were owned by federal, state, and local governments. The federal government alone had 600; see BPE 2001, El-Rufai (1999) and Zayyad (1992). Zayyad was the chairman of the TCPC.

**This figure was derived by deducting the 82 fully or partially privatized enterprises at the end of 1993 from the 600 at the beginning of 1989.

***This figure is from BPE (2001), but a paper by El-Rufai puts the figure at 590 (see El-Rufai 2001, 8). El-Rufai is the director general of the Bureau of Public Enterprises.

+E-mail correspondence dated 1 August 2001 from El-Rufai to the author.

++E-mail correspondence dated 30 June 2001 from El-Rufai to the author.

"golden shares" in the four large banks that had been privatized earlier: Union Bank of Nigeria, First Bank of Nigeria, Afribank and United Bank for Africa. The government subsequently abandoned this move but justified its policy on the grounds that it was pursuing a strategy of "guided privatization" in relation to the remaining public enterprises. Not surprisingly, there was no privatization during this period.

The third period of the privatization program was launched by the military regime that ruled from June 1998, to May 1999. The federal government had about 588 PEs at the beginning of this period and the total value of government investment in these PEs has been estimated at about US$100 billion (BPE, 2001:2). The departing military government only enacted the law without undertaking any privatization, leaving the incoming civilian government to implement the privatization program in the third period. The details of the privatization process are discussed below.

The Privatization Process in the Democratic Context

The new civilian government that came to power in May 1999, announced it would adopt the legal framework for the privatization program enacted by the last military government. The key features of the decree were the establishment of the National Council on Privatization (NCP) and a restructured Bureau of Public Enterprises (BPE). The NCP is a cabinet-level committee chaired by the vice president and includes the minister of finance, attorney-general of the federation and minister of justice, minister of industries, minister of national planning, secretary to the government of the federation, governor of the central bank, special advisor to the president on economic affairs, director general of the BPE, and four other members appointed by the President. The BPE, which is headed by a director-general, acts as the secretariat/technical arm of the NCP.

The composition of the NCP reflects a conscious policy to make the process of implementing privatization more inclusive. This effort was taken one step further by the establishment of ten sector steering committees for each of the sectors identified by the NCP. The line minister Chairs each steering committee and membership is drawn from the stakeholders in the public and private sectors, trade unions, academia, and NGOs. The NCP's main responsibilities are to provide overall strategic guidance for the direction, conduct, and management of the privatization program and to supervise the activities and approve the budget of the BPE.

Typically, the process of divestiture of a public enterprise consists of two stages. The first stage starts with the appointment of professional advisors with expertise in financial, legal, technical, valuation, and accounting.

This is followed by the placement of advertisements in the local and foreign newspapers offering sale of shares to qualified strategic or core investors. Prospective investors are given the opportunity to undertake due diligence on the companies to be privatized. Next is issuance of information memoranda and bidding documents to prospective, prequalified core investors. Bids submitted by prospective investors, are opened, followed by negotiations with short listed bidders (within 20% of the highest bids).

The second stage consist of an evaluation of the technical and financial proposals of prospective investors by the BPE and the technical committee of the NCP, which presents its recommendation to either the full NCP or to the vice president. The NCP then decides whether to approve or reject the recommendations and the announcement is made by the BPE.

As might be expected in a democracy, several actors are involved in or seek to influence the privatization program. Notably these include the executive, legislature, and interest groups such as labor, management/staff of public enterprises and investor groups, as well as international donors. Executive arm influence is reflected in the creation and composition of the NCP. A key feature of the current period of privatization is the political clout lent to the process by making the vice-president the chair of the NCP. This arrangement not only facilitates decision-making at the highest levels of government but also indicates the importance that the government attached to the privatization program. Thus, under the present civilian government, the vice president is the political champion of privatization program, which was not the case in the first and second periods. The arrangement has proved to be advantageous to the BPE especially in its relations with ministries that were reluctant to accept the privatization of public enterprises within their purview.

Even so, there have been some very public disagreements between the BPE and some supervising Ministries with respect to the privatization of Nigeria Airways and the Nigeria Telecommunications Company (NITEL). Indeed, it has been reported (*Financial Times*, 14 June 2001) that the removal of the minister of communications in the cabinet reshuffle of June 2001 had to do with the fact that "he often appeared to be working at odds with the government's policy of liberalization and had clashed on several occasions with officials running this year's privatization of the Nigeria Telecommunications Company (NITEL)"—a public enterprise under the ministry of communications. These incidents represent important instances of collision among some of the key actors.

Consistent with its ideological convictions and the interests of its members, it would be expected that the Nigerian Labour Congress would object to the privatization program. This is indeed the case in the general sense that it does not want the privatization program to result in unemployment of its members or transfer of control of strategic industries to foreign interests. However, the public posture of the NLC towards privatization has not been one of virulent opposition. This perhaps reflects the recognition that privatization may be a better option than allowing such enterprises to go out of business, since the government has lost interest in owning them. Even so, individual unions have made their objections very clear in cases concerning the enterprises in their sector. For example, in the case of the national airline, Nigeria Airways, the various unions representing the pilots, engineers, and aviation workers have reversed their strong opposition to the privatization of the airline, insisting instead that privatization should be undertaken after a turnaround of the now-moribund company. This conflicts with the position of the BPE, which prefers the option of outright liquidation before a new company is formed to serve as national carrier. In another example, the Nigerian Ports Authority, President Obasanjo took the sector unions to task for carrying antiprivatization placards during the 2000 May Day rally, charging them with being part of the reason for the privatization because they participated in running down their PEs. He stated on that occasion that there would have been no need to privatize if public enterprises were run properly. The workers responded in newspaper advertisements that if such were the case, the NPA should be exempted from privatization since it had been managed profitably since being commercialized in 1990.

The privatization program has attracted some criticism from the organized private sector. Participants at the seventh Session of the Nigerian Economic Summit—a forum that periodically brings together policy-makers from the public and private sectors to dialogue on Nigeria's economic, business, and financial policies—observed that the pace of program implementation was rather slow, although this was ascribed largely to an overambitious timetable in the first place. Similarly, the Nigerian Chamber of Commerce, Industry, Mines and Agriculture stated that survey conducted among its members indicated a general perception that the program was dragging on too long, quite apart from concerns about a lack of transparency and transfer of public monopolies to private monopolies.

In its most recent report, the BPE has responded to these criticisms, noting "Since its commencement in 1999, the [current] privatization program has been executed with all sense of transparency, accountability and professionalism consistent with the stance of the present administration" (BPE, 2001:24). Concerning delays, BPE has asserted, "All public offers, under phase 1 of the program, are on the verge of conclusion. As regards the commencement of the second phase, due to several delays, including unforeseen legal and technical issues arising from the due diligence process and those occasioned by the decision to seek the assistance of the

World Bank and other donors, the second phase has not proceeded as planned. However, the secretariat has now re-engineered the roadmap for the effective implementation of this phase of the program with a view to completing this phase in the next eighteen months" (BPE, 2001:24).

No analysis of the privatization process in Nigeria is complete without highlighting the role of international donors such as the international development institutions. The IDA—the concessional lending arm of the World Bank—has provided credits for the privatization of key infrastructure industries. The IFC has been retained as the advisor on the privatization of the Nigeria Airways. A strategic options report articulated three options for the privatization of Nigeria Airways: a joint venture national carrier to be created between the federal government and the winning strategic investor; the liquidation of Nigeria Airways, allowing private airlines to bid for routes covered by bilateral air service agreements; and the long-term turnaround of Nigeria Airways and subsequent privatization. After weighing the three options, the report recommended the liquidation of Nigeria Airways and the launch of a new national carrier. In addition, the World Bank is providing technical assistance for utilities sector reform and financial support of about US$50 million. USAID is providing about US$ 4.5 million; the U.K. government about US$5 million; and the Spanish government US$3 million (El Rufai, 2001:12). Assistance of more donors is being sought (BPE, 2001:31–34).

Public Perceptions of the Privatization Program

Notwithstanding the steady progress made since the inception of the new civilian government, the privatization program has been bedeviled by public perception of lack of consistency and by conflicting perceptions of political considerations. These perceptions have led to controversies, highlighted in the three transactions discussed below.

The unsuccessful first effort by Sadiq Petroleum Limited (SPL) to acquire 75% of the Government's shares in African Petroleum (AP) illustrate the public controversy concerning the perceived lack of consistency in the process. In this case, the National Council on Privatization (NCP) solicited bids from interested investors to buy majority shares in AP. Three firms indicated interest, but, only SPL submitted a bid. The announcement of the bid award to SPL was greeted with skepticism from the public as well as the House of Representatives, which adopted a motion to probe the technical ability, financial strength and managerial competence of SPL and called for a halt to the privatization process, pending a review of the existing legal framework.

The sale of the Benue Cement Company (BCC) to Dangote Industries Limited provides a striking illustration of the conflicting perception of political considerations in the privatization process. Some argued that NCP ignored its stated criteria of selling shares to core investors with proven experience when it sold BCC to Dangote Industries, a trading company without significant experience in cement manufacturing, rather than to Cementia Lafarge, which built and had operated BCC for many years. These critics argued that though Dangote might have passed the test of financial competence—the ability to pay a reasonable price for BCC—it lacked the technical expertise. They contrasted the BCC transaction with that of West African Portland Cement Company and Ashaka Cement Company, which were sold to Blue Circle Industries (U.K.), a reputable company with experience in cement production. On the other hand, some have suggested that because the selection of Dangote Industries had not received the support of the government and people of Benue state, the transaction was politically insensitive and the NCP's decision should not be based on business principles alone.

Finally, Ocean and Oil Services Limited's purchase of a 30% stake of the federal government's 40% shareholding in Unipetrol highlighted a controversy arising from the perception that an acquisition process may not have conformed to stated criteria. Ocean and Oil Services Limited was widely believed to lack financial resources to purchase the shares of Unipetrol. As a result, it borrowed from a bank to pay for the bid, implying Ocean and Oil would not add value to Unipetrol—a situation the government has been eager to avoid in the privatization process. The perceived irregularities of this transaction became a subject of public hearings by the privatization and commercialization committees of both the Senate and House of Representatives. No evidence of wrongdoing emerged from the hearings; however, they reflected public concern that the alleged lack of conformity with the agreed criteria would damage the credibility of the privatization program.

Conclusion

Privatization everywhere is marked by controversies, dogged by disagreements among the public officials involved in the process, and hemmed in by a variety of transitional issues. In this regard, the Nigerian experience has not been unique. Even so, the privatization experience under the current civilian administration has highlighted a number of issues with three main implications for the public policy process: the changing nature of both the criticisms leveled against the privatization program and government's response; the orientation of program implementation under the current democratic civilian administration; and the challenge of managing the transitional issues arising from privatization.

When privatization began about sixteen years ago under the military regime, the main public criticisms and concerns were that the government was selling off the nation's assets at very low prices, that privatization would result in resumed foreign domination of the economy, and that shares of the privatized enterprises would not be distributed equitably among Nigeria's states and citizens. To assuage these concerns, the military regime launched public awareness campaigns and designed measures to broaden public ownership of the privatized enterprises by selling shares in multiples of fifty and encouraging share ownership in different states. Under the civilian federal government, criticisms have arisen from the perception that the government has not rigorously adhered to the program rules and procedures it established and fears persist about lack of broad ownership. In response to the latter concern, in 2001, the Bureau of Public Enterprises negotiated an arrangement with several banks to lend money to Nigerians to buy shares of privatized public enterprises.

The issues falling within the second area include the fact that the new civilian government adopted the legal framework promulgated by the military to implement privatization program; the domination of the privatization by the executive arm; and the relative insulation of the program from political and public pressures. The new civilian government's decision to inherit the privatization and commercialization framework represents the triumph of pragmatism over idealism in the policy process. The ideal situation would have been for the government to either propose new legislation or resubmit the decree for review by the legislature. But the new civilian government saw much merit in continuing privatization under the previous legal framework because it allowed momentum to be restored—momentum that could have been lost had the legislature reviewed and reenacted the decree. It is worth noting that, in established democracies, it is not uncommon for an incoming administration to use the policy or legal framework of its predecessors, even from a different political party, if such a framework serves its purpose.

A closely related issue is that the pattern of policy-making that has emerged under the civilian administration has been marked by technocratic insulation, with the conduct and management of the privatization process slightly insulated from broader political and public pressures. This approach is not unique. The World Bank has noted, for example, that in some industrialized and developing countries with an effective public sector, "politicians have delegated macro economic and strategic policy coordination to capable, relatively autonomous central agencies, whose activities are guided by consultative processes that are transparent to outsiders" (World

Bank, 1997:81). By coopting representatives from the various segments of society in its sector standing committees and providing periodic briefings to the relevant committees of the legislature, the BPE is conforming to this model. Thus, if BPE can successfully pilot the privatization, it could hold interesting lessons for the future in combining relative insulation and operational flexibility with institutional accountability to relevant stakeholders in designing public sector agencies in Nigeria.

The third group of issues pertains to a host of transitional matters that must be addressed in the terminal phase of the privatization program. One of the most significant is establishing appropriate regulatory frameworks for privatized enterprises, which is especially important because privatization ineluctably separates the roles of government as owner and operator of public enterprises from that of regulator, with the regulatory role assuming greater significance (Otobo, 1998, 1997). Indeed, creating a regulatory framework is one of many transitional challenges that the BPE address. This needs to be pursued with great vigor, building on the work done in establishing a national communications commission for the telecommunications sector in 1992. The next phase is to design and establish new regulatory frameworks for the power, transport, and petroleum sectors.

Notwithstanding these criticisms there has been steady progress in the privatization program since the inception of the new civilian government. More importantly, this government has arguably shown itself more responsive than the military regimes to various public concerns and criticisms. Overall, progress in the privatization program can pave the way for a strategic economic objective of the new civilian government—the strengthening of a private sector–led economy in Nigeria.

References

Bureau of Public Enterprises. 2001. *Status Report on the Privatization Programme of the Federal Government of Nigeria, June 2001.*

Edozien, John D. and S. O. Adeoye. 1989. "Privatization in Nigeria." In *Privatization in Developing Countries,* ed. V. V. Ramanadham. London: Routledge.

El-Rufai, Nasir Ahmad. 1999. *The Second Privatization Programme: Opportunities for Investment.* Paper presented at *Financial Times* Seminar on Nigeria: Debt, Development and Democracy. 4–5 May 1999.

———. 2001. *The Privatization Programme: Institutional Framework and Implementation.* Presentation. 26 March 2001.

Federal Government of Nigeria. 1998 Budget Address by the Head of State. 4 January 1998.

Kuye, Omowale. 1990. "Problems and Prospects of Nigeria's Privatization and Commercialisation Programme." *Quarterly Journal of Administration* (Oct. 1990): 49–73.

Lewis, Peter. 1994. "Development Strategy and State Sector Expansion in Nigeria." Pp. 63–81 in *State-Owned Enterprises in Africa*, eds. Barbara Grosh and Rwekaza S. Mukandala. Boulder, Colo.: Lynne Rienner.

National Council on Privatization. 2000. *Privatization Handbook*.

Nellis, John. 1986. "Public Enterprises in Sub-Saharan Africa" World Bank. Discussion Paper No. 1. Washington, D.C.: World Bank.

Okigbo, Pius. 1981. *Nigeria's Financial System*. Harlow, Essex: Longman.

Otobo, Ejeviome. 1997. "Regulatory Reform in Support of Privatization: Patterns and Progress in Africa." *African Journal of Public Administration and Management.* 8/9(2): 25–50

———. "Nigeria" P. 294 in *Public Administration in Africa: Main Issues and Selected Country Studies*, ed. Ladipo Adamolekun. Boulder, Colo.: Westview Press.

———. "Privatization and Regulation in Africa: Some Key Policy Issues" *Development Policy Network Bulletin, Volume V, No. 1 December 1998.* P. 23–28

Ramanadham, V. V. 1993. "Privatization in Nigeria." P. 359 in *Privatization: A Global Perspective*, ed. V. V. Ramanadham. London: Routledge.

United Nations Development Programme and the World Bank. 1989. *African Economic and Financial Data*. UNDP New York and Washington D.C.: UNDP and World Bank.

———. 1992. *African Development Indicators*. New York and Washington, D.C.: UNDP and World Bank.

World Bank. 1997. *World Development Report: The State in a Changing World*. New York: Oxford University Press.

Zayyad, H. R. 1992. "Welcome Address by the Chairman of the Technical Committee on Privatization and Commercialisation." Pp. 9–11 in *Economic Democratisation: Report of the Proceedings of the International Conference in the Implementation of Privatization and Commercialisation Programme in Nigeria— An African Experience*, ed. H. R. Zayyad (Lagos Nigeria, Nov. 6–8 1990).

11

Governance, Institutional Reforms, and Policy Outcomes in Ghana

Joseph Ayee

This chapter assesses the efficacy or contribution of various key institutions to public policy making under the Rawlings civilian government in Ghana from 1993, to 2000. The chapter is divided into four parts. The first part deals with the nature, direction, and extent of governance reforms. The second part discusses the role of critical official and unofficial policy institutions. The part analyzes the relationship between policy processes and outcomes and the final part is devoted to the lessons learned.

Nature, Direction, and Extent of Governance Reforms

Policy Framework of Good Governance

Ghana's search for an enduring good governance framework started with the introduction of the Economic Recovery Program (ERP) in 1983. Apart from its economic benefits, the ERP's increased role for the private sector in the production and distribution of goods and services was characterized by improved partnership between the public and private sectors. A major decentralization program in 1988, enhanced grassroots participation in governance at the local level was also started. The gains from economic and political reform culminated in the promulgation of the 1992 Constitution, which provides the blue print for a national good governance agenda based on competition. In addition, the National Institutional Renewal Program (NIRP), which includes the Civil Service Performance Improvement Program, was launched in 1994, to promote good governance through the development of "value for money" public services and redefinition of the role of the state. In 1995, the government published

173

Ghana: Vision 2020—The First Step: 1996–2000, under which Ghana was to become a middle level country by 2020. It also provides a human-centered approach to development as a pragmatic means of improving good governance through support for democracy; decentralization and the devolution of government; liberalization of the economy; and reform of state institutions, their structures, roles, and procedures.

The Rawling Government's Understanding of Good Governance

Under the 1992 Constitution, the Rawlings government defined good governance as a neopatrimonial governance system consisting of:

- Highly centralized personal rule sanctified by periodic elections leading to personalism;
- The distribution of state-generated benefits to political followers leading to pervasive clientelism;
- The selection of public officials on the basis of personal rather than institutional loyalty; and
- The unmediated and uncircumscribed control of a coercive apparatus (Sandbrook and Oelbaum, 1997).

Rawlings governed largely as he saw fit and his supremacy derived partly from the 1992 Constitution, vests the entire executive authority of Ghana in the president, who is head of state, head of government, and commander-in-chief of the armed forces. The president appoints almost everyone to practically every key government institution at the national, regional, and local level. For instance, the chief justice and the justices of the superior courts are appointed either acting on the advice of the judicial council, in consultation with the Council of State and with the approval of the parliament and members of other constitutional bodies. Similarly, the president appoints the chief of defense staff and service chiefs as well as the inspector general of police acting in consultation with the council of state. In addition, most ministers of state appointed by the president with the prior approval of parliament, come from parliament. Although there are paper guarantees of limits to the powers of the president, they do not seem to pose a strong countervailing force.

Besides using his broad constitutional powers to build acquiescence, Rawlings sought to neutralize formal institutions that asserted their right to hold the government accountable. The legislature was hobbled by the near monopoly of parliamentary seats enjoyed by the Rawlings' National Democratic Congress (NDC), which had 133 seats out of the 200-seat Parliament. This notwithstanding, the committee system provided the opposition with a forum in which to criticize legislation and budgets. The opposition parties and the independent press voiced persistent complaints about government policies and behavior, but a lack of resources and periodic intimidation inhibited their impact. The Supreme Court and other judicial bodies delivered some courageous judgments, which sometimes seemed to circumscribe presidential discretion and reassert the formal rules of fair play.

The commitment to good governance by the Rawlings regime has been the subject of controversy. While some people, especially those closely associated with the government, thought that the Rawlings regime promoted good governance others especially academics and policy analysts, think otherwise. Proponents of government commitment to good governance argued that the government complied with virtually all the provisions of the 1992 Constitution, by establishing certain institutions, holding three generally "free and fair" elections in 1992, 1996, and 2000; making modest improvement in governmental accountability; and respecting the decisions of the Supreme Court in four separate constitutional cases in 1993, and 1994. On the other hand, the perceived government commitment to good governance is based on certain shortfalls such as undermining the independence of the judiciary by appointing judges with progovernment sentiments; its inability to repeal the Seditious Libel Law, which makes it a criminal offense to "publish a false report which is likely to injure the reputation of the state"; its inability to promote the right of and access to information and expression as enshrined in the 1992 Constitution, even though various pieces of legislation made it an offense for public officials to give information to anyone without prior authorization; the persistence of the culture of arbitrariness by security and law-enforcement agencies; its lack of commitment to its much-touted rhetoric of transparency, probity, and accountability in spite of the existence of anticorruption bodies; its inability to delink state affairs personnel and resources from those of the government; and its inability to address some of the problems of the private sector (such as infrequent dialogue between the government and the private sector, criticism of the morality of the profit motive and behavior of the business community, high interest rates, and inefficient practices public service practices (Ayee, 1999b; Prempeh, 1999; da Rocha et al., 1999; Kumado, 1999; Gyimah-Boadi, 1997, 1999b; Sandbrook and Oelbaum, 1997; Ayee, 2000a).

The Role of Critical Policy Institutions

A number of institutions both constitutional (formal) and extraconstitutional (informal) were involved in public policy-making under the Rawlings regime. The formal policy-making institutions are the cabinet, civil service and parliament, while the informal are the policy management group, political parties, and nongovernmental think-tanks. This presents a more dynamic picture in which events relating to the increasing democratization of the regime led to the greater involvement of other actors in the policy process. When they were not so involved, democratization made it possible for these other social actors (informal groups) to offer effective opposition that in some cases led to the failure or withdrawal of the policies themselves.

The Cabinet

The 1992 Constitution stipulates, "There shall be a Cabinet which shall consist of the President, the Vice-President and not less than ten and not more than nineteen Ministers of State." The main function of the Cabinet is to "assist the President in the determination of the general policy of the Government." Section 77 (1) enjoins that the President should summons the Cabinet and presides over all its meetings; or in his absence the Vice President.

How did the Cabinet assist President Rawlings in determining general government policy? The answer to this question is discussed below.

Cabinet meetings. The President presided over weekly meetings, but rumours were rife that in his two terms of four years in office he chaired the meetings only twice. For the first term, it was alleged that most of the meetings were chaired by the Presidential Advisor on Governmental Affairs (PAGA), P. V. Obeng, a noncabinet member who was part of Rawlings' Provisional National Defence Council (PNDC) military government. Indeed, one of the main reasons behind the squabbling between Rawlings and his first term Vice President Kow Arkaah was the latter's allegations that certain individuals had been allowed to attend cabinet meetings in an unconstitutional manner. The then Vice President was not allowed to chair the meetings because of his differences with the President, which led to his being assaulted by the President at a 1995 meeting. For the second term, it was again alleged that the Vice President John Mills, who was different from the first one, chaired most of the meetings. These rumours were denied by the chief of staff at the office of the president, who insisted that Rawlings chaired most of his cabinet meetings. These conflicting reports make it is difficult to judge the effect of his presence or absence on the cabinet's capacity to formulate public policies and programs.

Composition and skills of the cabinet. The composition of the Rawlings cabinet varied. During his first term, the Cabinet was made up of seventeen ministers while the second term had nineteen—the maximum stipulated by the 1992 Constitution. Two new ministries (National Security, and Planning, Regional Economic Cooperation and Integration) were created while two were restructured (Ministry of Information and the non-cabinet Ministry of Roads and Highways) to become Communications and Roads and Transport, respectively (Ayee, 1993).

More than three-quarters of the ministers appointed by the Rawlings government were not experts in their areas of responsibility. Deputy Ministers were supposed to be experts but in practice were not. The appointment of nonexperts did not affect deliberations at cabinet meetings when it came to policy issues that emanated from ministries, because ministers were well briefed on the issues by their chief directors before they attended cabinet meetings. Furthermore, technical personnel from agencies and departments of the ministries were invited to attend cabinet meetings with their ministries if technical issues were going to be discussed. For instance, in determining the criteria for disbursement of the District Assemblies Common Fund (DACF), the minister of local government and rural development invited the district assemblies common fund administrator to explain to the cabinet the technicalities involved in the criteria selection. Similarly, the minister of transport and communications in 1995, invited the director general of the Ghana civil aviation authority to attend a cabinet meeting that was scheduled to discuss an increase of the price of aviation oil and other issues affecting the aviation industry.

To enrich discussions at cabinet meetings and provide adequate information, three important measures were taken. The first is the directive by President Rawlings in 1995, that chief directors (the chief advisors to the ministers on all policies and other related matters) of ministries should accompany their ministers to cabinet meetings when policies concerning their ministries were going to be discussed—to give an informed opinion of policy issues coming from sector ministries. The presence of chief directors at cabinet meetings did improve the process of policy-making as well as the content of the policies made. The second measure, the use of visual aids and other teaching methods by technocrats and experts, enabled ministers to understand technical issues and problems before deciding on a policy or program. Third, an impartial discussion followed a minister's presentation of a policy memorandum. Indeed, cabinet meetings were referred to as a "vigorous discussion chamber." It was common for policy memoranda from a ministry to be sent back for revision if the presentation made by the minister and his team of technical experts was not convincing enough, not based on facts, or not complete.

Cabinet subcommittees. The Rawlings cabinet had four subcommittees, which thoroughly considered policies referred to it because of their technical nature and time constraints. They were:

- Finance and economic subcommittee, which dealt with policies and programs from the ministries of finance, economic planning, trade and industry, food and agriculture, lands and forestry, mines and energy, tourism, environment, and science and technology as well as issues relating to loans, donor support, and funding;
- Political, legal and security subcommittee, which was in charge of policies and programs from the ministries of justice, defense, interior, foreign affairs, local government, and rural development as well as constitutional matters, drafting of bills, screening of loan agreements, elections, public safety, and national security;
- Social sector subcommittee, which dealt with policies and programs emanating from the ministries of health, education, youth and sports, employment and social welfare, and communication as well as poverty reduction issues;
- Infrastructure and utilities subcommittee, which was involved in policies and programs from the ministries of roads and transport, works, and housing and issues relating to water and electricity.

The subcommittees, convened and chaired by the vice president, were made up of ministers of relevant portfolios. However, some ministers such as the attorney general and finance belong to all the subcommittees. The secretary to the cabinet and his secretariat facilitated the work of the subcommittees and reports were presented to the cabinet in the form of dossiers. At cabinet meetings the vice president verbally presented the subcommittee reports after which discussions were held on the issues raised. The work of the subcommittees facilitated cabinet policy decisions since knotty and controversial issues had been thrashed out.

Secretary to the cabinet. An institution that actively influenced public policy making was the cabinet secretary headed by the Secretary to the Cabinet, appointed by the President. Under the Rawlings presidency, the secretary to the cabinet summoned cabinet meetings under the authority of the president and, inter alia, performed the following functions:

- Coordinated the policy inputs from ministries, agencies, and departments for consideration by the cabinet as a whole;
- Briefed the president on all matters for discussion at cabinet meetings;

In performing these functions, he ensured that policy memoranda sub-mitted by ministries indicated all appropriate consultations made with key agencies likely to be affected by the policy proposals. Subsequently, the secretariat transmitted policy decisions to ministers for the required actions to be taken, and from time to time, monitored the implementation of those decisions.

One important way of influencing the public policy-making was that the secretary to the cabinet determined the agenda at meetings and also devised a format for ministers to present their policy memoranda. For instance, for bills to be submitted, the format required that a reference be made to pre-vious bills and that financial implications of the bills must be stated. For a policy proposal be considered by the cabinet, it was required to state the stakeholders consulted, the interministerial consultations held, probable repercussions for other agencies, and the policy proposal's financial impli-cations. In addition, the policy proposal had to be concise and clear.

The 1992 Constitution separated the positions of secretary to the cab-inet (SC) and head of the civil service (HCS), which has also improved the public policy-making process because the SC had more time to devote to follow-up action on cabinet decisions. Those in favor of separation of the two positions argue that the workload of the combined post is excessive and, therefore, government business is inadvertently slowed, resulting in stunted civil service management and reform while more urgent national and international issues become the major preoccupation (Ayee, 1994).

On the other hand, those in favor of the combination point out that separation would result in diffusion of authority in a vital area of govern-ment machinery where clear-cut authority is required. It is also argued that the person who has responsibility for the implementation of govern-ment decisions should as a matter of fact have full responsibility for deploying the personnel who will implement those decisions (Adu, 1973).

It must be pointed out that whereas the position of the SC is politi-cal, the HCS is a career post. Proximity to the leadership necessitates that the SC should share certain purposes and orientation with the members of the government. But the HCS involves responsibility for focusing atten-tion on the economy and efficiency of the service as well as expediting action on planning and improving administrative reforms. In other words, considering the multifarious nature of responsibilities of the SC who heads the focal point for directing and monitoring all government activities, it is clear that he cannot give full attention to or effectively manage the effi-ciency and effectiveness of the civil service (Amonoo, 1981; Ayee, 1994). For a regime intent on employing the civil service as an instrument for spearheading socioeconomic development, recognition of the distinct posi-tions and roles appears attractive and necessary. As the Okoh Commission rightly observed, the investment of responsibility in one man of the combined posts of secretary to the cabinet and head of the civil service "makes for too demanding a role within the context of our developing economy" (Ghana, 1977).

Press briefing on cabinet meetings. During President Rawlings' second term in office (1997–2000), a press briefing was sometimes held by the minister of communication to highlight cabinet decisions. During the briefing, the press were allowed to ask questions on the issues raised and seek clarifications. The role of the press briefing was to make the general public aware of cabinet decisions on policies and programs and thus to bridge the communication gap between government and the citizenry. It was also intended to make the public policy-making process transparent.

The Civil Service

Civil service functions. Under the 1993 Civil Service Law the main function of the Ghanaian civil service is "to assist the Government in the formulation and implementation of government policies for the development of the country." This function is carried out through sector ministries responsible for policy issues, manpower, and financial matters as well as exercising overall supervisory, monitoring, and coordinatory powers over technical departments (implementing programs and delivering services to citizens) in their respective sectors (Republic of Ghana, 1993).

Obstacle to civil service role in policy analysis. The functions of the civil service and sector ministries, coupled with their role as prime movers in formulating and evaluating policies that will deliver Ghana Vision 2020, entail the need for policy analysts with the requisite expertise and information. In other words, these functions need professionalization of the civil service and sector ministries. There are, however, few policy analysts in the civil service and the sector ministries a fact echoed by Ghana Vision 2020:

> Policy initiatives as well as programme design, implementation and monitoring have been handled by very few self-motivated and committed public sector officials who are over-stretched and over-used. . . . Most public service institutions lack expertise in critical areas such as policy analysis, planning, budgeting and accounting but are overstaffed at the lower semiskilled and functional levels. (Republic of Ghana, 1995:26)

This point is repeated by the HCS: "most of the existing personnel are generalist officers who may be suitable for perhaps one functional area, viz, Finance and Administration" (Dodoo, 1998:21).

Measures to enhance civil service capacity. To enhance the capacity of ministries and other central government agencies for public policy-making and analysis, the civil service law enjoins them to establish a planning, budgeting, coordination, monitoring and evaluation division and a research, statistics, public relations and information division. This requirement has not been met by most ministries and agencies. According to *Vision 2020:*

> In practice, the record is patchy. Some ministries have effective Planning Divisions, but in other ministries, the Planning Division and Research and Statistics Division are either non-existent or exist only on paper. There is also the tendency for Planning Divisions to be ignored. (Republic of Ghana, 1995:27)

The inability of the civil service and sector ministries to become a key policy-making actor is undermined by their inability to attract and retain professionals. This is due to

> poor conditions of service (including low remuneration and inadequate office facilities) which have created low morale and disincentives in the system, resulting in the loss of managerial and professional expertise to the private sector or foreign countries. (Republic of Ghana, 1995)

In spite of the initiation of the Civil Service Reform Program (1987–1993), the National Institutional Renewal Program (1994 to date), and its major offshoot the Civil Service Performance Improvement Programme (1994 to date)—all basically aimed at strengthening the capacity of the civil service and sector ministries, developing a culture of good governance, of efficiency and effectiveness in service delivery and of willing assistance to the private sector—equipping the civil service and sector ministries with policy analysts and other professionals is still far from accomplished. Most serving chief directors are generalists and were also recruited internally. However, a number of measures such as recruitment into the civil service through a specific line directorate and the gradual phasing out of generalist lines of promotion have been taken to rectify the situation and thereby develop the civil service as a paradigm of professionalism as envisaged by the programs (Dodoo, 1998).

In spite of the criticisms of the civil service, however, most Ghanaians perceive the few-top flight civil servants as endowed with the available knowledge and professional skills to provide sufficient inputs in the formulation of policies and programs. The bureaucrats come from a variety of social backgrounds, but most have university education. Apart from the chief directors, appointed on merit and political affiliation and who leave office with the government of the day, all other civil servants acquire official experience and neutrality in partisan politics, the overaching value system of the administrative class. This system entails the adoption of generalist rather than specialist orientation in solving of problems; the possession of a shrewd political sense; and a primary concern with the stability, growth, and tactics of the bureaucrats' organization rather than with its fundamental mission, values, or ideals. Regulations and conventions circumscribe the extent of the bureaucrat's involvement in political activities. For instance, he cannot hold office in a political party and must resign to contest political office. In addition, a bureaucrat cannot canvas support for candidates seeking political office or admission to the national legislature.

The pervasive and preponderant role of bureaucrats in public policy-making has been recognized by Riggs (1963:120) and supported by Abernathy (1971:1), who points out that senior civil servants in African countries exercise leverage in development planning, resource allocation, and the transition of plans into feasible projects and programs. However, in Ghana under the Rawlings regime, the government did not have access to top flight civil servants due to poor pay and remuneration, and so the the bureaucracy was unable to play a high profile role in policy-making.

The performance of policy analysts serving the public sector was uneven and often low. Public-sector institutions for policy analysis were inadequate in terms of their overall ability to cope with rapid changes in the environment as well as in terms of their ability to present an integrated approach to problems facing Ghanaian society. Moreover, the knowledge and database available for policy formulation and analysis in Ghana was inadequate. The relative degree of information at the disposal of policy analysts was a decisive factor in the determining priorities, and like other African countries, data for policy analysis was rudimentary or nonexistent. As result, policy analysts and reformers were compelled to rely extensively on "guesses, intuitions, ideological preferences, or hunches; by contrast, the existence of a body of reasonably accurate data in some developed countries enhances the capacity of their planners to form more efficacious collective choices" (Rothchild and Curry, 1978:23).

The National Development Planning Commission

Another institution established to enhance policy analysis is the National Development Planning Commission (NDPC), which prepares national development plans and monitors, evaluates, and coordinates development policies, programs, and projects (Republic of Ghana, 1994). For the NDPC to perform these functions, its membership is drawn from relevant areas and roles pertaining to development, economic, social, environmental and space planning, statistics, finance, banking, population studies, and gender.

In spite of its wide array of expertise, NDPC's performance in policy analysis—apart from formulating Ghana Vision 2000 and the First Medium-Term Development Plan (1997–2000) has not been encouraging. The NDPC has admitted its inability to marshal data for the formulation of the First Medium-Term Development Plan of Vision 2020, especially with respect to development indicators, development targets, and estimated cost of programs (Republic of Ghana, 1998:17).

A number of reasons explain this poor performance. First, the role of the NDPC, like any planning agency, is primarily to receive impart and organize information. The NDPC cannot work alone, since it depend on information supplied by ministries, departments, agencies, district assemblies, and the private sector. The problem is that the ministries, departments, and agencies also do not have the information. Second is the rather sour relationship between the ministry of finance (MOF) and the NDPC. Certain conflicts of interest have arisen between the MOF on one hand, which is traditionally conservative, cautious, and restrictionist in policy orientation and the NDPC, on the other hand, whose functions are essentially expansionist in outlook. For example, the economic planning functions of the MOF were supposed to be transferred to the NDPC. But the MOF has not relinquished some of its planning functions. Like all finance ministries, the MOF is notoriously jealous of its power of budgetary control. Only through the backing of the president can the NDPC hope to influence the budgetary process. Third, in spite of the background of the NDPC members, appointments are still made on political grounds rather than on merit. Consequently, the NDPC has become the dumping ground for political casualties while some regard it merely as an occupational transit institution.

Parliament

Under the 1992 Constitution, the Parliament plays a key role in public policy formulation and is mandated to debate the president's state of the nation address and approve the financial policies and programs, including loans, taxes, and the national budget, which are initiated mostly through bills and legislation by the executive branch. Even though the law-making power of Ghana is expressly vested in parliament, the executive branch, under the Rawlings government as elsewhere, both initiated and influenced legislation. In fact, the executive had an advantage over parliament in introducing legislation, for two reasons account. First, the amount of information, expert advice, and technical drafting that usually go into the preparation of a bill were often not easily available to Parliament. Parliament had (and still has) a small library and few research assistants, which were inadequate for giving members of parliament (MPs) sufficient information on bills to make an informed input during debate. Moreover, MPs did not have (and still do not have) offices in which they could read and prepare for parliamentary debates. Second, MPs could not count on the backing of their parties to get a bill through Parliament to the same degree as the executive can. In fact, under the Rawlings period, no private member's bill had gone through. Under the circumstances, instead of initiating bills, MPs found themselves exercising, for most part, their power to changes bills sponsored by the executive. In the absence of a tradition of broad consultation and public discussion of policy before a bill gets to Parliament, a heavy burden was placed on the MPs to exercise good judgment in the public interest before considering bills.

Under the Rawlings government, most public policy proposals such as funding of tertiary education, value-added tax, national wage policy, land policy, decentralization, and a national health insurance scheme adopted by either the cabinet or minister affected existing legislation. Consequently, draft bills accompanied the memoranda to the cabinet and were submitted to Parliament for discussion and adoption. Unlike a bureaucracy where hierarchy of authority is of central importance, MPs had equal vote at the voting stage. Also, except in a few special instances, discussion of the policy proposal took place in the open. Furthermore, when Parliament was going to debate bills from the cabinet, with the exception of the appropriation bill, the relevant parliamentary standing committee invited memoranda from stakeholders by announcing in the press its meeting place and time. The outcome of such Parliamentary deliberations was almost invariably a law on the policy problem.

Parliament's role as an effective formulator of public policies and programs through passage of bills and legislation was severely undermined by:

- the size of Rawling's party in Parliament, one seat short of a two-thirds majority—enough to amend the Constitution. MPs the Rawlings' NDC party usually voted along party lines because none of them wanted to incur the displeasure of the president. Parliament was therefore perceived as a "rubber-stamp" body;
- the generally partisan nature of debates from both sides of the political divide;
- the stipulation by the 1992 Constitution that most ministers of state should be appointed from among MPs;

- the lack of office accommodation and poor library facilities for MPs;
- the inadequate information at the disposal of MPs, made worse by employment of only a few research assistants.

Nonetheless, the sixteen select committees (such as these on food, agriculture and cocoa affairs, health and education, subsidiary legislation, and constitutional and legal) influenced public policies because almost all bills presented to Parliament were referred to them while they performed investigatory functions such as hearing witnesses, assembling facts, and conducting enquires. The various parliamentary committees were able to churn out more than 213 bills such as the Ghana Education Service Bill, Local Government Bill, Ghana Education Trust Fund Bill and the Export Development and Investment Fund Bill. One of the several merits of the parliamentary committee system is the opportunity for dialogue between legislators and the public, especially civil society organizations. For instance, the passage of the Criminal Code (Amendment) Act of 1995 generated much intense lobbying and consultation between the Committee on Subsidiary Legislation and women's advocacy groups such as the National Council on Women and Development and the Federation of International Women Lawyers. Through this act the penalties for rape and defilement of a female below fourteen years of age were increased. Stakeholder participation through dialogue and consultation is an important aspect of good governance. Because most bills passed by Parliament had substantial input from stakeholders they did not encounter resistance from the target groups.

Political Parties

The role of political parties in shaping public policies and programs cannot be overemphasized. Through political education, political parties can help generate reliable information, which can raise the standard of knowledge and of the intelligence of the electorate. Even though Parliamentary opposition was outnumbered by the NDC, the minority leader, "shadow" minister, and parliamentary spokesmen for various government ministries and departments raised the tone of public discussion and improved the quality of public policy. For instance, the government's human rights record and legal reforms were constantly scrutinized by the opposition spokesman on justice while its economic policies were put under the microscope by the spokesman on finance.

A number of other measures were taken by the opposition to influence public policy. First it held press conferences on policies, programs, and issues, which it felt the government had not adequately explained to the public, and presented an alternate view. In 1996, for instance, the minority group held a press conference to outline its alternate budget after the national budget was presented. Most of the time, documents relevant to the policies and programs that were not available to the press were copiously quoted to buttress points made. With questions from the media and responses from the opposition spokesmen, a search-light was directed at the policies. After the opposition press conferences, the Rawlings government would respond, accepting or denying the issues raised. Even if the press conferences did not have a direct impact on public policy, they at least compelled the government to discuss some policies in the public domain.

Second, the opposition boycotted parliamentary proceedings for some days to highlight their objections and to attract the maximum public attention. For instance, in the discussion of the VAT Bill 1995, the opposition staged a walkout because it thought that the tax would bring hardship to most Ghanaians. The boycott, however, did not have much effect because the government still had the majority to carry on with business.

Third, on some occasions the opposition went to court to seek interpretation to government acts of omission or commission. For instance, the minority leader in January 1997, asked the Supreme Court to give a true and proper interpretation of certain provisions on the constitutional status of retained ministers of state and deputy ministers in the second Parliament of the Fourth Republic. The view of the minority group was that as of January 7, 1997, when the second Rawlings administration was inaugurated, there were no ministers of state or deputy ministers in Ghana. The 1993–1997, appointees had, like their appointing authority himself, exhausted their mandate. The view of the majority, however, was that ministers and deputy ministers appointed upon the approval of Parliament in 1993–1997, continued to exercise their functions at the president's pleasure. The ruling on 28 May 1997, was ambivalent. By a unanimous decision the court ruled that "every presidential nominee for ministerial appointment, whether retained or new, requires prior approval of Parliament." Accordingly, on the inauguration of a fresh term, all Ministers and deputy ministers nominated for office need the prior approval of that new Parliament, whether or not the nominee was a minister or deputy minister in the previous term. The court, however, decided by a majority of four to one that the term "prior approval" is not a term of art. In other words, "prior approval" does not connote "consideration and vetting" and the no court can question how Parliament goes about exercising its powers of approval (Ayensu and Darkwa, 1999).

The role of the minority group in Parliament in influencing public policy has often been underestimated as not being effective because of the large number of government MPs. Yet, it is equally true that the input of the minority group—especially in financial, constitutional, and legal issues—refined most of the bills laid before Parliament. Holding an alternative view is part of good governance and the minority's alternate views on policies and programs of the Rawlings regime could be described as one of the building blocks in the process towards achieving good governance.

The Policy Management Group

Under the Rawlings government the political elite was guided in policy formulation by the party's manifesto. As in previous civilian governments, policy issues were submitted to committees and the plenum of Parliament for discussion and debate prior to their crystallization into concrete policies. The importance of policy formulation by the political elite was so crucial to the Rawlings government that a policy management group (PMG) was created in 1996. The formation of the PMG is also the result of the failure of the civil service and the National Development Planning Commission (NDPC) to offer appropriate policy analysis. The PMG was made up of mostly presidential advisers at the office of the president and came from diverse disciplines such as political science, public administration, sociology, law, economics, and English. The PMG was chaired by the presidential advisor on governmental affairs, a noncabinet and nonconstitutional position that performed the duties of a prime minister. Some PMG members attended Cabinet meetings. The number of PMG membership is not known but it was started as a small group of five people and later increased in number, making it too unwieldy to perform the functions entrusted to it (Ayee, 2000b). This is not surprising because in such a neopatrimonial system of government, informal institutions (such as the PMG) even though they shape political behavior and expectations and influence public policies, are not publicly acknowledged for fear of criticism that the formal constitutionally-mandated institutions are being privately circumvented.

The PMG served as a think-tank, giving second thoughts to policy proposals before they were considered by the cabinet and reviewing policies to assess their effectiveness. It was supposed to serve as the focal point the crystallizing and reconciling thought on intended government policies. It was also charged with the development of a central framework within which the government's policies and programs as a whole could be more effectively formulated. The basic role, then, of the PMG was that of a catalyst in policy-making and analysis but not the final determiner. It is difficult to assess the PMG performance in policy analysis since it worked behind the scenes with no information concerning its output (Ayee, 2000b).

Nongovernmental Organization Think-Tanks

The work of a few policy analysts outside the governmental sector such s the Centre for Democracy and Development (CDD), Institute of Economic Affairs (IEA), Centre for Policy Analysis (CEPA), and universities and research institutions has been enduring and fruitful. These nongovernmental organization think-tanks conducted research projects on policy-related issues and organized roundtable conferences and seminars to disseminate their findings regularly in publications such as *Legislative Alert, Govenance, and Critical Perspectives*. Some of these findings contradicted those of the government: for instance, a 1998 publication of CEPA and the University of Ghana's Institute of Statistical, Economic, and Social Research (ISSER) *State of the Ghanaian Economy Report* contradicted government statistics on economic issues such as money supply and the rate of inflation.

The contribution of nongovernmental policy analysis units was impaired by two factors. First is the NDC government's inability to take seriously recommendations made by the nongovernmental policy analysts, who were branded either as opposition elements or as enemies whose recommendations must be taken with a pinch of salt. This lack of respect for advice offered by local professionals is typical of all Ghanaian and many other African regimes. Second, nongovernmental policy analysts were constrained by sensitive matters and the secrecy of some types of official information. In spite of the constitutional stipulation of the right to information, government institutions still withheld information relevant to policy development and analysis as distinct from information relating to the government's own internal deliberations on policies and programs.

Policy Processes and Outcomes: Case Studies

The relationship between policy processes and outcomes is conditioned by the level of consultations and stakeholder participation. Where stakeholders had prior discussion of policy proposals the policy tends to be implemented without considerable opposition. However, with inadequate consultation of stakeholders the policy faces resistance and opposition, leading to its eventual withdrawal. The following two cases illustrate these points.

The Value-Added Tax

In March 1995, with little public debate, the government introduced the value-added tax (VAT) with a standard rate of 17.5% and a zero rate, after the passage of the VAT bill in December 1994. The government dismissed opposition misgivings on the VAT because it regarded the opposition as a section of embittered pressure groups (Osei, 2000). Similarly, the misgivings of other civil society organizations (CSOs) such as the Trades Union Congress, Association of Ghana Industries, Chamber of Commerce, and Employers Association fell on deaf ears. In fact, these CSOs publicly declared that they were not consulted by the government. The VAT was also condemned by then Vice President Kow Arkaah, who asked the country to revolt against it during his speech to the country's workers on May Day, 1995. Later revelations by the Vice President were that the 17.5% VAT policy, as implemented in March 1995, was not the policy he presided over at a cabinet meeting, indicating an inner core of policy-makers that excluded the Vice President (Osei, 2000). Eventually when the VAT was introduced in March 1995, there was massive public outcry and indignation against it because traders took advantage of it and increased prices of their wares including food items which were supposed to be excluded. In May 1995, a CSO called Alliance for Change organized a massive demonstration, which led to the loss of four lives. The government was finally forced to withdraw VAT.

National Economic Forum

In September 1997, a National Economic Forum was held in Accra to deliberate on issues such as the reintroduction of the VAT, creation of jobs, regaining and maintaining macroeconomic stability for accelerated growth to energize the private sector, and confronting the challenges involved in the pursuit of the country's development path. In other words, the main purpose was to bring together people from the private sector, public sector (Government) and the general Ghanaian community to participate in a dialogue on the current state and future prospects of the economy, in order to achieve a national consensus on pragmatic policy measures for accelerated growth within the framework of *Ghana Vision 2020* (Ghana, 1997). Participation of key stakeholders was fundamental to the organization and deliberations. Accordingly, the planning committee responsible for organizing the National Economic Forum included representatives from the Private Enterprise Foundation, Trades Union Congress, majority and minority groups in Parliament, and the Ghana Export Promotion Council. Deliberations were enriched by the views of representatives of the various political, religious, ethnic, and development groupings including researchers, public officials, formal-sector private business operators, state-owned enterprises, organized labor, Parliament, representatives of farmers, traders, political parties and a myriad of professional and academic associations (Ghana, 1997).

The forum accepted in principle the reintroduction of the VAT based on the realization that a severe revenue crunch lay ahead, propelled by escalating development costs. While the spirit of discussion regarding the VAT was acceptable, there was need also to develop the letter of that discussion. In developing that discussion, issues of grave concern to participants needed to be addressed as a way of facilitating the reintroduction and implementation of VAT. Taking into consideration these concerns, the forum made the following proposals:

- VAT must have "no winners" and "losers".
- VAT must not be politicized.
- VAT must be considered as part of an entire package of reforms that aim to achieve macroeconomic stability.
- VAT must introduce opportunities for amnesty in its implementation, with regard to earlier tax laws infringements.
- All persons engaged in the design and implementation of VAT must exhibit good faith and commitment.
- Public education program on VAT must be broad or all-inclusive, in-depth, and comprehensive.
- Discussion must be enhanced through wider and deeper participation in the process, for example having the subgroup enlarged for continuous debate that will inform the VAT Oversight Committee (Ghana, 1997).

As a result of the forum, the government reintroduced the VAT in December 1998, without any opposition. The ceiling was reviewed upward to 15% in 2000, after another forum was held to discuss the funding of tertiary education. It was agreed at the forum that the 5% increase be used to establish an education trust fund for tertiary education.

The attempt to build a consensus on policies by consulting stakeholders through seminars, conferences, workshops, and brainstorming sessions has certainly improved the implementation of public policies and programs in Ghana. This contrasts with Grindle's assertion that a large portion of individual and collective demand making, the representation of interests, and the emergence and resolution of conflict occurs at the output stage (1980:15).

Conclusion: Lessons Learned

The analysis has shown the involvement of multifarious institutions in public policy making in Ghana. A number of issues in public policy-making have been reinforced:

- A certain level of public participation improves the chances of success of public policies and programs. Consultation of stakeholders not only refines the policy proposals but also forestalls resistance from interest groups. This also improves the level of public transparency and accountability.
- Exclusive politics deprives the nation of expert contribution from outside the ruling party in public policy-making.
- "Policy space" is not only the preserve of political elites such as politicians and bureaucrats but also of civil society organizations. The boundaries of the Ghanaian policy space have been constricted because policy elites had to contend with societal groups and stakeholders that can promote and defend their interests. Consequently, the policy elites did not have enough room to maneuver the capacity to influence the content, timing, and sequence of policy initiatives (Grindle and Thomas, 1991).
- Even though policies seem to be rational, some of them are politically clouded because the alternatives are often dominated by crisis situations, values of the political leadership, and considerations of power enhancement criteria.

Finally, public policy-making by the institutions was not perfect in spite of the generally consultative process that most policies were subjected to. Hence, the Rawlings government launched in 1996 the national policy process and cabinet process reforms, which were managed by the National Institutional Renewal Program (NIRP). The reforms were meant to develop capacity to enhance cabinet business and to design a framework for policy formulation and coordination and its link to resource allocation. The outcome of these initiatives was the defeat of the Rawlings government in the general elections of December 2000.

References

Abernathy, D. 1971. "Bureaucracy and Economic Development." *Africa Review* 1: 1–14.

Adu, A. L. 1973. *The Public Service and the Administration of Public Affairs in Ghana.* Accra: Ghana Academy of Arts and Sciences.

Amonoo, B. 1981. *Ghana, 1957–1966: The Politics of Institutional Dualism.* New York: Allen and Unwin.

Appiah, F. 1999. *In the Throes of a Turbulent Environment: The Ghanaian Civil Service in a Changing State.* School of Administration Monograph Series. Accra: University of Ghana.

Ayee, J. R. A. 1993a. "Enhancing the Public Policy-Making Process: The Executive President under Ghana's 1992 Fourth Republican Constitution." *Journal of Management Studies* 10 (December–January): 1–9.

————. 1993b. "Complexity of Joint Action: The Implementation of Restructuring of Ministerial Organizations under the PNDC." *African Journal of Public Administration and Management* 2(2): 25–43.

————. 1994. "Civil Service Reform in Ghana: An Analysis of the 1993 Civil Service Law." *Journal of Management Studies* 11: 13–26.

————. 1998. *The 1996 General Elections and Democratic Consolidation in Ghana.* Accra: University of Ghana.

————. 1999a. "Ghana." Ch. 15 in *Public Administration in Africa: Main Issues and Selected Country Studies*, ed. Ladipo Adamolekun. Boulder, Colo.: Westview.

————. 1999b. "The Survival of Constitutional Rule." Paper presented at the Programme of Public Lectures and Symposia, "Critical Issues and Challenges of the 21st Century." Accra, 15–19 November.

————. 2000a. "Good Governance for Sustainable Growth and Development in Ghana." Ch. 8 in *The State of the Ghanaian Economy in 1999.* Accra: ISSER.

————. 2000b. "Saints, Wizards, Demons and Systems: Explaining the Success or Failure of Public Policies and Programmes." Inaugural Lecture. Accra: University of Ghana.

Ayensu, K. B., and S. N. Darkwa. 1999. *The Evolution of Parliament in Ghana.* Accra: Institute of Economic Affairs.

Da Rocha, B. J. et al. 1999. *The Right to Information and Freedom of the Media in Ghana's Fourth Republic.* Accra: Institute of Economic Affairs.

Dodoo, R. 1997. "Performance Standards and Measuring Performance in Ghana." *Public Administration and Development* 17: 115–21.

————. 1998. "Country Paper Ghana." Paper delivered at the Second Biennial Pan African Conference of Ministers of Civil Service: "Public Service in Africa: New Challenges, Professionalism and Ethics." Rabat, Moroco, 13–15 December.

Dror, Y. 1968. Public Policy Making Re-examined. New York: Chandler.

Ghana, Republic of. 1977. *Main Report of the Commission on the Structure and Procedures of the Ghana Civil Service: 1974–76.* Accra: Ghana Publishing Corporation.

————. 1978. *The Proposals of the Constitutional Commission for a Constitution for the Establishment of a Transitional (Interim) National Government for Ghana* (Government Printer: Accra).

————. 1982. *Report of the Committee on the Restructuring of the Civil Service Machinery.* Accra: Government Printer.

————. 1992. Constitution of the Republic of Ghana, 1992. Tema: Ghana Publishing Corporation.

————. 1995. *Ghana Vision 2020: The First Step: 1996–2000.* Accra: Government Printer.

————. 1997. *National Economic Forum Report.* Accra: Worldwide Press.

————. 1999a. *First Draft Comprehensive Development Framework Towards Ghana Vision 2020.* Paper presented at the 10th Consultative Group Meeting. November 23–24, Accra.

————. 1999b. *Sessional Address by H.E. Flt. Lt. J.J. Rawlings (President of the Republic of Ghana) on the Occasion of the State Opening of the Third Session of the Second Parliament of the Fourth Republic, 14th January 1999.* Accra: Government Printer, Assembly Press.

Grindle, M. S. 1980. "Policy Content and Context in Implementation." In *Politics and Policy Implementation in the Third World*, ed. Merilee S. Grindle. Princeton: Princeton University Press.

———. 1991. *Public Choices and Policy Change: The Political Economy of Reform in Developing Countries*. Baltimore: Johns Hopkins Press.

Gyimah-Boadi, E. 1997. "Ghana's Encouraging Elections: The Challenges Ahead." *Journal of Democracy* 8(2): 78–91.

ISODEC. 1995. "Focus on NGO Bill." *Public Agenda* (Accra), June 30–July 6, 1995.

Osei, P. D. 2000. "Political Liberalisation and the Implementation of Value-Added Tax in Ghana." *Journal Modern African Studies* 32(2): 255–78.

Owusu-Ansah, K. A. 1978. "Public Policy-Making and the Ghana Civil Service." *Greenhill Journal of Administration* 4(3–4): 1–40.

Pinkney, R. 1972. *Ghana under Military Rule*. London: Methuen.

Prempeh, H. K. 1999. *The Ghanaian Judiciary and the 1992 Constitution: A Problem of Asymmetrical Jurisprudence*. Accra: Centre for Democracy and Development.

Rawlings, J. J. 1994. *State of the Nation Address*. January 1994. Tema: Ghana Publishing Corporation.

Riggs, F. 1963. "Bureaucrats and Political Development." In *Bureaucracy and Political Development*, ed. J. La Palombara. Princeton: Princeton University Press.

Rothchild, D. and R. L. Curry. 1978. *Scarcity, Choice and Public Policy in the Middle East*. Berkeley: University of California Press.

Sandbrook, R. and J. Oelbaum. 1997. "Reforming Dysfunctional Institutions Through Democratisation? Reflections on Ghana." *Journal of Modern African Studies* 35(4): 603–646.

UNDP. *Ghana Human Development Report, 1997*. Accra: UNDP.

World Bank. 1996. *Towards a Public Sector Management Strategy for West Central Africa*. Washington, D.C.: World Bank.

12

Economic Policy Research, Governance, and Economic Development: The Case of Namibia

Dirk Hansohm

Sub-Saharan Africa (SSA) continues to lag behind the growth of other regions (Collier and Gunning, 1999). The average SSA country is poorer than the average low-income country and getting poorer. SSA's declining importance in the world economy has given rise to diagnoses of the "marginalization of Africa" (Collier, 1995), and there is an almost universal pessimism about its economic prospects.

Four categories of explanations for Africa's economic performance can be distinguished, differing in two dimensions: those focusing on domestic versus external factors, and those emphasizing exogenous "destiny" factors versus policy factors (Collier and Gunning, 1999).

The role of external factors, i.e., the degree and kind of SSA's integration into the world economy, has always played a prominent role in the discussion on its development. Marxist and neo-Marxist authors have ascribed SSA's development malaise to its alleged high and exploitative integration into the world economy (see Rodney, 1972). More recently, others argue that the economies of SSA are characterised by a low rather a high degree of international trade integration(Ng and Yeats, 1997). Accordingly, many analysts identify the lack of openness of trade regimes as the most crucial and immediate reason for SSA's disappointing growth performance (Sachs and Warner, 1995; Ng and Yeats, 1997). However, more recent analyses broaden the perspective and include issues of good

Helpful comments by Tekaligne Godana on a draft of this chapter are gratefully acknowledged.

governance in the list of prescriptions for development (see Ng and Yeats, 1999; Wohlmuth, 1998).

This chapter argues that the quality of governance, in particular the role of economic research, are key missing links within the development process and supports this view with evidence from Namibia. The first section shows that despite the creation of a favorable framework, economic growth remains insufficient to overcome poverty and inequality in Namibia. The next section discusses the link between governance, economic research and development as a foundation for the discussion of the Namibian case. The third section looks at the specific case of the Namibian Economic Policy Research Unit (NEPRU), the final section draws some policy conclusions.

Namibia's Development Experience

After independence, the Namibian government put in place favorable conditions for healthy economic development: a peaceful transition from a highly inequitable apartheid system to a democratic society, reversion of discriminatory legislation, and independent judiciary and the rule of law, a free press, a market-oriented economic policy, and high investments in education and health.

How has economic development fared since independence? The Namibian government has defined as its four key development objectives growth, employment, poverty reduction, and equality. However, the first and foremost indicator for economic welfare remains economic growth—it is the precondition for sustainable achievement of all the other objectives. Namibia's growth record has been favorable in comparison both with neighboring countries and with the preindependence decade (see Figure 12.1).

However, in the context of high population growth, economic growth on a per capita basis has been clearly insufficient (see Figure 12.2). Average growth has not been higher than population growth, meaning that average per capita incomes have stagnated.

Official figures may underestimate real per capita growth basis to some extent, as they are based on population projections, which do not take into account the impact of the HIV/AIDS epidemic. The UNDP estimates that do so would show a slightly higher per capita growth.

Another fact qualifying the high average income figure is the huge discrepancies within Namibia. The Gini-coefficient measures the degree of income inequality from zero (totally equal income distribution) to one hundred (totally unequal income distribution). It was calculated at seventy for Namibia (UNDP, 1998:9), meaning that around 2% of the population controls

Figure 12.1 Growth (%) of Namibia's Economy (GDP) Compared to sub-Saharan Africa (1980–90 and 1990–97)

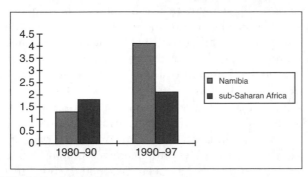

Source: World Bank (1999b).

Figure 12.2 Namibia's Growth in Historical Perspective (1990–97)

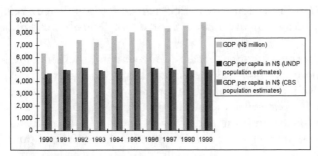

Source: Central Statistics Office (1996), UNDP (1998) for 1998, and 1999, NEPRU (1999a).

approximately 65% of the economy. The origins of this inequality are the discriminatory apartheid system as well as the mineral economy with its economic distortions (Auty, 1995).

Due to this highly skewed income distribution in Namibia, poverty is prevalent despite the high per-capita income. More than 55% of the population is reported to live in poverty (less than US$2 a day). The high unemployment rate of 34.5% (using the broad definition that includes people who are available for work but are not actively looking for employment) contributes to the incidence of poverty. Although data are insufficient to track the development of equality and poverty in Namibia over time (Schade et al., 1995), it is clear that both remain major challenges. There is also not sufficient information on the development of employment.

However, data suggest that unemployment remains a severe problem (Hansohm, Venditto, Ashipala, 2000).

The disappointing growth performance can be explained to some extent in terms of special circumstances, such as adverse climatic conditions (affecting fisheries and agriculture), and falling commodity prices (reducing mining output). However, there is a more worrysome underlying trend. As the development of total factor productivity (TFP) shows, for every unit of capital invested in the economy, less and less output is earned (see Figure 12.3). This reflects the mature mining sector, the high share of the public sector, and inefficiencies in the economy. As a result, returns on investment fall, and savings flow out of the country.

All in all, the record of economic development and of attaining Namibia's development goals has been insufficient, both in light of the expectations of the population and of economic theory. The following sections suggest an answer to this puzzle.

The Link Between Economic Policy Research, Governance and Economic Development

When the former colonies became independent, their income levels were generally poor, but political leaders and development experts expected that increased welfare would follow independence. The experience of the following decades, however, did not bear out this hope. While a few countries achieved industrialization and growth (newly industrialising countries, emerging economies), most developing countries remained poor or became even poorer.

Figure 12.3 Development of Total Factor Productivity in the Namibian Economy (1991–97)

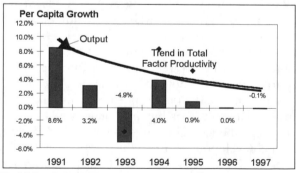

Source: World Bank (1999a).

Economic theory has not been able to explain this convincingly. According to the assumptions of traditional growth theory, poor countries achieve higher growth than rich countries and thus catch up. This "old growth" theory, based on very restrictive assumptions, is contradicted by the absence of general convergence. The "new growth" theory, relaxing some of these assumptions, incorporates obstacles to convergence. However, the new growth theory does not predict that the most rapid growth will occur in a subset of low-income countries.

The Importance of Governance

In addressing the question why some countries are rich why others remain poor, Olson (1996, 2000) has advanced a powerful argument that does not include geographical location, availability of raw materials, climate, knowledge, or culture.

Raw materials are increasingly unimportant, as most economic activity can now readily be separated from deposits of raw materials and arable land. Knowledge is now for the most part available to poor countries, at a relatively modest cost. Culture can explain only a small part of the huge differences in per capita income between rich and poor countries.

Eliminating all other possible causes, Olson identifies the quality of governance, in particular economic policies and institutions, as the only plausible explanation for the vast and increasing differences in wealth among countries. He argues that this explanation also fits the relationships between levels of per capita income and rates of growth better than either the old or the new growth theory. Poor countries cannot be anywhere near the frontiers of their aggregate production functions—otherwise their marginal product of capital would be many times higher. The encouraging message is that any poorer country that adopts relatively good economic policies and institutions can catch-up to a considerable degree to the richer countries.

The African growth experience also fits Olson's approach well. Earlier approaches to development followed classic development theory and implemented a strategy of state-led import substitution. This was followed by the other extreme of market-led, export-led development in the course of structural adjustment programs (SAPs). The critique again explained low growth focused by structural factors as negative terms of trade, low capital transfers, and limited access to markets of industrial countries. Neither of these views can provide a consistent explanation of Africa's economic trends. Even where adjustment policies have been rigorously implemented, they have failed to establish sustained growth and development, and one can certainly argue that nowhere else have SAPs been applied as intensively and as frequently as within SSA. At the same time, many countries are now locked into a permanent adjustment process. Growth has surged in some countries, but has hardly been sustained. In many, economic collapse soon became a self-reinforcing process. It is clear that many policy errors have been made during both the import-substituting industrialization and the adjustment periods. In each period, pragmatism has been trumped by ideology.

Attention must be turned from the policy orientation towards its quality. Countries in SSA currently lack the basic institutional capacities to undertake complex economic policies. A major lesson from East Asian experience is that these capacities are built up through a learning process. Reforms are needed to create a competent and independent state bureaucracy and to build close ties between this bureaucracy and an emerging business sector (Akyüz and Gore, 2001).

Botswana—comparable to Namibia in many respects—is a case in point for Olson's arguments (Acemoglu, Johnson, & Robinson, 2001; Hansohm, 2001a). There is wide agreement that Botswana exceptional growth rate (7.7% annually between 1965, and 1998) is due to good policy and good institutions. Global integration and ensuing development were not achieved by a policy of aggressive openness, but by an emphasis on the quality of economic policies and institutions. A policy of managed openness and of effective use of imported resources (including aid and skills) was a part of this approach. Integration was thus not the result of a policy of openness, but rather a product of sensible policy.

Thus, this chapter argues that the focus of Africa's development perspectives should move from the question of policy choice to the broader set of the quality of economic policies and institutions, which can be discussed under the heading of governance.

Governance is a broad concept with many definitions (see Wohlmuth 1998). It includes, but goes well beyond, government and its role. It also refers to other actors such as the private sector, nongovernment organizations (NGOs), and community-based organizations (CBOs), as well as the interactions between these actors. Thus it refers to the quality of organizations and institutions in the wider sense (Rodrik, 1998). It is also related to issues such as transaction costs, in particular information (Stiglitz, 1988).

Governance in poor countries is often characterized by:

- Unaccountable governments
- Weak civil societies
- Low levels of freedom and civil liberties
- Weak enforcement of property rights
- Limited role for the rule of law

- Low levels of cooperation between the public and private sectors
- Sets of economic policies not based on systematic application of economic analysis

The Role of Economic Policy Research and Advice

An important, but as yet little researched area is the impact of economic research. Virtually all industrialized countries and NICs have systems of economic information and analysis in place that feed inputs into the economic policy-making process. Most developing countries are characterized by the absence of these systems.

Economic policy research and advice is important first because it provides data about the economy and its expected development. Second, on this basis, it helps interpret these data according to economic principles. This is the basis of an informed process of decision-making, of a discussion of the pros and cons, costs, benefits, and risks of particular courses of action. Third, a public informed about the economy and policy options allows public discussion and thus can strengthen governance.

Industrial countries possess a sophisticated structure of economic policy research, based on a solid foundation of basic academic economic research, with clearly defined channels of transmission of economic advice to policy-makers. A vast literature has developed describing and analyzing this area (see Haveman, 1989; Peacock, 1991; Aaron, 1992; Eizenstat, 1992; Hamilton, 1992; Klein, 1999; Mohr, 1999). Important lessons highlighted by this literature include:

- Policy-makers and economic policy researchers operate in two different worlds, a fact that is often not acknowledged. This is bound to lead to systematic problems of understanding.
- Thus, economists need to formulate their lessons using clear and nontechnical language.
- In their analysis, economists need to take account of the actual process of policy-making and of the constraints under which policy-makers operate.
- Value judgments must not be presented as scientific truths, but must be made explicit.
- The degree of certainty of advice, and the areas of important disagreement (the pros and cons of particular actions) need to be made clear.
- Different options and their risks need to be explained.
- Good economic advice may test the limits of what is politically feasible but should not fly in the face of political reality.

- Economists should avoid the danger of concentrating their advice on areas of comprehensive analysis and where disagreements are most likely. Often, the application of the more basic economic principles is more important.

Many of these lessons have still to be learned, particularly in developing countries, most of which have a limited capacity for economic management and policy research. However, achieving national social and economic goals requires a well-developed economic management capacity within the public sector and beyond to effectively employ human, financial, and material resources. A comprehensive strategy for training government economists to use the tools of economic analysis provides the opportunity to fully develop this capacity. This needs a national economic capacity building strategy (van Niekerk, 1995).

Research systems of poor countries are generally characterized by:

- weak institutions for economic research;
- little systematic research on the economy being done;
- little reception of recent international insights of economists.
- economic policy interventions being minimally based on the prescriptions of these theories. (Goldsmith, 2001; Wohlmuth, 1998)

However, in SSA due to internal and external factors the policy environment has changed in the course of economic reform leading to higher demand for economic research. Internally, most African political systems are in a process of liberalization, with the end of public monopoly of policy analysis and an increased domestic public scrutiny of policy action (Ndulu, 1997). On the external front, donors are also increasingly interested in using and promoting local economic research capacity. More importantly, in the context of globalization of economic activities, there is an increasing need for economic policy analysis, as matters become more sophisticated and change more rapidly. This is not only important as an information input for policy-makers, but also as input for an informed public discussion on economic policy matters.

From these points arise two arguments about the need for research institutes that are independent from the direct control of government bureaucracy:

- Independent agencies can be expected to operate more flexibly, efficiently and effectively.
- They have higher credibility, both to government (rather than departments evaluating themselves), and to the public.

Economic Policy Research, Governance and Economic Development in Namibia

Namibia, as discussed above, has a democratic government, is governed by the rule of law, has a participative system of policy-making, it follows a market-based economic policy, and invests heavily in human resource development. However, the quality of many institutions is still weak. Economic policies are not yet based on the systematic application of economic analyses. Cooperation between the public and private sectors is still limited. Relations between private business, labor, and government are often controversial—there is a low level of social capital (Fukuyama, 2001). The civil society is not strongly developed, and its participants have little access to economic information and analysis. While there is a well-developed press, reporting on and analysis of economic matters is poorly developed and economic issues are generally perceived through a political lens.

This section briefly discusses the role and capacity of institutions, both in the public and private sector, to formulate, execute, and monitor economic policy and discusses some examples of policy-making. Overall, the economic policy is characterized by a refreshing degree of autonomy. Namibia is not subject to externally imposed economic reform programs (structural adjustment) and looks critically at policy proposals by international organizations. In this sense, its policies are home-grown. At the same time, its cadre of indigenous economists is extremely limited. This results in a mixture of two drawbacks:

1. Policy is not based on a consistent set of economic information, analysis, and policy choices.
2. There is a high degree of dependence on expatriate advisors, mostly on a short-term basis. This tends to lead to at least three problems:
   a. No long-term relationship exists, so there is little opportunity to build a relationship of trust, which is essential for knowledge transfer.
   b. Consultancy services tend to take the form of turnkey reports, limiting the ability of government officials to make effective use of them.
   c. Little if any local capacity for policy analysis is built up in the public sector.

After ten years of independence, Namibia still faces a serious shortage of trained economists (as analyzed in 1995, see van Niekerk, 1995). This threatens the successful implementation of Namibia's development plan. Many ministries have failed to fill important economic management and planning positions with qualified economists. Often positions had to be filled by expatriate technical advisors. There has been little transfer of skills from expatriate advisors to Namibian counterparts. Skill transfer has not been satisfactory for a number of reasons. One key reason: very few Namibian economists have been employed in economic policy management positions. Expatriate advisors have been required to carry out line functions rather than to train their counterparts to perform these duties. Furthermore, the training gap between expatriate advisors and Namibian counterparts has often been too wide to allow the counterpart to effectively absorb the skills and lessons of experience from the advisor. The time the advisors must spend providing basic technical training in computer skills, quantitative methods, and economic principles significantly reduces the opportunity to train counterparts in more sophisticated techniques of economic management and planning.

Namibia's educational system has not yet been able to provide sufficiently the economic training required for competent government economists. Furthermore, public sector salaries are not competitive with the private sector. The prime institution for tertiary education, UNAM, faces difficulties attracting qualified and senior staff through adequate and appropriate remuneration packages. Donor-provided fellowships to government economists for training abroad have significantly increased the country's economic management capacity, but not in a comprehensive fashion (van Niekerk, 1995).

The following provides some instances of the impact of economic research on policy-making and discusses institutions involved in economic research.

National Development Planning

Government has invested significant resources in its development planning process. The First Development Plan (NDP1) covered 1994–1999, while NDP2 covers 2001–2005. Each plan comprehensively covered the economic and social sectors and presented a wealth of economic data. In particular NDP2 was designed to be participative through a number of workshops. Both NDP1, and NDP2 are not subject to external pressure and are really home grown. Efforts have been made, especially in NDP2, to involve nonstate domestic institutions in the design process, with limited research inputs. NDP1 has been subject to a mid-term review. These plans compare favorably with those of many other countries.

Nevertheless, the plans' actual impact has been limited. Problems faced include:

1. a deficient information base;
2. limited reference in the process of actual policy-making to the plans;
3. limited consistency of plan elements that are written by different agencies;
4. lack of prioritization among objectives;
5. high dependence on expatriate assistance in the design process;
6. high resource demands competing with other tasks of the planning administration.

Policy on Poverty

The reduction of poverty was one of the four major goals of the First National Development Plan (NDP1), but the mid-term review of NDP1 revealed that the sector-based strategies were not sufficient to reach this objective (Republic of Namibia, 1998b). Therefore, the government opted for an integrated, research-based approach to address poverty: the Poverty Reduction Strategy (Republic of Namibia, 1998a). Two local institutions—NEPRU and the Social Science Division (SSD) of UNAM—were part of an international research team.

However, severe capacity constraints limit the effectiveness of planned policies. The mid-term review of NDP1 concluded that poverty was poorly conceptualized by many ministries. None of the sectors or ministries had devoted sections specifically to poverty reduction. Until now Namibia's poverty situation has not been monitored, and no comprehensive and consistent data are available. These data are necessary to monitor the extent and characteristics of poverty over time. Without these data we do not know if the extent and severity of poverty have improved or worsened during the last ten years. Consequently, the success of measures to reduce poverty is not known (Schade et al., 1998). This is a severe shortcoming, as poverty is widespread and its reduction is a key policy objective. This deficit has been recognized and monitoring poverty is envisaged in the Poverty Action Plan (Republic of Namibia, 2000).

Industrial Policy

The limitations of policy implementation by capacity limitations affect Namibia's industrial policy, as articulated in the 1992 White Paper (MTI, 1999). A review of this policy identifies human and resource capacity of the line ministry as well as virtually all other involved bodies as key stumbling blocks. Monitoring of progress in industrialization and industrial policy implementation is difficult because of the lack of data.

Employment Policy

This is a key area of Namibian policy-making, as the creation of employment is the most important instrument to reduce poverty and inequality. The first constraint to the formulation of employment policy is the quality of data. In fact, it can be argued that the data on employment are the most deficient of all statistical data. The data on employment are limited (in particular on the informal sector), while data on incomes are incomplete and unreliable (Hansohm, Venditto, & Ashipala, 2000; NEPRU, 2001). The information on key indicators such as employment, wages, and productivity is also insufficient. Data are not collected regularly, are available only long after the survey dates, and the categories are not consistent with those of the national accounts—making calculations of important economic productivity indicators impossible. Macro-level data are generally outdated, and very limited information exists on the micro level (NEPRU, 2001).

Factors contributing to this state of affairs include the lack of professional staff to generate, process, and disseminate data in a regular and timely manner (NEPRU, 2001). Another factor is the lack of a clear mandate for any one institution to collect and process data on employment.

Nonstate Actors

A number of bodies represent different parts of the private sector: the Namibian Chamber of Commerce and Industry (NCCI), the Namibian Employers Federation (NEF), and the Indigenous People Business Council (IPBC). No one group can claim to be the voice of the private sector in its entirety, nor does any group have the capacity to analyze economic policy. There have been occasional consultations between these private sector organizations and senior government members.

The formal labor force is represented by the trade unions under their umbrella organization National Union of Namibian Workers (NUNW). They are in a better position with their own small research institute, the Labor Resource and Research Institute (LaRRI).

NGOs also have an umbrella organization: the Namibian Nongovernmental Organization's Forum (NANGOF). Its mandate is to involve itself in policy formulation that affects the interests of the poor and marginalized (Hansohm, Venditto, & Ashipala, 2000). Its policy advisory unit that monitors the development of bills within ministries as well as in parliament, informs the communities affected, and gathers the grassroot opinions. In some cases, consultants are employed to enable NANGOF to submit recommendations accordingly.

Economic Policy Advice and Research Institutions

On the economic advice side, there are two legally constituted bodies: the Bank of Namibia (BoN) with a large research department and the National Planning Commission (NPC) with its secretariat (NPCS). The BoN produces regular reports on economic developments, particularly in the monetary area. It has also a mandate to advise the government on request; however, has not been used much. The NPC has a mandate to advise the government on economic policies, particularly in development policy and planning. The economics department of UNAM and a number of small research institutes and individuals also carry out economic research.

In 1997, the government established the President's Economic Advisory Council (PEAC). Its overarching aim is to promote exchange of information and strengthen cooperation, collaboration, and coordination between Namibia's public and private sectors to arrive at a mutual understanding of the economy and longer-term economic development. This strengthens governance through better information exchange and building of trust. However, its contributions remain as yet limited and are not based on a systematic analysis (NEPRU, 2001).

The Case of the Namibian Economic Policy Research Unit

The Namibian Economic Policy Research Unit (NEPRU), set up in 1990, is the leading independent institute for economic research in Namibia. NEPRU is an autonomous institution, governed by a board of trustees. Its main objectives are:

1. To assist the government of independent Namibia through applied research for policy formulation and decision-making in strategic economic and socioeconomic areas;
2. To build an information resource base on socioeconomic issues with regard to Namibian affairs; and
3. To train Namibians in relevant research skills.

The last two objectives arise from the first. All are destined to support the economic policy process in a direct or indirect, but not less important, way. A strong board of trustees, including high profile members of government and civil society, governs NEPRU. This secures a degree of government influence but also connects NEPRU to private sector decision-makers.

The following discusses the three objectives and how they contribute to the policy process and governance in a wider sense.

The Research Record

The most important means to influence and improve governance is through research. NEPRU's primary client is the government, including the National Planning Commission and various line ministries. Other clients include multilateral and bilateral development organizations, and to a small degree the private sector and NGOs. Although NEPRU's work concentrates on Namibia, the institute is increasingly involved in research in the Southern African region. NEPRU cooperates with other research institutions in the region and beyond. It is part of various regional research networks, including the Southern and Eastern Africa Policy Research Network (SEAPREN) with six institutes from Botswana, Namibia, South Africa, Tanzania, Uganda, and Zambia.

The changing structure of the kind of projects NEPRU executes reflects its growing relevance (NEPRU, 2000b). Its first projects consisted mostly of speech writing, workshop reports, descriptive reports, and opinion pieces. More analytical work, if any, was done by academics attached to the unit on a short-term basis. As it grew, however, it took on projects of an increasing relevance:

1. Joint projects with government agencies, so that skills are transferred in the work process
2. Joint projects as local partners of international consultants, so that skills are transferred to NEPRU staff
3. Projects involving elements of public consultation
4. Projects involving quantitative analysis
5. Projects involving monitoring and evaluation.

NEPRU's research is predominantly driven by demand, ensuring the relevance of its research activities. However, this leaves little opportunity to move the research agenda forward and to deepen competence in identified fields of importance. To overcome this problem, the institute is developing research programs in identified key areas. NEPRU has developed research competence particularly in the following fields:

- macroeconomic planning, policy analysis, and governance
- fiscal policies
- poverty and employment
- rural development, agriculture and land

- trade, regional integration, industrial policy, and small enterprise promotion.

NEPRU transfers its research results into the policy-making process not only by providing research reports, but also through targeted policy briefings, participation in numerous government committees, advice to and interaction with senior government officials, information to the public, and public seminars. An important step in more systematically providing policy analysis and advice was the signing of a cooperation agreement with the NPC in late 2000.

The Training Objective

In the process of doing research the institute trains Namibian economists. NEPRU's training activities concentrate on Namibian bachelor's degree holders in economics, with the aim of producing professional economic researchers. They are employed as junior researchers and in the first phase are part of research teams in various fields. Later they attend master's-level courses in economics at first-class universities abroad. After this they are given extended responsibilities in project management. At the end of this period they are promoted to researchers.

NEPRU also trains clients in economic policy and research methodology. However, this function, envisaged as a major activity, has remained in its infancy. Only in 2001, with the employment of a training coordinator, was this task given systematic attention. Two important elements are an internship program for middle-level policy researchers and managers, and a regular series of policy seminars. In addition, over the years, many Namibian and foreign students and guest researchers have been attached to the unit, resulting in additional publications (a separate series *Occasional Papers*), seminars, and skills transfer through joint projects.

Information to the Public

No less important is the information for the public about economic developments. NEPRU has published close to 200 documents, including research reports, working papers, travel and meeting reports, briefing papers, viewpoints, occasional papers, and books. It regularly produces *Quarterly Economic Review* and *Namibian Economic Review and Prospects* (annual). The institute also produces irregularly published viewpoints on topical issues. Recently a series of policy briefings, directed at policy-makers, was launched. All new publications are presented by press releases and in some cases by press conferences. NEPRU's library with some 6,000 titles and an extensive stock of information includes grey literature on Namibia, current literature on economics, and key periodicals. The library is also available for the public. NEPRU also has an economic data base and an expanding literature data base. Its expanding Web site provides information about past, current, and upcoming activities; staff; employment opportunities; publications; and press releases. The *Working Papers*, *Viewpoints*, *Quarterly Economic Reviews*, and the *Newsletter* can be downloaded from the Web site. Abstracts of other publications are available. Selected information is continuously sent by e-mail to interested parties.

Outlook

NEPRU has played an increasing role in research, training, and information provision. However, it has still not reached fully the objectives set by its founders. The vision of NEPRU is to raise its profile as a leading economic policy research institute in Namibia and the Southern African region. Indicators for the attainment of this goal are

- To become the leading policy advisor of the Namibian government
- To participate in the national, regional, and global economic policy debate through quality economic research
- To have a strong Namibian research staff.

Conclusion: Strengthening Governance Through Economic Policy Research

As discussed above, Namibia has not yet reached the model of a society where economic policy is based on a consistent set of economic information, analysis, and advice. Reflecting on the previous discussion, the following elements would help strengthen the link between economic policy-making and research:

1. Raising policy-makers' awareness of the benefits of economic policy advice based on research
2. Raising the awareness about existence of domestic research capacity, its comparative advantages (local knowledge, long-term availability), and the benefits of building it up
3. Closing the cultural gap between researchers and policy-makers through more systematic interaction and finding a common language
4. Raising awareness among researchers of the constraints under which policy-makers operate

5. Raising donors' awareness of the existence of a domestic research capacity, its comparative advantages, and the importance of its input to strengthening governance.

References

Aaron, Henry J. 1992. "Symposium on Economists as Policy Advocates." *Journal of Economic Perspectives* 6(3): 59–60.

Abdel Rahim, Aisha. 1996. "Review of Public Enterprises and Parastatal Bodies in Namibia." NEPRU Research Report No. 14, September.

Acemoglu, Daron, Simon Johnson, and James A. Robinson. 2001. An African Success Story: Botswana. Unpublished manuscript, 11 July.

Akyüz, Yilmaz, and Charles Gore. 2001. "African Economic Development in a Comparative Perspective." *Cambridge Journal of Economics* 25: 265–88.

Allison, Caroline. 1988. "Study of Namibian NGO Capacity and Development." Report sponsored by NANGOF and USAID.

Auty, Richard M. 1995. "Economic Development and the Resource Curse Thesis." Pp. 58–80 in *Economic and Political Reform in Developing Countries*, eds. Oliver Morrissey and Frances Stewart. Houndmills: Macmillan.

Bräutigam, Deborah, and Kwesi Botchwey. 1999. "The Institutional Impact of Aid Dependence on Recipients in Africa." Chr. Michelsen Institute, Working Paper 1999: 1.

Central Statistics Office. 1996. *Statistical Abstract 1996*. Windhoek, Namibia: CSO.

Coase, Ronald H. 1999. "Economists and Public Policy." Pp. 33–52 in *What Do Economists Contribute?*, ed. D. Klein. New York: New York University Press.

Collier, Paul. 1995. "The Marginalisation of Africa." In *International Labour Review*, 134(4–5): 541–57.

Collier, Paul, and Jan-Willem Gunning. 1999. "Why Has Africa Grown Slowly?" *Journal of Economic Perspectives* 13(3): 3–22.

Dollar, David, and William Easterly. 1999. "The Search for the Key: Aid, Investment, and Policies in Africa." Washington, D.C.: World Bank, Policy Research Working Paper 2070, March.

Eizenstat, Stuart E. 1992. "Economists and White House Decisions." *Journal of Economic Perspectives* 6(3): 65–71.

Fukuyama, Francis. 2001. "Social Capital, Civil Society and Development." *Third World Quarterly* 22(1): 7–20.

Goldsmith, Arthur A. 2001. "Risk, Rule and Reason: Leadership in Africa." *Public Administration and Development* 21: 77–87.

Gulhati, Ravi. 1990. "The Making of Economic Policy in Africa." World Bank. Washington, D.C.

Hamilton, Lee H. 1992. "Economists as Public Policy Advisers." *Journal of Economic Perspectives* 6(3): 61–64.

Hansohm, Dirk. 2001a. "Integration and Development through Good Economic Policies and Institutions: The Case of Botswana." *African Development Perspectives Yearbook*, forthcoming.

———. 2001b. The Namibian Economic Policy Research Unit (NEPRU) and Economic Policy Making in Namibia. Presented at the African Policy Institute Forum. 21–22 June 2001, Harare.

Hansohm, Dirk, Bruno Venditto, and John Ashipala. 2000. *Economic Reform Programmes, Labour Market Institutions, Employment and the Role of the Social Partners in Namibia.* Harare: International Labor Organization.

Haveman, Robert. 1989. "Economics and Public Policy: On the Relevance of Conventional Economic Advice." *Quarterly Review of Economics and Business* 29(3): 6–20.

Hayek, Friedrich A. 1999. "On Being an Economist." Pp. 133–49 in *What Do Economists Contribute?*, ed. D. Klein. New York: New York University Press.

Hope, Kempe Ronald, Sr. 1998. "Development Policy and Economic Performance in Botswana: Lessons for the Transition Economies in sub-Saharan Africa." *Journal of International Development* 10(4): 539–54.

Klein, Daniel B., ed. 1999. *What Do Economists Contribute?* New York: New York University Press.

McCloskey, D.N. 1999. "The Common Weal and Economic Stories." Pp. 104–18 in *What Do Economists Contribute?*, ed. D. Klein. New York: New York University Press.

Ministry of Trade and Industry. 1999. "Review of the 1992 White Paper on Industry Policy." Windhoek, Namibia: MTI.

Mohr, Ernst. 1999. *The Transfer of Economic Knowledge.* Cheltenham/Northampton: Edward Elgar.

National Planning Commission. 1998. "National Capacity Assessment Report."

Ndulu, Benno J. 1997. "Editorial: Capacity for Economic Research and the Changing Policy Environment in Africa." *World Development* 25(5): 627–30.

NEPRU. 1999a. *Namibia: Economic Review and Prospects 1998/1999.* Windhoek, Namibia: NEPRU.

NEPRU. 1999b. "Taking Advantage of Global Integration." Windhoek: NEPRU Viewpoint.

———. 2000a. Press release on Board of Trustees retreat. September 2000.

———. 2000b. Project analysis. Unpublished internal report.

———. 2001a. Employment and Poverty in Namibia. Unpublished report for the ILO.

———. 2001. "Reform of the President's Economic Advisory Council (PEAC)." Confidential Report, 31 August.

Ng, Francis, and Alexander Yeats. 1997. "Open Economies Work Better! Did Africa's Protectionist Policies Cause its Marginalisation in World Trade?" *World Development* 25(6): 889–904.

———. 1999. "Good Governance and Trade Policy: Are They the Keys to Africa's Global Integration and Growth?" World Bank Policy Research Working Paper 2038, January.

Olson, Mancur. 1996. "Big Bills Left on the Sidewalk: Why Some Nations are Rich, and Others Poor." *Journal of Economic Perspectives* 10(2): 3–24.

――――. 2000. "Governance and Growth: A Simple Hypothesis Explaining Cross-Country Differences in Productivity Growth." *Public choice* 102: 341–64.

Peacock, Alan. 1991. "Economic Advice and Economic Policy." *Companion to Contemporary Economic Thought,* ed. David Greenaway et al. London: Routledge.

Prakash, Aseem. 2001. Grappling with globalisation: Challenges for economic governance in Republic of Namibia. 1998a. *Poverty Reduction Strategy for Namibia.* Windhoek: National Planning Commission.

――――. 1998b. *Mid-Term Review of First National Development Plan, Review Volume 1.* Windhoek: Office of the President.

――――. 2000. *National Poverty Reduction Action Programme 2001–2005, First Draft.* Windhoek: National Planning Commission.

――――. 2001. National Development Plan II. Volume 1. Windhoek, NPC.

Rodney, Walter. 1972. *How Europe Underdeveloped Africa.* Dar es Salaam and London: Tanzania Publishing House and Bogle-l'Ouverture Publications.

Rodrik, Dani. 2000. "Institutions for High-quality Growth: What They Are and How to Acquire Them." NBER, Working Paper 7540.

Sachs, Jeffrey D., and Andrew Warner. 1995. "Economic Reform and the Process of Global Integration." *Brookings Papers on Economic Activity* 1: 1–18.

Schade, Klaus, et al. 1998. Overview of Poverty in Namibia. Windhoek. NEPRU (unpublished).

Schelling, Thomas. 1999. "What Do Economists Know?" Pp. 119–24 Klein in *What Do Economists Contribute?* New York: New York University Press.

Stiglitz, Joseph E. 1988. "Economic Organization, Information, and Development." Pp. 93–160 in *Handbook of Development Economics,* eds. H. Chenery and T.N. Srinivasan. Volume 1, .

United Nations Development Programme. 1998. Namibia Human Development Report 1998.

Van Niekerk, Ingrid, and Michael Samson. 1995. "Discussion Document for a Namibian Economic Policy Capacity Building Strategy." Unpublished.

Wohlmuth, Karl. 1998. *Good Governance and Economic Development. New Foundations for Growth in Africa.* Bremen: University of Bremen.

World Bank. 1997. "Namibia: Rising to the Challenge of Poverty Reduction." Technical paper for preparation of poverty reduction strategy for Namibia.

――――. 1999a. Namibia. Recent Economic Developments and Prospects." June 8, Report No. 19403-NAM.

――――. 1999b. *World Development Report 1999/2000.* Washington, D.C.: World Bank.

Ministry of Trade and Industry. 1999. "Review of the 1992 White Paper on Industrial Development." Windhoek, Namibia: MTI.

World Economic Forum. 1998. *The Africa Competitiveness Report.* New York: WEF.

13

Governance and Local Government Reforms in Zambia's Third Republic

ROYSON M. MUKWENA AND PETER K. LOLOJIH

Zambia gained independence from Britain in 1964. From 1964, to December 1972, Zambia followed a multiparty system of government. This period came to be known as the First Republic. On December 13, 1972, Zambia was proclaimed a one-party state, ushering in the Second Republic, which lasted until December 1990, when multiparty politics were re-introduced ushering in the Third Republic. The return to a multiparty political system entailed changes in the operations of, among other institutions, the legislature, the judiciary, the cabinet, and the public service. To reorient some of these institutions to the new political dispensation, the government embarked on governance and institutional reforms, launching the Public Service Reform Program (PSRP) in November 1993, to improve the quality, delivery, efficiency, and cost-effectiveness of public services to the people of Zambia.

The three main components of PSRP are a restructuring of public services, management and human resources improvement, and decentralization and strengthening of local government. This chapter focuses on the strengthening of local government, for two reasons. First, local government in any society plays a key role in service delivery and facilitation of development; second, it promotes good governance in any society.

Inevitably, local government reforms in Zambia have impacted policy processes and outcomes in local government. This chapter analyzes these impacts, focusing on key players in local government, namely councillors and officers, in an attempt to assess the extent to which local government reforms have enhanced or reduced the inputs these actors make into the policy-making process. Specific issues analyzed are:

- Nature, direction, and extent of local government reforms;
- Quantity and quality of the reforms;

215

- Perception of the skills possessed by councillors and officers for policy-making
- Roles assigned to the key actors in the policy process.

Analysis of any reform process is inconceivable without briefly highlighting the historical background and development of the process in question.

Zambian Local Government
Prior to the Third Republic

Local government in Zambia prior to the Third Republic can be divided into two phases: from 1965 to 1980, and from 1981 to 1991.

Phase One: 1965–1980

The local government system that operated in Zambia between 1965, and 1980 was based on the Local Government Act 1965. This English style of local government, adapted from Zambia's former colonial master, Britain, was suitable to a multiparty system of government, which Zambia embraced at independence. The 1965 Act provided for three types of local authorities: two urban (municipalities and townships) and one rural. The president of Zambia was empowered to confer the title of "city" on a municipal council.

The municipalities, township, and rural councils were divided into wards, each of which elected a single councillor who served for three years. However, the minister responsible was empowered to appoint persons to a council provided that the number of appointed councillors did not exceed three (or if a municipality adjoined a mine township, did not exceed five). The Act also permitted a municipal council to appoint as alderman any person who had been a member of that council for not less than ten years, provided that the number of aldermen was not more than a third of the whole council. For each municipal and city council there was a mayor and deputy mayor, and for each rural and township council there was a chairman and a vice chairman elected annually by councillors from among themselves. Local authorities had departmental chief officers under the control of a chief executive (a town clerk for municipal councils and a secretary for township and rural councils).

In 1970, the 1965 Act was amended to give the responsible minister powers to appoint the mayor and the deputy mayor of every municipal council and the chairman (and vice chairman) of every township and rural council from among councillors. This amendment was repealed in 1975, and from 1976, the pattern reverted to the pre-1970 position (Mukwena, 1998). The original amendment can perhaps best be understood in the context of the 1970 local elections, at which the United National Independence Party (UNIP) failed to make its hoped-for breakthrough in the rural districts of Southern Province, and had also surrendered ground in Western Province to the opposition African National Congress (ANC) (Mukwena, 1998). Thus, as Mukwena (1998:108), observes, "To avoid the election of chairman from councillors who were ANC members in those areas, the UNIP government amended the Act. As Mukwena (1998:108) again observes, "The repeal of this amendment in 1975, was not surprising either, since by that time UNIP was no longer under threat from any opposition following the introduction of the one party system."

Phase Two: 1981–1991

In January 1981, the Local Administration Act of 1980 replaced the Local Government Act of 1965, which was repealed because local government under that Act proved ineffective due to lack of integration and cooperation between different levels and institutions, such as the state administration, party organs and local councils. Officially the 1980 Act had three principal objectives. The first embodied the publicly expressed desire of the government and the ruling UNIP to decentralize power to the people. The second objective was to "ensure an effective integration of the primary organs of local administration in the district" (Zambia, 1980:127). As a result, district party and council structures were fused (Mukwena, 1999a). The third objective was to enable district councils to play a more direct and substantial role in the development process than they had been expected to undertake in the past (Mukwena, 1999a).

We should also look at the reforms in the context of the Zambian leadership's desire since independence to increase and cement political control over local government (Mukwena, 1992; Chikulo, 1981). Indeed as Mukwena (1992:244) has observed, "A careful examination of the provision of the 1980 Act reveals that the hidden objective of the Act was that of increasing political control over local councils and other organs and creating benefits for local party functionaries in order to revive the demoralized and ineffective UNIP organisation at grassroots where unpaid local party officials felt they had received next to no benefits from independence."

Following the passage of the 1980 Act, all existing city, municipal, township, and rural councils came to be known as district councils. If districts had both township and rural councils, the two were merged to form new district councils. As stipulated in the Act, each district council consisted of:

- The district governor as chairman;
- The district political secretary;
- Two district trustees appointed by the UNIP provincial committee and approved by the UNIP central committee;
- All chairmen of UNIP ward committees in the district;
- All members of parliament of the district;
- One representative from each of the officially constituted mass organizations operating in the district;
- One representative from each of the trade unions operating in the district;
- One representative from each of the security forces;
- One chief elected by all chiefs of the district (Zambia, 1980:105).

The president appointed the district governor and district political secretary. UNIP members elected the chairmen of UNIP ward committees. The representatives of mass organizations, trade unions, and security wings were chosen by their respective organizations. The Act also established a secretariat for each district council under the supervision of a district executive secretary.

Although the institutional capacity of local authorities in Zambia had been in decline for some time, especially since the introduction of the one-party state in 1972, the imposition of inappropriate local government structures under the 1980 Act intensified this decline during the period 1981 to 1991. For instance, merging the local party structure with the local council opened avenues for rampant financial mismanagement and diversion of council resources to party activities (Mukwena, 1999b). It also institutionalised political interference in the day-to-day operations of local authorities (Mukwena, 1999b).

Local Government in the Third Republic

Following Zambia's return to a multiparty political system in December 1990, the Local Government Act of 1991, replaced the 1980 Act in December 1991. The major changes that came with the 1991 Act were the clear institutional divorce of party structures from the council, the abandonment of the integrative role of the district councils, and the reintroduction of representative local government based on universal adult suffrage. Under the 1991 Act the responsible minister is empowered to establish in any district a city council, municipal council, district council, township council, or management board provided that a township council or management board can only be established on the recommendation of the appropriate city, municipal, or district council (Zambia, 1992a). There are currently seventy-two local authorities in the country.

The council is composed of elected councillors representing wards, members of parliament (MPs) in the district, and two representatives of the chiefs in the district, appointed by all the chiefs in the district. The inclusion of MPs and chiefs' representatives on the list of councillors came later, following amendments to the 1991 Act. When amending the Act in early 1992, to provide for their membership to councils, MPs argued that the change would enable them to efficiently and effectively serve the residents in their constituencies. Contrary to the MPs' argument, Mukwena observes, " . . . the amendment was aimed at ensuring political control over the new councils by national politicians—control that might provide access to local resources and facilities that might potentially be used to reward supporters and hence consolidate one's political position—for instance, the allocation of residential and commercial plots, council houses, and market stalls" (2001:24).

The 1991 Act also provides for a mayor and deputy mayor for city and municipal councils and a chairman and vice chairman for district councils, who are elected by the council from among elected councillors (Zambia, 1991a, 1992a). Such council leaders are elected annually, with no person allowed to hold such positions for more than two consecutive terms (Zambia, 1991a).

District councils have three departments: Administration, finance, and works. The heads of the administration, finance, and works departments are the deputy secretary, treasurer, and director, respectively (Zambia, 1992b). Municipal and city councils, on the other hand have six departments: Administration, finance, engineering, housing, and social services, legal services, and public health, headed by directors (Zambia, 1992b, 1992c). The town clerk is the chief executive for a municipal or city council, while the council secretary is the chief executive for a district council (Zambia, 1992b, 1992c). Chief executives and their heads of departments constitute the council secretariats (Zambia, 1992c). The key actors in the local government policy process include the minister of local government and housing, the councillors, and the appointed officials who constitute council management. The minister is responsible for laying down broad policy guidelines for the permanent secretary and his or her team to implement. The secretary is accountable to parliament for all acts of omission or commission of officials. The councillors, headed by a mayor or chairman, constitute the legislative wing of the council. They represent their constituents and are responsible for policy-making and supervising policy implementation. The appointed officials, headed by a town clerk or council secretary, constitute the executive wing of the council and are responsible for rendering technical advice to the councillors as well as implementing policies.

Capacity of Local Authorities in the Third Republic

The 1991 Act outlines up to sixty-three functions that local councils are supposed to perform. These functions are divided into nine broad categories: general administration, advertisements, agriculture, community development, public amenities, education, public health, public order, and sanitation and drainage. Due to several factors, however, local authorities in Zambia are not cable to efficiently and effectively perform their functions countrywide. The first problem relates to finance. Most councils have not developed a culture of independence from central government funding. Most, if not all, local authorities have exhibited lack of initiative to execute economic activities that can enhance their revenue base with a view to freeing themselves from financial dependence on central government. This situation is characteristic even of local authorities such as the Lusaka city council that have a reasonable number of well-qualified staff in key positions and more than adequate potential sources of local revenue. Since central government is not able to regularly disburse sufficient funds in the form of grants, local authorities do not have the financial capacity to carry out their functions. The housing empowerment policy that has resulted in the sale of council houses and the transfer of the responsibility to provide water and sewerage services from councils to companies has robbed councils of a sure source of income.

Soon after assuming power in November 1991, the new MMD government reestablished links with the IMF and the World Bank and began pursuing an economic stabilization and adjustment program with the multilateral financial institutions. Structural adjustment reforms have been couched within a policy framework whose aims included a commitment to a balanced budget, more effective resource mobilization, and a far more efficient system of resource allocation. Sharp reductions of public sector expenditure, removal of various consumer subsidies, raising of domestic interest rates to market levels, and foreign exchange rate liberalization have been effected in a bid to realize these objectives. Yet the adoption of stringent austerity measures under the economic reform program has, in the short term, led to an intensification of the very economic ills they were supposed to eliminate.

Among the most serious consequences of the new policy initiatives have been a high level of inflation and the erosion of the buying power of the kwacha. Real national revenue has also continued to decline, resulting in a steady drop in public expenditure in areas such as local government (World Bank, 1995). Moreover the MMD government's policy emphasis on reducing public expenditure as a proportion of Gross Domestic Product has also worked to further reduce the funding that could be made available to local government. Increased interest rates have likewise made it difficult for local authorities to borrow from domestic financial institutions. The introduction of the so-called cash budget system in 1993, had severe repercussions for the financial position of local authorities. This system, a key measure adopted by the government at the insistence of the IMF in order to reduce domestic inflation, operates on the principle that revenues must be collected and 'in the bank' before they are spent; thus, under this arrangement the government can no longer finance its deficit by printing money (i.e., borrowing from the Bank of Zambia) (Zambia, 1995:35; Mukwena, 1998). For local government this has meant at times there have been no funds in government accounts at the central bank, and the Ministry of Local Government and Housing has not received the money due to it from the Ministry of Finance (Mukwena, 1998). Other government departments have also experienced difficulties in paying the money owed to local authorities, a situation that needless to say has been a serious additional source of disruptions for local government operations (Mukwena, 1998).

Approximately 53% of the 2001 budget was financed by the donor community (Zambia, 2001), clearly demonstrating the extent of the central government's financial incapacity. Dependence on central government funding has, on many occasions, resulted in local council workers going without a salary for several months. The permanent secretary for local government, in fact, noted that most councils had no capacity to sustain themselves financially and needed new policy direction for survival. He observed that all councils were unable to meet salary demands, resulting in numerous strikes by unionized workers. He also admitted that after the sale of council houses, the revenue base for local authorities had been eroded.

Second, poor service conditions make it very difficult to attract qualified staff. It may, therefore, be argued that the few qualified staff who are available in key positions in some of the local authorities lack the necessary motivation. Given the high levels of unemployment in the country, it is plausible to assume that most of the qualified staff working for local councils are doing so because greener pastures are not readily available. Dedication to duty and the willingness to initiate efforts to ensure an efficient and effective local government system cannot reasonably be expected to come from such workers.

Third, it is an open secret that most councillors, in most local councils, have very low levels of education. It is very unlikely that persons of such caliber can initiate and pass policies tailored to enhance social and economic development in their communities. They are also not likely to command adequate respect and cooperation from appointed officials, a scenario that has often resulted in tension and conflict between the two groups. A commission of inquiry noted that operations in councils had been hampered by the inability of some councillors to understand their functions and responsibilities as policy makers. To enhance their caliber, the commission recommended that the local government elections Act of 1991, be amended so that a person wishing to stand as councillor should not only be conversant with the English language, but should have passed Grade 9 or Form 2. The government rejected this recommendation (Zambia, 1994a).

Finally, inadequate or absent capital equipment and poor infrastructure is yet another contributing factor to the dismal performance of local councils in Zambia. The road network in most parts of the country is inadequate, and the few roads available are in very poor condition and usually impassable during the rainy season. Most local authorities own a fleet of dilapidated vehicles that are beyond repair, and they have no graders to service roads within their jurisdiction. This has led to ineffective communication between the local authority and subdistrict structures. Councillors, for example, find it very difficult to regularly interact with their constituents, meaning that issues discussed in council meetings, more often than not, do not reflect contributions from the local communities they are meant to serve.

Government Efforts to Reform Local Government

In line with the 1991 Act, important steps were taken to rationalize the administrative set-up of local authorities in the Third Republic. For example, the commercial, industrial, and social departments of district councils were abolished, and their staff were incorporated into the finance and administration departments, respectively. In the case of municipal and city councils, only the commercial and industrial department was abolished and its employees absorbed into the finance department. The social department was split into two departments: social and housing, and public health. As a result, district councils have emerged with three departments (administration, finance, and works), while municipal and city councils have six (administration, finance, engineering, housing and social services, legal services, and public health) (Zambia, 1992d). This rationalization was on balance a progressive measure, especially for district councils, since it has reduced council departments to a more manageable number and resolved functions overlap among departments under the previous system, notably between the commercial and industrial and the finance departments, which resulted in tensions among department heads in several local authorities.

In another bid to revitalize the administrative capacity of local authorities, the minister of local government and housing amended the Local Authorities Superannuation Fund Act. Under this Act, councils must retire employees with twenty-two years' service in local government (Zambia, 1991b). The object of this Act was to ensure that: councils retained young, energetic, and professionally qualified personnel; all excess staff was laid off; and councils had manageable numbers of employees whom they could pay adequately (Zambia, 1993a:2). However, due to lack of funds to pay retirement and retrenchment packages, local authorities were not able to weed out excess staff (Zambia, 1993b:26).

Although the urban local authorities are generally stronger financially than their rural counterparts, due to the severity of the country's economic crisis the differences in their economic status tend to blur. In fact the failure of local authorities to pay salaries for several months is faced by almost all urban and rural authorities. Thus, it is difficult to categorize Zambian local authorities according to economic classes.

The 1991 Act reduced political controls over the executive officers of local authorities and hence lessened the problems of political interference in the day-to-day running of council affairs, but the continued membership of local MPs on the councils has contributed to tension between MPs and elected councillors as well as council officers. The MPs tend to dominate council proceedings and some MPs, for example, have taken a leading role in deciding whom the council should employ at senior levels (Mukwena, 1998).

Another political development that has undermined the role of local government is the creation of constituency funds for development projects in parliamentary constituencies (Tordoff and Mukwena, 1995). Under this initiative, the government allocates development funds annually to all constituencies. Properly channelled and controlled, these additional funds undoubtedly would benefit local authorities and the communities they serve. The problem, however, is that MPs have sought to divert funds to projects that further their political careers to the detriment of other, more useful projects, fueling tension between MPs on the one hand and councillors and officers on the other. Channeling constituency development funds through local authorities would boost the finances of local authorities and enhance their role in local development.

The capacity of the Ministry of Local Government and Housing to promote the role of local government has been limited. The weaknesses at the ministry level, which adversely affected the performance of local authorities in the Third Republic, included shortage of skills and lack of coherent policy guidance, planning capacity, and resources, particularly finance (Tordoff and Mukwena, 1995; Zambia, 1994b; Zambia/ODA, 1995).

To facilitate the role of the ministry in guiding and monitoring the operations of local authorities and helping them acquire institutional capacity, the 1991 Act provided for the appointment of a provincial local government officer (PLGO) for each province (Zambia, 1991a:351). To underscore the importance of the role of the PLGO's office in the development of local government, the ministry sought to appoint staff of quality and experience to these positions. The qualifications required for appointment to this position of PLGO were a bachelor's degree or membership (at the level of fellow or associate) of the Institute of Local Government Administrators of Zambia (Ministry of Local Government and Housing, 1994). The responsibilities of the PLGO included, among others:

- Providing support and professional advice to District Councils generally including organization and management of training workshops where necessary and when resources occur;
- Monitoring, on behalf of the Ministry of Local Government and Housing, the general activities of local authorities, including development, finance, management, and providing services;
- Providing financial, technical, and management advice to district councils where possible;
- Auditing, all district councils in the province and ensuring that their activities are properly conducted and in accordance with statutory requirements, regulations and directions, and with sound management principles and practice, and taking such action as may be necessary on the basis of such audit and other reports;
- Coordinate and support technical assistance (as opposed to capital support) given to district councils in the province by donor agencies (Provincial Local Government Officer, Southern Province, 1994: 1–2).

Generally, PLGOs have not been able to effectively discharge their functions due to several constraints, such as lack of funds and transport and the shortage of professionally qualified support staff, especially in the audit section (Provincial Local Government Officer, 1995; Senior Local Government Auditor, 1995). One other weakness in the PLGO offices was that the only finance staff available were local government auditors, who were involved in many aspects of financial administration and advice to the councils, in addition to having an audit function (Zambia/ODA, 1995). Not only was their independence at risk of being compromised by their other work, but the latter inevitably limited the time available for the former (Zambia/ODA, 1995).

Public Sector Reform Program

The local government component of the Public Sector Reform Program (PSRP) was to incorporate the following potentially ambitious set of proposals:

- Structural changes to allow greater autonomy;
- Introduction of better management systems across the board;
- Reintroduction of the pre-1980, provincial and district government system, which would include the role of coordinating the function of all government agencies
- Introduction of national, provincial, and district institutions to improve the coordination of development and program planning, implementation, and monitoring, and to improve sensitivity to local needs and opportunities; and
- Introduction of measures to ensure proper financing of local government (Zambia, 1993c:24–5).

The overall intent of this PSRP component was to make the operations of local government efficient, cost-effective, and responsive to the needs of local communities (Zambia, 1993c). Its objectives also included efforts at the national level to enhance the capacity of the Ministry of Local Government and Housing to provide support to local authorities in policy formation, implementation, evaluation, and improved organizational management to better coordinate development activities through a National Development Co-ordination Committee (Zambia 1993c:25–6).

The envisaged reforms under the PSRP experienced considerable delays in getting underway. In the first place, more than two years elapsed before the ministry received authority to implement the reorganized structure drawn up in early 1993 (Tordoff and Mukwena, 1995).

Even after approval was given, the program was adversely affected by lack of funds, making it impossible to implement most of the PSRP proposals. The local authorities, for example, were not able to obtain sufficient financial resources to fund the retrenchment exercise that was an important aspect of the reforms. Inadequate funding for local government reforms should be seen in the context of the economic crisis the country is going through. In view of poor economic performance, real national revenue has continued to diminish, resulting in a steady drop in public expenditure in local government.

Political Power Sharing at the Local level

The December 1998, local government elections registered a 9.8% increase of non-MMD members on councils countrywide, from 21.1% in the 1992 elections to 30.9%. In terms of partisan representation MMD's share of elected councillors fell from 78.9% in 1992, to 69.1% in 1998, (FODEP, 1999). The insignificance of the 30.9% non-MMD councillors can, however, be more appreciated when recognizing that the number is not only split among the seventy-two councils countrywide, but also that it is composed of members representing different political parties and independents.

The ruling party (MMD) took the lead in the election results in eight of the country's nine provinces except in the Eastern Province where the former ruling party, the United National Independent Party (UNIP), took the first slot. Independent candidates maintained the third position in all except in the North Western Province, where they got the second position with 14.2% of the votes cast, and in the Western Province where they were relegated to the fourth position by Agenda for Zambia (AZ), which got 13.72% against their 7.91%. In the Southern Province a relatively new political party, United Party for National Development (UPND), scooped the second position with 10.42% of the votes cast, and UNIP slid to the fourth position (Electoral Commission of Zambia, 1999). Out of the seventeen political parties that contested the 1998, local government elections countrywide the top three slots were occupied by the MMD, UNIP, and the Independents in all except in the Western and Southern Provinces.

On average six political parties contested the 1998, local government elections in each province save for Lusaka and the Copperbelt provinces where thirteen and eleven political parties, respectively, participated. According to the consolidated national totals of the election results, only five political parties and the Independents got more than 1% share of the votes cast while the share of the rest ranged between zero and 0.5%. The ruling party (MMD) scooped the top slot (60.13%), UNIP (23.72%), Independents (6.83%), UPND (3.59%), AZ (1.43%), and National Christian Coalition-NCC (1.28%) (Electoral Commission of Zambia, 1999). The domination of the ruling party and by extension the fragmentation of the opposition is clearly not debatable considering that the total share of the top five opposition contestants adds up to only 37% of the national total.

Councillor–Officer Relations

In Zambia, as in most other countries, political authority takes precedence over administrative authority. In many instances this has caused tension and conflict between politicians and bureaucrats especially on financial matters. Prior to the appointment of district administrators towards the end of 1999, no one at the district level could be referred to as a political appointee representing the central government. The district administrators have supposedly been appointed to coordinate activities at the district level as the most senior civil servants at that level. Activities of these political appointees coupled with the lack of specified minimum educational and professional qualifications has enhanced speculation that the district administrators are merely the ruling party's watchdogs strategically placed to increase its chances of winning the 2001, national elections. Some district administrators, for example, openly joined calls for the Zambian constitution to be amended to allow the President Chiluba to contest the 2001, elections for the third term, calls that were viewed by many people as partisan. During by-elections some district administrators have been involved in campaigns, an activity that is not expected of a senior civil servant. One businessman and activist for the MMD, for example, hailed the appointments of district administrators for three districts in the Eastern Province, describing them as hard working party cadres. Singling out one of the appointed administrators the businessman went on to say that even after losing elections for provincial chairmanship in 1996, the appointed administrator soldiered on to work for the party, enduring a lot of pressure in the process (*Times of Zambia*, 24 February 2000). The district administrators have, among other duties, taken over the chairmanship of the District Development Coordinating Committees (DDCC) from the council secretaries or town clerks. Given the nature and role of these committees—i.e., promoting decentralized development planning and coordination at the district level—senior council officials and civil servants at that level resent these appointments. The appointment of district administrators has undermined the roles of elected councillors and council officials at the local level.

According to Ismail et al. (1997) contributing factors to poor working relations between councillors and officials include the councillor-official dichotomy, poor communication, poor caliber of some councillors, and the difference in work orientation. It is generally prescribed that councillors are the policy makers while officials are the policy implementers. This somewhat rigid division of duties can easily lead to one group perceiving the actions of the other as being detrimental to its efficient and effective operations. Efficient and effective service delivery to the local communities requires various critical preconditions to characterize the administration of local government. A good working relationship between the elected and appointed officials of the local authority is one important precondition. A local authority characterized by tension and conflict between the two groups will find it difficult to adhere to the values and principles of local government, which include the promotion of a high standard of professional ethics, efficient and effective use of resources, promotion of public participation in the management of its affairs, transparency, and the capacity to respond to the needs of its local people (Ismail et al., 1997). Poor working relations among and between the councillors and the appointed officials have generally characterized local authorities in Zambia since 1991, when the system of elected councils was reintroduced.

Although in theory the new Act had separated political controls over the executive members from the day-to-day running and execution of council affairs, in practice the mayors, chairmen, and councillors continue to act as political overseers of the council executives, leading to friction and, in the case of some councils, to near paralysis (Mushota, 1994:162). Most councillors are preoccupied with the idea of being the employers and have consequently tended to overemphasize their authority, to the dismay of many appointed officials. This state of affairs has had a negative impact on the capacity of many of the authorities to deliver the needed services to their communities.

Illiteracy and ignorance, suspicion, wrong perceptions about the role of councillors, failure to comprehend levels of authority, and different party allegiances characterize the operational tensions at all levels of local authority (Mushota, 1994:162; CDD, 1999; *Times of Zambia* 5 September 2000; Chiteba, 1996).

The need to institute deliberate measures at national and local levels aimed at improving the working relations between councillors and officials cannot be overemphasized. Unfortunately, however, most councils lack the resources required to design and mount effective workshops or seminars to educate officials and councillors on their roles and on the need for the two groups to work as a team. There are also no significant efforts at the national level aimed at addressing the problem, although central government does acknowledge its existence. Speaking at the installation of Kabwe municipal council mayor, the then-minister of Central Province, Jeston Mulando, noted government's concern over squabbles among councillors and chief officers as a contributing factor to the poor delivery of services. He urged councilors and officials to expend their energies towards their civic responsibilities instead of squabbling, and that government would not tolerate tribal divisions in the councils nor would it condone camps or divisions when development was suffering (*Times*, 7 November 2000).

Conclusion

So far government's commitment to ensuring a well functioning local government system can best be described as mere rhetoric. The government should want to see vibrant local authorities capable of rendering efficient and effective service delivery. Ironically, however, policies and directives are passed that, in effect, not only deprive the authorities of the necessary revenue but promote and sustain their financial dependency on the central government. The government directive to local authorities to sell their houses and the policy to transfer the responsibility to provide water and sewerage services from local authorities to companies are some of the policies that have narrowed the revenue base of councils. This has led to inability to deliver, which in turn has led to significant levels of resistance from local communities to paying market levies, land rates, and so on. Further, as earlier mentioned in this paper, some of the measures that government has introduced have ended up undermining the roles of elected councillors and council officers and have created tensions in local authorities and fueled frustrations among elected councillors and councils officers. The measures in question include the continued membership of MPs on councils, the introduction of constituency development funds under the control of MPs, and the appointment of party cadres to the position of district administrator. The government should show its commitment to improving local government performance by reversing its habit of giving priority to political concerns over administrative ones.

On the other hand, it should be noted that Zambia's poor economic environment has significantly hampered efforts to strengthen local government. For instance, the poor economic performance has made it difficult for government to provide attractive conditions of service to local government staff. And local government reforms cannot succeed if the reforms are not supported by good conditions of service that attract and retain qualified, experienced staff and motivate them to perform at desired output levels. In fact, in Zambia, most local authorities have not been able to pay workers' salaries for several months (*Times of Zambia* 3 April 2000). For example, it was recently reported that Luanshya Municipal Council had not paid staff salaries for eleven months (*Times of Zambia* 22 October 2001). Local authorities also failed to effect the 40% salary increment that was awarded to local government workers in 1999 (*Times of Zambia* 3 April 2000).

Further, most local authorities are overstaffed and government would like to reduce staffing levels as a way to decrease recurrent expenses, an exercise that clearly requires a lot of financial resources to implement. The government is willing but not able to finance retrenchment and early retirement packages for council workers. The deputy minister of local government and housing recently admitted, " . . . the only constraint in implementing the restructuring programme was the lack of funds to meet retrenchment packages" (*Zambia Daily Mail* 24 October 2001). Consequently, local authorities have no choice but to keep even workers who have volunteered for early retirement on payroll. Finally, most councils lack the resources required to design and mount effective workshops and seminars to educate councillors and officers on their roles and the need for them to work as a team.

References

Chikulo, B. C. 1981. "The Zambian Administrative Reforms: An Alternative View." *Public Administration and Development* 1(1): 55–65

Chiteba A. C. 1996. "Wrangles in Councils in the Third Republic." *The Institute of Local Government Administrators of Zambia Journal* 11(7).

Commissioner of Town and Country Planning. 1995. Interview with W. Tordoff and R. M. Mukwena. Lusaka, 19 April.

Cooperation for District Development. 1999. Preliminary Report (Unpublished).

Electoral Commission of Zambia. 1999. Summary of Local Government Elections— 1998. Final Results.

Foundation for Democratic Process. 1999. FODEP Report.

German Technical Assistance to Zambia. 1998. "Strategic District Development Planning." Concept Paper GT2.

Ismail N. S. Bayat and I. Meyer. 1997. *Local Government Management.* Johannesburg, International Thomson Publishing.

Ministry of Local Government and Housing. 1994. "Job Specification for Provincial Local Government Officer." Lusaka.

Mukwena, R.M. 1992. "Zambia's Local Administration Act, 1980: A Critical Appraisal of the Integration Objective." *Public Administration and Development* 12(3): 237–47.

———. 1998. "The Role of Local Councils in Rural Development: A Study of Gwembe and Kalomo District Councils, Zambia, 1981–1995." Ph.D. Thesis, University of Manchester, Manchester.

———. 1999a. "Can Local Government Performance Be Measured? Lessons from Zambia." *Africanus* 29(1): 45–58.

———. 1999b. "Building the Institutional Capacity of Local Authorities in Zambia in the Third Republic: An Assessment." *African Administrative Studies* 53: 105–31.

———. 2001. "Situating Decentralisation in Zambia in a Political Context." *African Administrative Studies* (forthcoming).

Mushota, R.T. 1994. "Municipal Development Programme (MDP) for Sub-Saharan Africa, Country Study: Zambia, Local Government in Zambia: A study of Human Resources Development, Management and Utilization." Lusaka: MDP.

Permanent Secretary, Ministry of Local Government and Housing. 1995. Personal conversation with R.M. Mukwena. 10 July, Lusaka.

Provincial Local Government Office, Southern Province. 1994. "Revised/Updated Allocation of Duties in the Local Government Department." Livingstone: PLGO.

Provincial Local Government Officer, Southern Province. 1995. Interview with R. M. Mukwena. 15 March, Livingstone.

Senior Local Government Auditor, Southern Province. 1995. Interview with R. M. Mukwena. 15 March, Livingstone.

Times of Zambia, 12 May 1998.

————. 24 February 2000.

————. 3 April 2000.

————. 5 September 2000.

————. 7 November 2000.

————. 22 October 2001.

Todoff, W. and R. M. Mukwena. 1995. "Decentralisation and Local Government Reform: An Assessment." Lusaka: GRZ/ODA, Local Government Support Project.

World Bank. 1995. "Republic of Zambia Public Expenditure Review." Confidential Report No. 13854-ZA. Southern Africa Department, Africa Region, New York: World Bank.

Zambia Daily Mail, 24 October 2001.

Zambia, Republic of. 1980. *Local Administration Act, 1980.* Lusaka: Government Printer.

————. 1991a. *The Local Government Act, 1991.* Lusaka: Government Printer.

————. 1991b. *The Local Authorities Superannuation Fund (Amendment) Act No. 27, 1991.* Lusaka: Government Printer.

————. 1992a. *Local Government (Amendment) Act, No. 19, 1992.* Lusaka: Government Printer.

————. 1992b. *Local Government (Creation and Abolition of Government Posts) Regulations, 1992.* Lusaka: Government Printer.

————. 1992c. *Local Government (Council Secretariat) Members' Functions Order, 1992.* Lusaka: Government Printer.

————. 1992d. *Statutory Investment No. 53 of 1992.* Lusaka: Government Printer.

————. 1993a. "Action-Taken Report on the Report of the Parliamentary Committee on Local Administration for the First Session of the Seventh Assembly Appointed on 5 December 1991" (Confidential). Lusaka: MRLGH.

————. 1993b. "Addendum to the Action-Taken Report on the Report of the Committee of Local Administration for the First Session of the Seventh National Assembly Appointed on 27 January 1993" (Confidential). Lusaka: MRLGH.

————. 1993c. Cabinet Office Circular No. 103/26/5, 18 March 1993. Public Service Reform Programme. Lusaka: Cabinet Office.

————. 1994a. *Government Paper No. 1, 1994.*

————. 1994b. "Report on the Restructuring of the Ministry of Local Government and Housing." Lusaka: Management Development Division.

Zambia, Republic of/Overseas Development Administration. 1995. "Local Government Support Project, 1st Six-monthly Report." Hunting Technical Services, Hemel Hempstead; PMTC International Ltd., Bedfordshire; Development Administration Group, University of Birmingham; Price Waterhouse, Management Services Board, Lusaka.

————. 2001. *Budget Speech. Minister of Finance.* 26 January.

About the Contributors

Joseph Ayee is Professor of Political Science at the University of Ghana. He is also currently UNESCO Professor of Leadership Studies. His published works include *An Anatomy of Public Policy Implementation: The Case of Decentralization Policies in Ghana* (Avebury, 1994), *Ghana's 1996 Elections* (1999) and *Saints, Wizards and Systems* (Ghana University Press, 2000)

Julius Court is Programme Officer at the United Nations University in Tokyo, Japan. His research interests include comparative development in Asia and Africa; governance and public administration; income inequality; and Japan's foreign aid. His main publications include *Water, Peace and the Middle East*, co-edited with J.A. Allan (I.B. Tauris, 1996); *Asia and Africa in the Global Economy*, co-edited with E. Aryeetey, M. Nissanke, and B. Weder, (UNU Press forthcoming).

O.P. Dwivedi is Professor of Public Administration, University of Guelph, Ontario, Canada. He has served as a consultant to the World Bank, WHO, UNESCO, and United Nations Department of Economic and Social Affairs. He is the author of several books including *Bureaucracy and the Alternatives in World Perspectives* (co-editor) (Macmillan, 1999); and *Where Corruption Lives* (Kumarian Press, 2001), co-edited with Gerald E. Caiden and Joseph J. Jabbra.

Dirk Hansohm is Director of the Namibian Economic Policy Research Unit (NEPRU) in Windhoek, Namibia. He is an economist and his areas of specialization include macroeconomics, industry, trade, poverty, labor and small enterprise promotion. Previously he has worked at the University of Bremen and for international organizations in Nigeria, Sudan and Zimbabwe. His published work includes two books: *Small industry development in Africa. Lessons from Sudan* (Lit Verlag, 1992) and *Schwarz-weiße Mythen. Afrika und der entwicklungspolitische Diskurs* (Lit Verlag, 1993).

Goran Hyden is Distinguished Professor of Political Science at the University of Florida, Gainesville, Florida, U.S.A. His research interests include democratization in a comparative perspective with special emphasis on Africa; governance and sustainable development; the role of foreign aid agencies in national development in Africa; and comparative public administration. His main publications include *African Perspectives on Governance*, co-edited with H.W.O. Okoth Ogendo and Dele Olowu (Africa World Press, 1999); *No Shortcuts to Progress* (University of California Press and Heinemann, 1983); *Beyond Ujamaa in Tanzania: Underdevelopment and an Uncaptured Peasantry* (University of California Press and Heinemann, 1980).

Peter K. Lolojih is a Lecturer in the Department of Political and Administrative Science at the University of Zambia. He has also worked as Assistant Registrar (Administration and Personnel), and Administrative Assistant to the Dean, School of Humanities and Social Sciences. He is Chair and member of various committees at the University. His main area of research interest is promoting local democracy and enhancing administrative capacity.

Paschal B. Mihyo is Senior Lecturer in Labour Studies at the Institute of Social Studies, The Hague, The Netherlands. Before joining ISS he was Associate Professor of Law at the University of Dar es Salaam, Tanzania. His main areas of research interest are human rights; labour law; and world trade. His publications include *Non-Market Controls and The Accountability of Public Enterprises in Tanzania* (Macmillan, 1994). *African Youth in the Information Highway* (IDRC, 2000).

Vasant Moharir retired as Senior Lecturer in Public Policy and Administration at the Institute of Social Studies, The Hague, The Netherlands where he worked for thirty years. He has been involved in teaching, research and consultancy at ISS and in University of Witswatersrand, South Africa, University of Harare, Zimbabwe, the University of Khartoum, Sudan and the University of Namibia, as part of ISS projects of collaboration with those universities. He has published articles on administrative reforms, public policy analysis, public enterprise management, decentralization, a book on Administrative Reforms and Development Planning in Sudan and co-edited a volume on *Management for the Next Millennium*.

Royson M. Mukwena is an Associate Professor in Public Administration at the University of Namibia and also Dean of the Faculty of Economics and Management Science at the same University.

Gene Ogiogio is currently Manager, Knowledge Management at the African Capacity Building Foundation (ACBF). Prior to that he was ACBF Manager of Programs and also doubled as Program Team Leader overseeing the Foundation's interventions in Eastern and Southern Africa. Before his appointment as Manager of Programs, Ogiogio was Operations Advisor for the Partnership for Capacity Building in Africa, a position he held after serving as Principal Program Officer in charge of capacity building programs in Anglophone Africa. Ogiogio specializes in econometrics, development economics as well as capacity building and institutional development. He is widely published in the areas of institutional and economic policy reforms, exchange rate management strategies and policies, and capacity building. He holds a Ph.D. degree in economics, and is a member of several research and development management networks.

Dele Olowu teaches at the Institute of Social Studies (ISS) at The Hague, The Netherlands. He was professor of public administration and local government studies at Obafemi Awolowo University and has also served as adviser to a number of African governments on public sector management reforms, including Nigeria (his home country), Ethiopia, Sierra Leone and Mozambique. He was a resident consultant/adviser to the United Nations Economic Commission for Africa on governance and capacity building from 1995, to 1998, after which he joined the ISS.

Grace Atieno Ongile is programme officer, Eastern and Southern Africa at the African Capacity Building Foundation (ACBF), Harare, Zimbabwe. She has extensive experience in institutional and individual capacity building issues in Africa. Her research interest is in development economies focusing on the impact of structural adjustment policies on economic development in Africa, gender and development, small-scale firm growth and gender and trade liberalization in Africa. Her publications include *Gender and Agricultural Supply Response to Structural Adjustment Programmes in Kenya: A Case Study of Smallholder Tea Production in Kericho-Kenya* (Nordic African Institute, 1999), and a chapter in Eva Haxton and Cleas Olsson (eds.) *Gender focus on the WTO* (Global Publications Foundations, International Coalition for Development Action, 1999).

Ejeviome Eloho Otobo is Principal Economic Affairs Officer in the Office of the Special Coordinator for Africa and Least Developed Countries in the Department of Economic and Social Affairs at UN headquarters in New York. He most recently held the position of Chief of Policy Planning and Programme Development Section at the Economic Commision for Africa. His main areas of research interest are business-government relations and public management. He has written on issues of public enterprise management; regulation of privatized enterprises; economic governance and corporate governance. He contributed the chapter on Nigeria in Ladipo Adamolekun (ed.) *Public Administration in Africa: Main Issues and Selected Country Studies* (Westview Press, 1999).

Soumana Sako is the Executive Secretary of the African Capacity Building Foundation. An economist by profession, Sako, a Malian national trained in the United States, has a wealth of national and international experience in government, development management, economic reforms, community services, as well as in academia, development cooperation and international consultancy. Sako has in the past held several senior positions in Government, including serving as Minister of Finance and Commerce, and Prime Minister, Head of the Transitional Government of Mali. He has also served as the United Nations Development Programme (UNDP) Senior Economist for the Central African Republic, Madagascar and the Comoros. He was also a visiting Professor and Regent Lecturer at the University of California Los Angeles, as well as Professor of Public Finance and Development Economics at the National University of Mali. Sako holds a Bachelor of Arts degree from the National School of Administration, Mali, an MPA in Project Planning and Management and a Ph.D. in Public Policy Research and Analysis in Economic and Social Development from the University of Pittsburgh. He is married with four children.

M. A. Mohamed Salih is Professor of Politics of Development, Institute of Social Studies, The Hague, The Netherlands and the Department of Political Science, University of Leiden. His books include *Environmental Planning, Policies and Politics in Eastern and Southern Africa* (Macmillan and St. Martin's Press, 1999) and *Environmental Politics and Liberation in Contemporary Africa* (Kluwer Academic Publishers, 1999), *African Democracies and African Politics* (Pluto Press, 2001) and *African Pastoralism: Institutions, Conflict and Government* (Pluto Press, 2001).

Index

237

Also from Kumarian Press...

Kumarian Press, located in Bloomfield, Connecticut, is a forward-looking, scholarly press that promotes active international engagement and an awareness of global connectedness.